Charles Furst is with the Neuropsychiatric Institute, University of California, Los Angeles. He has taught at Dartmouth College and at California State University at Northridge.

Origins of the Mind

Mind-Brain Connections

Charles Furst

A SPECTRUM BOOK

Prentice-Hall, Inc., Englewood Cliffs, New Jersey 07632

Library of Congress Cataloging in Publication Data

FURST, CHARLES.
    Origins of the mind.

    (A Spectrum Book)
    Includes bibliographical references and index
    1. Brain   2. Mind and body.   3. Conscious-
ness.   I. Title.
QP376.F85   153   78-23185
ISBN 0-13-642777-4
ISBN 0-13-642769-3 pbk.

For Frieda and Lou

©1979 by Prentice-Hall, Inc., Englewood Cliffs, N.J. 07632

A SPECTRUM BOOK

Printed in the United States of America

10 9 8 7 6 5 4 3 2 1

Editorial/production supervision and interior design by Maria Carella
Cover design by Al Pisano
Manufacturing buyer: Cathie Lenard

PRENTICE-HALL INTERNATIONAL, INC., *London*
PRENTICE-HALL OF AUSTRALIA PTY., LIMITED, *Sydney*
PRENTICE-HALL OF CANADA, LTD., *Toronto*
PRENTICE-HALL OF INDIA PRIVATE, LIMITED, *New Delhi*
PRENTICE-HALL OF JAPAN, INC., *Tokyo*
PRENTICE-HALL OF SOUTHEAST ASIA PTE., LTD., *Singapore*
WHITEHALL BOOKS, LIMITED, *Wellington, New Zealand*

MAR 15 '80

Preface

Is there any principle in all nature more mysterious than the union of soul with body? ... Were we empowered, by a secret wish, to move mountains, or control the planets in their orbit, this extensive authority would not be more extraordinary, nor more beyond our comprehension.

David Hume, *Enquiry Concerning Human Understanding*, 1748.

You've told me a lot
'Bout the forebrain and hindbrain.
So now tell me this:
Where or how is the mindbrain?
Anonymous

This is a book about the mind and the brain and how they relate to one another. It used to be that the question of the mind–brain relationship was one of the important concerns of psychologists. In this century, the question has been put aside, partly out of philosophical despair of ever coming up with an answer, and partly because it became lost in the day-to-day business of

v

making science about the brain and about human behavior. Since my own interest in psychology was born out of a naive pondering of the mind–body problem, I thought that it might be useful to others to review the current state of scientific knowledge about the brain in the context of this ancient, though perhaps unsolvable, question. To this end, I have taken a naive, or at least an open, stance on the issue, disregarding caveats by philosophers and others that the mind–brain question is dead or was never live-born.

The book is written for the interested nonspecialist. It assumes little or no previous knowledge about the working of the brain and so might be useful in introductory courses in psychology or the neurosciences. The selection of topics was guided by my concern for presenting the findings of contemporary brain science which are most relevant to understanding conscious mental experience. My aim is to be provocative, rather than comprehensive or precise. However, some precision is required of the reader in trying to understand some mechanisms which have been proposed as underlying this or that mental ability.

Since the book is for a general audience, I have taken great liberties in simplifying complicated issues and in summarizing disparate facts. I beg the indulgence of more hard-nosed colleagues who might object to my simplifications of the prevailing neuro-mythology. More fastidious readers will also notice that I use some terms rather loosely (such as "theory" for "hypothesis") to conform to nontechnical usage and to avoid formality.

This book has benefited from the comments and criticisms of a number of colleagues and friends. Donald Walter was especially generous and helpful with his comments (mostly acerbic, but good-natured). Other reviewers of large or small parts of earlier drafts included Barbara Furst, Adam Wechsler, Tora Kay Bikson, James Tweedy, John Polich, Gregory McHugo, Augustin de la Peña, William Newman, Edward Sadalla, Thomas Bikson, Roger Sperry, and Jason Brown. I am grateful to all of these for their help. They are all, of course, blameless for what appears here in printed form.

Part of the book was written while I was on a sabbatic leave from Dartmouth College. Thanks to Margaret Westlake, Margaret Thomlinson, and Ann Nietzke for typing portions of the manuscript, and to Bennett Kashdan for help on details. Sharon Belkin and Nabuko Kitamura executed the original line drawings. I am grateful to Barbara Furst for her encouragement and support throughout this project.

CHARLES FURST
Los Angeles, California

Contents

Introduction

There is a science fiction novel called *Donovan's Brain*, in which a physician with mad-scientist leanings secretly removes the brain from a plane-crash victim and keeps it alive by pumping enriched blood through it as it floats in a tank of water. Eventually, the doctor establishes communication with the brain,

1

tapping Morse code messages on the side of the tank and receiving direct replies by mental telepathy.[1] Although medical technology has not quite reached the point where these experiments can actually be done, the premises seem entirely plausible—especially if we substitute another form of communication for ESP, say the recording of nerve signals from electrodes implanted in the brain. The plausibility of the story illustrates something about our beliefs, namely that consciousness is a property of living brain tissue. Also, whatever it is that makes another entity a person, we believe he or she could exist without any of the usual trappings of personhood, such as arms, feet, lungs, a heart, or a face. What is crucial is that a person have a mind, and for this we regard having a brain as prerequisite.

Mind and Brain

One of man's basic intellectual concerns has been to ask questions about the nature of mind. People have ever wondered about such things as the immortality of the soul. But even prior to this is the question about the peculiar relationship between an individual's soul—or mind, as we call it today—and the particular physical entity, the person's body, which it seems to inhabit, or at least to which it seems more than fortuitously attached. Despite reports by people who claim to travel outside of their bodies as incorporeal spirits, for the vast majority of mankind the experience of oneself is bound up with the particular corporeal entity of one's physical body. Persons are not identical to their physical beings, but they attend the same cocktail parties.

What is the nature of this relationship? It turns out that most of us have a pretty definite idea. Our mind *lives inside* of our body, somewhere in the region of the brain. It receives information from our sense organs and controls the workings of the brain which, in turn, controls the workings of our glands, our vocal apparatus, our skeletal musculature, and all the other parts which make us act like ourselves.

This conception, which has been dubbed the "ghost in the machine," is usually associated with the seventeenth-century philosopher René Descartes, who formulated the position most explicitly. Despite the fact that it seems like a natural way to view the mind–body relationship, this belief, as we shall see later, is not without its critics.

What kind of events are these that we attribute to "mind"? Certainly they include such things as perceiving, reasoning, feeling, intending, planning, and meaning. Although it is extremely difficult to give a definition of what we mean by "mental," it is clear that there is something very basic and elementary to our experience to which these terms all refer. The term "consciousness" has come to stand for all of these things.

There are various senses in which the word "consciousness" is used. Some writers, for example, use the term in a more restricted meaning of "awareness of self" or "awareness of awareness"—so that consciousness would be something which could be attributed mainly to persons. Here, we will use the term more generally to denote just "awareness" or "sentience," leaving open the likelihood that consciousness is a state which we share, at least to some degree, with other animals. "Consciousness" stresses the primitiveness of awareness, as personal identity and personal experience. It is distinguished from states of *un*consciousness, like sleeep, and from automatic episodes which are performed habitually.

We believe that the conscious mind is located in the brain. Like all other obvious truths, this one deserves scrutiny. Clearly, the first evidence is the fact that if you cut off someone's arm, he may suffer some change in personality, but says that he feels to be pretty much the same person as before. His memory, perceptions, and beliefs are recognizable both from within and from without. Not so if one of his temporal lobes becomes diseased or is destroyed by the surgeon's knife. Although large amounts of brain tissue can be destroyed with surprisingly little change in a person's experience of self, fundamental changes in personality and intelligence often occur.

If someone's temporal lobe is removed, changes may occur in his memory for events and people, perhaps in his appetite for food, or in his capability to find his way home. But, could not the same argument be used to assert the belief of many primitive peoples that the mind is located in the heart? Certainly, removing a person's heart would put an end to his personal identity. Yet heart transplants are now common, and we know that the patient following such surgery is much the same person as he was before. The thought of some breakthrough in medical technology which would permit the transplantation of a living brain from one human to another raises more profound questions of identity. For example, whose house does the patient return to upon release from the hospital?

But more important, our localization of the mind in the brain makes sense to us because it fits with everything we know about the functions of different bodily organs. And we know a great deal. We know what the heart does: it pumps blood through vessels so that the body's tissues can receive oxygen and nutrients and rid themselves of wastes. The brain, though, is connected to sense organs and skeletal muscles through networks of nerves, and because we believe that the workings of mind receive sensation and result in behavior, we ascribe mental functions to the brain. This much was obvious a long time ago.

The most compelling reason for our belief in the connection of mind to brain is this: The human brain, with its interconnecting networks of 10,000 millions of neurons and its largely unknown symphony of biochemical and biophysical interactions, is the most complex system in the known universe. In terms of the quantity of information it handles, the brain is far more complex than any computer. Our brains have the capability for being in an immensely large number of potential states, and it is this complexity above all else which we would like to associate with the workings of mind.

Many psychologists have shown that unconscious processes in perception and thought are perhaps more important for understanding mind than those processes that reach consciousness. Unconscious processes are the background on which the play of consciousness unfolds. It is likely also that most of the brain's activity never manifests itself in conscious experience. To study the brain—to find out what enables a person to walk or to become hungry—is largely to study unconscious processes. In this book, we undertake a more limited study of the brain. Specifically, we limit ourselves to the consideration of those brain processes which bear strongly on the nature of conscious mind. What follows in this first chapter is an introduction to the philosophical problem that guides this search. We will survey from a modern perspective some of the main currents of Western thought on the question of mind's relationship to physical matter, hoping to give along the wayha feel for the subtleties involved in this issue—an issue which may in the end turn out not to be a factual question at all.

Descartes and the Ghost in the Machine

The mind–body issue was most clearly stated for modern thinkers by René Descartes, the great philosopher, scientist, and mathematician of the early seventeenth century. A primary intellectual concern of this period in history was the discovery of truth by rational (i.e., logical, deductive) thought. Since the faculty of Reason was clearly man's highest achievement, and the one which set him off from lower animals, it seemed only natural that the proper route to knowledge should be through rational thought. Metaphysics, the philosophical discovery of the furniture of the universe and its interrelationships, was the highest form of rational thought, and Descartes was its leading practitioner.

Descartes tried to establish a metaphysics based on certainty, and to do this he set out to accept only those things which he could not doubt. At the outset, he could hold on to this one truth only: that *he* existed. For even to doubt this simple proposition was proof that there was someone who was doing the doubting. Now, what was the nature of this person, this I, who existed? Certainly not Descartes's physical body, because he could conceive of his existence (as a doubting being) without it. This did not necessarily mean that Descartes's independence from his physical body was an actual fact—that he could at some point in time fly away from his corporeal self—only that it was conceptually thinkable. Therefore, Descartes concluded, he had a clear and distinct idea of himself as an essentially thinking, nonmaterial thing, entirely different from his body. Viewed from an historical perspective, Descartes was rationalizing what had been the prevailing religious and popular belief in Western civilization for centuries.

What Descartes had reasoned was not that mind and body were actually seperate entities, but only that they were conceptually separate. Descartes actually believed a human being to be an "intimate union" of mind and body. The question that was formulated by Descartes had to do with the nature of this union. His question has been one of the key issues in philosophy ever since.

Descartes's solution, as we shall see, involved an interacting causal system, with mental events influencing physical events and *vice versa*. But in the terms in which the question is formulated, other possibilities clearly existed: causalities going in only one direction, or a causal correlation—and each one of these positions has had a philosophical champion.

For example, another solution to this problem, proposed by the German philosopher Leibniz (1646–1716), is known as *psychophysical parallelism*. In this view, both the physical and the mental are independent, self-contained realms. They happen to coincide by a "pre-established harmony" set in motion by God.

It is just as with two clocks which keep perfect time: if they are set initially to the same time they will continue to agree. To an observer they might appear to be causally related; movement of the hands of one clock would *appear* to cause the other's hands to move without there being any actual causal influences between them. Mental events and physical events will continue to coincide because they operate independently but in parallel. Today, this solution to the mind–body issue seems antique.

Descartes's solution has been called *interactionism*. The mind and the body interacted at some particular place, which for Descartes was the pineal body at the base of the brain. Interactionism means that the causation could go either way: sensory events influenced the soul, which in turn decided what to do and activated the muscles to effect appropriate actions. How mental stuff, which is in essence spatially dimensionless ("unextended substance" was Descartes's term), could ever be in any particular *place* is one of the ambiguities of Cartesian philosophy. Indeed, it is the crux of the puzzle we are dealing with here: thoughts, perceptions, and desires do not, properly speaking, exist *anywhere* at all.

Descartes used the soul to explain intelligent brain function: there is something like an intelligent creature in your brain which sees what needs to be done and then pulls the right strings (see Figure 1-1). Descartes did not concern himself with the question of just how intelligence works in a physical sense, since at that time intelligence was regarded as a purely spiritual property.

As many writers have pointed out, it was the scientific advances of the nineteenth century, most notably the theory of the evolution of species and the principle of conservation of matter and energy, which annihilated Descartes's soul. For, if the universe was a closed system, as nineteenth-century physics revealed, with the total amount of stuff in it constant, then intelligent action should be explainable on the basis of pieces of matter in motion, without recourse to a nonmaterial soul. And

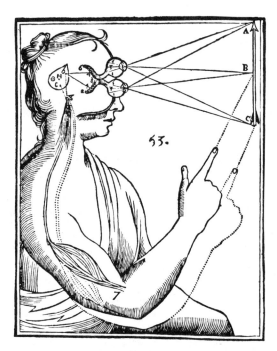

FIGURE 1-1. Descartes's diagram illustrating his mechanistic theory of brain functioning and the mind–body interaction. Light reflected from an object (ABC) is imaged on the retinas of the eyes. The image is then conducted by the optic nerves to the brain, where it is apprehended by the soul at the pear-shaped pineal body, which Descartes regarded as the site of interaction of mind and body. Movement is initiated at the pineal and is effected by "animal spirits" which travel down motor nerves to the arm muscle, which the spirits inflate. Although Descartes was wrong on some points of anatomy (hollow tubes for nerves and inflatable muscles), his theory contains the elements of the modern concept of reflex action. (Copyright 1972 by Edwin Clarke and Kenneth Dewhurst; reprinted by permission of the University of California Press.)

if man evolved as a continuous extension of the animal kingdom, as nineteenth-century biology proposed, then he should, in principle, be as easy to figure out as a flatworm. The challenge to Descartes came in the form of scientific materialism, the view that soul or mind was unimportant for a naturalistic understanding of man. The vehicle for this materialism was a movement in psychology called Behaviorism.

Behaviorism

The method Descartes used to ascertain the duality of mind and body is known as *introspection*—a looking inward to discover knowledge about the contents of mind. To accept, as Descartes did, that we have this faculty of knowing our own minds first of all and knowing all other things only secondarily, presents the problem of explaining how it is that we can ever know that other people have mental events like our own, or even that other minds exist at all. It would certainly be conceivable that one's own conscious mind is the only reality in the entire universe and that the rest is just a fantastic delusion. This conceptual knot, known as *solipsism*, is a position which philosophers have taken pains to avoid by supposing that we know of the existence of other minds by an argument from analogy. Argument from analogy is an inductive inference of the following form: if X and Y share properties a, b, c, and d; and if, further, X is observed to have the property e; then it is likely that Y will also have e. As applied to the existence of other minds, the claim is that since other people share many physical resemblances to me (they have one head, two arms, two legs, etc.), and since they behave like me in situations in which I know I have mental experiences (they say "ouch" when pricked by a pin), then it is reasonable to infer that they have mental experiences like my own, even though I cannot directly observe these experiences.

The issue of the knowability of other minds was at the root of Behaviorism, the most influential psychological movement in modern times. Behaviorism championed the view that the proper scientific study of mind was through overt behavior. We can never know other minds directly, but only infer them in others from their behavior. Since scientific propositions deal with publicly observable events (i.e., those which can be verified by more than one person), then, the Behaviorists argued, the only concepts and laws proper for an objective science of mind are concepts and laws dealing with behavior itself.

Behaviorism was associated initially with John Watson, the psychologist who sought to elevate the conditioned reflexes of Pavlov to a general theory of all human behavior.[2] The movement culminated in the "learning theories" of the 1940's and 1950's, most notably in the baroque postulate system of Clark Hull, who elegantly explained all human and rat behavior in terms of learned habits motivated by biologically based drives.[3] Viewed historically, Behaviorism was a product of the times. The nineteenth-century achievements in physics and biology dethroned man from his seat at the feet of God and placed him within the rest of Nature. It was therefore proper to study man as one would study a newt or a molecule and to explain his workings mechanistically, without recourse to soul or vital spirit. Behaviorism came into being at a time when introspective methods, which had dominated academic psychology, appeared to be at a dead end. The derisive term "armchair psychology" suggested to Watson's contemporaries the futility of this approach.

Watson's position on the mind–body issue was that mental events were merely fortuitous by-products of bodily processes—not themselves of much significance and completely without causal influence. It was a position which has been termed *epiphenomenalism*—meaning that mental events were merely secondary to underlying brain events, but it implied that mind did not reflect anything very important about the brain.

Watson went to some length to explain thought in terms of peripheral events in the body. Small, covert muscle twitches in the lips, tongue, and throat produced subvocal speech, which for Watson subsumed most of human thinking, as he saw it. He and his followers were able to demonstrate that there were indeed such muscular accompaniments of thinking, and subsequent investigations have revealed that there are many interesting muscular correlates of thinking.[4] However, it is now known that muscular contractions themselves are not necessary for the internal events we call thinking. The most telling evidence against this theory comes from experiments with *curare,* a paralytic drug used by South American Indians as a poison. Curare blocks the transmission of impulses from motor nerves to the muscles which they control. An injection of the drug can cause complete paralysis of all skeletal muscles (including the muscles controlling the chest and diaphragm, making artificial respiration necessary during these experiments). Persons injected with curare, while often experiencing profound and terrifying effects, nonetheless report that they have no interruptions in consciousness. Watson's theory, in its strong form, at least, does not hold up.

Behaviorism dominated American psychology in this century until only very recently. There are a number of historical reasons for its domination, but primarily it was because Behaviorism was correct about science being a public enterprise. It is true that all of our inferences about the mental events of others must be made from their observable behaviors, including their verbal utterances. The behaviorism engendered by this proposition alone is less extreme than the one which denies altogether the importance of mental events. This less extreme position is called *methodological behaviorism,* to distinguish it from the earlier radical behaviorism of Watson. In the methodological sense, most modern scientific psychologists are behaviorists (with a small "b") since they no longer use introspective methods to test their hypotheses. It was partly the failure of the Behaviorists to account for the most interesting aspects of human activity in terms of conditioning and learning which led to its demise. But also, it was due to a growing realization that among the genuine concerns of psychology was its earliest: to account for thinking, perceiving, remembering, planning, and all those other events which we call "mental." The Behaviorists had thrown out the baby with the bath water.

Modern psychology, while behavioristic in the methodological sense, tries to deal with mind in terms of mechanism. The recent emergence from the Behaviorist era has seen a new growth of attempts to explain mind in mechanistic ways: the search for brain mechanisms underlying cognition, the use of information-processing systems as models for memory and attention, the simulation of intelligence by computers. Philosophically, the most challenging issue to arise from these mechanistic cognitive approaches is the question of whether it is possible to explain mind completely as a machine.

Can Machines Be Conscious?

For Descartes, the question of machine consciousness would be absurd, since God gave spirit to man only. True, animals were only mechanisms, not possessed of souls—but neither were they conscious beings. The human body itself, Descartes thought, was nothing but a machine without the soul to guide it, but the soul did guide, and that was how Descartes explained intelligent actions.

Today, however, the question of machine consciousness seems not quite so preposterous, because it is a fact today that there are machines—digital computers—which can play credible games of chess, make intelligent management decisions, or prove mathematical theorems. *Artificial intelligence,* as this discipline is called, demonstrably exists.[5] We use intelligent acts to infer sentience in others. Can we not, then, ask whether an intelligent artifact like a computer could ever have consciousness?

One objection to this line of speculation is that a computer's intelligence is severely limited by its not being able to do anything it has not been programmed to do. In a paper entitled "Computing Machinery and Intelligence," A.M. Turing gave a well-reasoned justification for not denying intelligence to machines. To the above objection, he replied that it could be justifiably argued that people, too, could not do anything they were not programmed to do, since the human brain is also "programmed" by its genetically determined state at birth and by the education and experience it subsequently receives. He asked, "Who can be certain that 'original work' that he has done was not simply the growth of the seed planted in him by teaching, or the effect of following well-known general principles."[6]

Many kinds of computer programs go beyond the specific instructions programmed into them, by learning to modify their behavior on the basis of experience with a task environment. One highly successful checker-playing program adjusts its strategies against human opponents, and it improves its play in this manner. Programs such as these invent lines of play that often surprise their originators. In fact, over a decade ago, checker-playing computer programs were available which could beat a human checker champion.[7]

Other games, and most real-life problems, are not so easy. Consider the problem of deciding upon which move to make at some point in a game of chess. You can make any one of, say, 15 alternative moves, and for each of these your opponent can make perhaps 15 different moves of his or her own. To each of these, you can reply in any one of 15 ways, etc. This situation is diagrammed in Figure 1-2.

FIGURE 1-2. Simplified decision tree for playing chess. At each point in the game, a player can choose from among 15 alternative moves (the actual number for a real chess game depends on the positions of the pieces at a particular point in the game). The task of evaluating all possible outcomes (branches) several moves ahead becomes enormous. (After E. A. Feigenbaum and J. Feldman, Computers and Thought, New York: McGraw-Hill, 1963.)

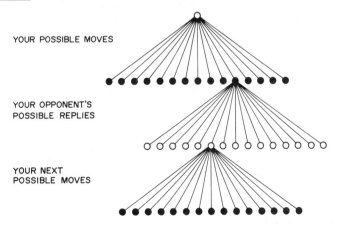

YOUR POSSIBLE MOVES

YOUR OPPONENT'S POSSIBLE REPLIES

YOUR NEXT POSSIBLE MOVES

This figure is what is known as a "decision tree." In this drawing, only one branch at each stage is depicted, but actually each node has an almost equal number of branches coming from it. It can be seen that even for a few moves ahead, all the potential consequences of any given move are enormous. A complete chess game of 50 moves, in our example, would generate a tree with 15^{50} distinct paths (the actual estimates, with more than 15 possibilities at each junction, are around 10^{120}), which is a very large number indeed.[8] It is so large, in fact, that no existing computer, or any computer possible to envision at present, could ever decide the best move to make in a human lifetime by searching the tree exhaustively. Chess-playing computer programs do what people must do: limit the number of moves which are considered at each level and also limit the depth of search (the number of moves ahead that you consider). This limiting is done in the computer by various rules of thumb, or heuristics, which prune the tree by considering only the moves which seem important. For example, one good chess heuristic is: don't explore very deeply any paths which place the queen in danger of capture.

Today we seem to be only a few years away from having computer programs which are impressively intelligent. As long ago as the early 1960's some computer scientists wrote and demonstrated the "General Problem-Solver," a program which solved many different kinds of logical and mathematical problems by incorporating problem-solving heuristics which transcend specific tasks. These techniques were derived from psychological studies which found certain general heuristic methods people use when they think through similar problems. For example, the program would try to prove theorems by deducing backwards from the statement to be proved to the known axioms, a technique many mathematicians say they use. Another heuristic was "means-end-analysis," in which the program tried to go from an ititial state to the target state by setting up a series of intermediate stages which bridge the difference between these states; then, work would proceed on realizing these intermediate goals. It is hard to see what differences there might be between this machine's thought processes and those of a college student working on the kind of problems which we use to judge the latter's intelligence.[9]

In use today are computer-operated devices which can read a page of text and translate it into human speech sounds. Several computer programs "understand"—i.e., parse— a wide range of English sentences and can respond to human questions with relevant and grammatical replies. Granted, the current state of the art of building smart robots is not very advanced by science fiction standards. But here, too, the future is almost upon us.

"Shakey" is a robot who lives in the rooms and corridors of the Stanford Research Institute in California. He is a complex electronic artifact with motor-driven wheels, touch-sensitive feelers, an optical range-finder, and a TV camera for eyes (see Figure 1-3). His "brain" is a large digital computer which communicates with Shakey's smaller "on-board" computer via radio-telemetry. The robot has remarkably good abilities to "perceive" and to manipulate objects in its environment. Given a room arrangement, Shakey can detect the location and shape of objects and barriers and construct a visual model of the room for its computer memory. This model is then used to guide it in navigating around the room and responding to problems typed into its computer. Given a problem such as "place the wedge next to the north face of the cube," Shakey can decipher the meaning of the command, locate the relevant forms in the room, and perform the requested action.

While it might seem that Shakey possesses no more of a mind than a trained chimpanzee, even this level of performance is extremely complex in terms of the millions of computer instructions which must be executed.

In principle, it would be possible to build a more impressive robot by incorporating the abilities of the most successful artificial intelligence projects into one machine. A true state-of-the-art robot would have Shakey's abilities to perceive and

FIGURE 1-3. "Shakey," a computer-controlled mobile robot, developed at the Stanford Research Institute. Shakey picks up visual information from range-finders and a TV camera, and tactile information from feelers. The robot is controlled remotely via a radio link to a digital computer, which acts as its brain. (Photo courtesy of SRI International.)

manipulate its physical environment, plus the abilities to solve many kinds of mathematical and logical problems, to decode a good deal of human speech and also to speak it grammatically and meaningfully, to read printed text, and to play a reasonably good game of chess.

Would the fact of this robot, if it were built, signify anything more than that man's own mind is clever enough to invent clever machines? Is Shakey to be regarded in the same category as an electric toaster? Are computers really intelligent, or do they just appear to be so?

There are semantic problems with this question, since the answer depends largely on how you define "intelligence." What is a fair definition? Must it involve "purpose"? If so, there are similar semantic difficulties, since it is commonplace to build purposive action into machines. An example is a thermostat.

A way out of this dilemma was suggested in the previously mentioned paper by Turing. *Turing's Test*, as it came to be known, was to put the machine in one room and a real person in a second room. A questioner would be able to communicate with either of these rooms, and, to make the game fair, assume that the communication is via teletypewriter. The questioner is free to ask any questions of either the machine or the real person (without, of course, knowing which was in which room). Such an interchange might go as follows:

Q. Please write me a sonnet on the subject of the Forth Bridge.
A. Count me out on this one. I never could write poetry.
Q. Add 34957 to 70764.
A. (Pause about 30 seconds and then give as answer) 105621.
Q. Do you play chess?
A. Yes.
Q. I have K at my K1, and no other pieces. You have only K at K6 and R at R1. It is your move. What do you play?
A. (After a pause of 15 seconds) R–R8, mate.[10]

Turing's Test involves deciding, through such interrogation, which room contains the machine and which the person. Turing argued that if one can't reliably decide, then the machine passes the test. Turing's Test is an *operational definition* for intelligence. That is, it's a definition in terms of the operations you would perform to determine the presence or absence of the quality "intelligence."

The larger question, however, is not one of intelligence in machines, but of the possibility of consciousness in machines.

Although what we mean by "conscious" or "sentient" can perhaps be separated from what we mean by "intelligent," we usually infer consciousness from observing intelligent actions. If we are to take seriously the possibility that mind can be explained in terms of mechanisms, then it would follow that it must be possible to build a machine which is conscious.

Is this even conceptually possible? Or is consciousness the sort of thing which relates only to biological tissue? Certainly, if you restrict the definition of consciousness to beings which have hair, or a body temperature near 98.6° F, or DNA, then, trivially, machines could never be conscious. But the same argument from analogy which we use to infer consciousness in other people can be applied just as well to the case of machines. Turing's Test furnishes a criterion for ascertaining one property of the analogy.

Can we ever know that a machine is conscious? Not with certainty, but we can't even know this for another human being. Still, it is interesting to ponder the future impact of the computer revolution on how humans conceive of consciousness. With the appearance of ever more intelligent artifacts which will converse with us, the temptation might be strong to regard mind as a property of complexly organized matter.

Philosophical Behaviorism

In this century, there has been a profound change in philosophical writings on traditional problems. Twentieth-century philosophers have been largely concerned, in one way or another, with the workings of language. This interest is entirely understandable, in view of the fact that language is the vehicle for communication of philosophical ideas.

In 1959 an Oxford philosopher named Gilbert Ryle published a book called *The Concept of Mind,* which came to be extremely influential in intellectual circles. In it, he attacked the whole mind–body issue as a pseudo-problem, a misunderstanding engendered by the improper use of language. Ryle's argument suggested that it was the structure of Indo-European languages (a class of which English and French are members) which caused this false issue to be drawn. In our language it is possible to refer to "the mind" and "the body" as if they were two separate and independent entities, like apples and pears. Ryle says that "mind" and other words which refer to mental events are different sorts of things altogether than physical objects, and that a mistake arises from using these categories as if they were of the same logical type. It would be like a foreigner coming to a college campus and, after seeing the library, offices, classrooms, and athletic fields, then asking, "But, where is the college?" Mind and body, Ryle says, are not two separate entities, but rather two ways of describing the same thing. Descartes's separation of the two, which Ryle satirizes as the "ghost in the machine," arises because of a category mistake, an improper use of the language.

For Ryle, what we know about other people's minds are always inferences from their behavior. Ryle is thus the philosophical counterpart of a Behaviorist.

Among other things, Ryle tried to show "that when we describe people as exercising qualities of mind, we are not referring to occult episodes of which their overt acts and utterances are effects; we are referring to those overt acts and utterances themselves." He extends this to an analysis of the concept of intelligence as a faculty of the mind: "The absurd assumption made is this, that a performance of any sort inherits all its title to intelligence from some anterior internal operation of planning what to do." In other words, Ryle says that most people believe in a myth that intelligent actions are merely the result of some intelligent mental operation just prior to the actions themselves. He continues: "What distinguishes sensible from silly operations is not their parentage but their procedure, and this holds no less for intellectual than for practical performances . . . 'thinking what I am doing' does not connote 'both thinking what to do and doing it.' When I do something intelligently, i.e., thinking what I am doing, I am doing one thing and not two. My performance has a special procedure or manner, not special antecedents." This is, of course, similar to the point made by Turing.[11]

It is the same, Ryle argued, with other mental concepts—they refer to observed actions, not really occurrences in a private place.

A major problem with Ryle's approach is that it cannot deal with what we call imagination. When I conjure up a mental picture of a racing car—one would say, "in my mind's eye"—this is a very private event and one which I know about very definitely. I know, for example, that it looks different than a mental image of an elephant or a bicycle. It is an event to which neither you nor any other person besides myself could have immediate access. In fact, the experience is every bit as real and definite for me whether or not I tell someone else about it. So, Ryle's argument is not universally true. Not all mental terms can be reduced to statements about behavior or dispositions to behave. Some kinds of mental experiences do not manifest themselves publicly.[12]

Wittgenstein and the Faculty of Introspection

Although subsequent philosophers have taken different positions from Descartes on many aspects of the mind–body issue, in this century a focus has been, as it was for Ryle, to question the basic distinction. Most philosophers have tacitly accepted the principle that one can have direct introspective knowledge of one's own inner thoughts, feelings, memories, intentions, etc., and that this kind of knowledge is more immediate and in some sense more basic than our knowledge of external things.[13] Introspection was said to be a faculty of the mind, and it was accepted as such by most philosophers and psychologists. Descartes's problem was formulated in terms of a Christian "soul" which could survive death and which could, therefore, exist in a disembodied state. The philosopher Ludwig Wittgenstein saw that this possibility rested on the assumption that one could have direct knowledge of one's own mind, knowledge which was logically prior to knowledge about all other things. If we did not have the faculty of introspection, then Descartes's separation of mind and body (on the basis of how we come to know about each) would become a fiction and the whole issue would disappear.

Wittgenstein's objection rested on his conviction about the importance of language in structuring human thought. He believed that language conditions all thought and forms its basis. He rejected the assumption that there can be direct introspection of one's own mind, because this kind of knowledge would then be independent of the influences of language, and that was an impossibility.

Most psychologists and philosophers would hold that we learn what mental words like "pain" mean by first observing, through introspection, occurrences of various headaches, backaches, toothaches, etc., and then associating the word "pain" to all these occurrences. Wittgenstein said this conception is false. He argued that we actually learn the concept of pain by learning the language, which includes the correct uses of the word "pain" and all of the social contexts in which the word may be applied.

He attacked introspection by attacking the notion that there ever could be such a thing as a "private language," by which he meant the conception of learning the meaning of mental terms, like "pain," from a private assignment of meaning to inner experiences. All concepts derive from language, which is necessarily a social product. Therefore, Wittgenstein argued, we cannot know concepts about our own mental processes before we have a language in which to describe them. And since language is a public and social enterprise, we learn about our minds by learning the language developed by a community of physical human beings.

So mental events are not known directly by introspection, but rather they are known indirectly through the filter of a language, which construes raw experience. By reversing the steps through which we learn about our mind, Wittgenstein tried to remove the basis for believing that mind could ever exist separate from the body. This would seem to remove the mystery of the relationship of mind to matter, because mind would be no longer a ghostly thing, but something altogether different.

For Wittgenstein, mental events are inherently impalpable. If you leave your house intending to go to the store but instead, out of habit, drive absentmindedly to work, then what exactly is the content of your "intention"? Wittgenstein would say that we use the term "mental" or "inner" here to point to the event's impalpability. It is a metaphor, a picture of something hidden and therefore unknowable. This is in contrast to the usual usage of the term "mental" to refer to a spiritual substance.[14]

A good example of how the terms we use influence how we think about our mental experiences was provided by the psychologist Theodore Sarbin. Sarbin researched the linguistic history of the concept "anxiety" and found that it was introduced into the English language from *anguisse,* a thirteenth-century French term which meant a painful sensation in the throat. Sarbin reasoned that the term was originally borrowed as a metaphor—that is, someone wishing to describe his particular emotional state referred to the feeling one gets when a fishbone is caught in one's throat. The expression caught on, and as it was spread further from the time and place of its origin, its original metaphorical meaning was lost. "Anxiety" was thus reified as a particular mental state. Sarbin saw this process as myth-making; anxiety as a concrete mental state was a myth when it was divorced from its metaphorical origin. He believed that such a "metaphor-to-myth transformation" characterizes the development of many mental-state concepts in human language. The implication is that our conceptions of many of our mental experiences are structured by the language we use to describe them, learned from a community of language users who all describe their "inner" experiences the same way. Divorced from their original underpinnings, the metaphors become opaque, and we accept the terms as concrete attributes of mind.[15]

Wittgenstein's position as a whole is hard to grasp. Is he saying that we can experience only things which we have words to describe? Is all of our knowledge verbal, propositional knowledge—knowledge which can be spoken, written down, or expressed in a logical statement?

The emphasis on language is understandable historically. The intellectual climate in the first half of this century was influenced greatly by anthropological and linguistic studies of primitive languages. The discovery by anthropologists that other people seemed to conceive of things a bit differently than we did was one of the strongest intellectual influences on this period. The person associated most closely with this idea was the linguist Benjamin Whorf. In one instance, Whorf found that Eskimo languages had many words for different kinds of snow (hard-packed white snow, hard-packed snow that looked like it had thawed and refrozen, etc.), and he argued that this meant that they must *perceive* and *discriminate* snow in a more sophisticated manner than we who must make do with one word, modified if necessary by a cumbersome string of adjectives.

In another study Whorf showed that some languages tend to structure events in terms of complicated actions where we would use a noun. For example, in the Hopi Indian tongue, the equivalent of "look at that *wave*" would be a phrase like "slosh," which described a complicated motion. Whorf claimed that this meant these people perceived the natural structure of physical events to be fundamentally different than the one which we perceive: composed not of constant and enduring objects, but rather as transient and ever-changing happenings, always in process, always becoming something else.

The view that language structures our perceptions of reality, a position known as "linguistic determinism," does not require that all thinking be in the form of words. Whorf said that most thought is an unconscious manipulation of "linguistic paradigms" or whole word classes "behind" or "above" the level of individual words themselves. This seems to say that it is the structure of the sentences in our language and its basic semantic categories which have the most profound effect on our thinking. Although Whorf's arguments are intriguing, much of the research that has been generated on the issue has failed to substantiate his hypothesis in its strong form.[16]

What, then, are we to make of Wittgenstein's assertion about the role of language in knowing our own minds? How much of our perception of our mental events is structured by the words we learned as children to describe our states of mind? It is a difficult issue, and one which seems impossible to settle on empirical grounds alone. There is now ample evidence, to be described later in this book, that a good deal of the cognitive machinery of our brains is devoted to nonpropositional, nonlinguistic kinds of knowledge—knowledge which could be described as visual or spatial. If this is so, then clearly not all of our knowledge is based on language or linguistic paradigms.[17]

Wittgenstein did not deny the inner event itself. He was rather more concerned with the meaning of the terms we use to describe these events, and so his concern was with how we conceive of these events. The fact remains that there are these events. Above all, there is the bare fact of consciousness itself which seems to call for explanation in its relationship to the material world.

Consider the not unlikely possibility that some day in the future medical experts will be able to extract an intact brain from a dying person and keep it alive *in vitro*. A special fluid in a large bowl would oxygenate and nourish it. It could be attached to wires which would mimic sensory messages, and other wires would lead from the motor areas of the brain and could provide outputs. It might even be possible, given proper knowledge of the speech code, to translate verbal messages into neurological codes and vice versa, and so talk to this disembodied brain and receive replies. The question is, would it be possible to say that the brain "felt a pain"? Or that "Harvey is angry"?

Linguistic philosophers such as Wittgenstein or Ryle would deny the meaningfulness of such a statement, because for them statements about mental events are meaningful only when spoken in relation to persons—to living, breathing human beings. Of course, it would be possible to regard Harvey's brain as a person, and most of us, after having a sensible conversation with it, would probably do so. We would have little trouble in attributing consciousness to Harvey's brain, and this in itself attests to the plausibility of regarding consciousness not as a linguistic construct but as a curious property of living brain tissue.

The Identity Theory: Consciousness as Brain Process

Materialism is a class of philosophical theories which dispense with the duality of mind and matter by holding that the universe is composed only of physical objects and their relationships. For a materialist, living beings are ultimately nothing but physical mechanisms.

While materialism is especially attractive as a scientific philosophy, it has always been troublesome for materialists to explain consciousness. However, one current version of materialism deals directly with the problem by regarding conscious experiences as being the same as some brain process. This view has been called the *identity theory*: it holds that mental processes and physical brain processes are one and the same thing—that is, they are identical to each other.

The meaning of this theory is not immediately obvious. How can a mental event—a desire, an intention, a toothache—be the *same* as the discharge of a group of neurons, say, in some particular physical region of the brain? U.T. Place, a leading advocate of this theory, said that it is the same sort of statement as "A cloud is identical with a mass of small particles in suspension" or "Lightning is in reality the motion of electric charges." What we have on the one hand is a phenomenon observed on a macroscopic level (cloud), and we determine, through scientific observation, that it is identical to, and explained by, some microscopic phenomenon (suspended particles).[18]

This does not mean that the identity of consciousness and brain process is a logically necessary one. Being afraid, for example, does not *mean* something occurring inside one's skull. Rather, the theory states that the identity is an empirical possibility, a scientific proposition which cannot be ruled out on logical grounds alone.

What identity means here, above and beyond mere correlation or causality, is that the two events said to be identical should occur in the *same place* and at the *same time*. This is the sense in which we say that a cloud is a mass of particles in suspension. So, the crux of the problem is: could it ever be determined that someone's thought or someone's pain occurred *inside his skull?* The philosopher J.A. Shaffer argues against identity theory in this way: "It would be as absurd to wonder whether that thought had occurred in my foot, throat, or earlobe as it would be to wonder whether that thought might have been cubical or a micron in diameter."[19] This puts us back to the distinction formulated by Descartes. Mind, being "unextended" stuff, needs to be explained in its relation to extended, material substance. Clearly, sensations are not the sorts of things that can be observed to be in a particular place. They are not, in fact, the kinds of things which can be "observed" at all. Rather, they are "experienced" or "had." So, one criterion for determining identity is impossible. We can observe correlations between brain processes in time and space, and mental experiences in time. If they are simultaneous and of the same duration, then a type of strong correlation is established—a coincidence of events in time, but not, strictly speaking, an identity.

Perhaps the matter can most fruitfully be put aside for the moment by regarding the identity theory as a working hypothesis, which is what most brain scientists seem to do anyway. Few of us today would deny that processes in the central nervous system in some sense underlie our mental experiences. And few of us, at least in our own personal experience, have any evidence of the occurrence of disembodied mind.

Yet, from time to time there are reports from people who claim to have left their bodies on occasion, sometimes to travel great distances as disembodied spirits. One of these reports, described in a recent book by Robert Monroe titled *Journeys Out of the Body*, describes many such experiences. While disembodied, Monroe claimed, he would eavesdrop on conversations of his friends, which he could then later reproduce to them to verify his story.[20]

Are we to tell Monroe, as Ryle would, that he was the victim of a category mistake? To do so would be to deny his experience, which for him was probably quite real. Of course, to be objective about the matter, neither would we accept his testimony unchallenged. The rarity of such experiences would induce us to try to explain them as dreams or, less charitably, as hallucinations. But some of us might still be bothered by the possibilities raised by these experiences, especially if they were to happen to us.

Even without considering disembodied consciousness, the mind–body issue is not put to rest by linguistic philosophical approaches like Ryle's or Wittgenstein's. Although the ways in which we construe our conscious experience are undoubtedly influenced by our language, there is just as undoubtedly a conscious experience that needs explaining. The mind–body question boils down to the fact of bare consciousness. How is it that all *this*, my experience of sitting in this chair and feeling its form around by body, viewing my desk and the paper on which I'm writing, hearing the singing of my child in the next room—how is it that all this *awareness* can arise from the motion of physical particles in three-dimensional space? Perhaps the very impossibility of even imagining the form of an answer to this question illustrates that it is beyond human abilities ever to understand the nature of the universe in scientific terms. But perhaps, also, an expanded knowledge about the workings of the brain might shed some light on the question—or at least mark the limits of the physical knowability of mind.

If the mind–body issue turns out ultimately to be one of those great insoluble questions, it does not at any rate appear to this writer at this point in time to be a meaningless one. The psychologist-philosopher William James once remarked that a glimpse into the mind–brain relationship would be "the scientific achievement before which all past achievements would pale."[21] It still may be that someday an increased knowledge of brain functioning will permit a greater understanding of this mystery. This book is a progress report.

These, then, are the kinds of issues which guide the organization of the book: What brain events occur when consciousness is present and when it is absent? Are there definable states of consciousness between the extremes of sleeping and waking? What neural mechanisms enable a cat to see prey or a human to see another human's face? How might thinking be carried on, and what parts of the brain specialize in what forms of thought? What is known about the physical basis of remembering?

In undertaking this quest for mind, no attempt will be made to be comprehensive about what is known about the brain. We will not say anything, for example, about the neural regulation of hunger and thirst, about which a good deal is known. Nor will we deal in any depth with emotions. While the selection of topics is always arbitrary, a survey of the issues raised in this section will hopefully benefit from a circumscribed treatment.

A Little Neurology

NOTE: *The final section of this chapter presents a brief introduction to the gross architecture and elemental components of living brains. Readers already familiar with these basics may skip to the next chapter.*

Figure 1-4 shows an overview of the human brain. The two *cerebral hemispheres,* which constitute the *forebrain,* are recent evolutionary developments which grew out of and which sit upon the much older and more primitive *brainstem* (thalamus, pons, medulla). The brainstem is a series of bumpy enlargements which form the upper end of the spinal cord. Incoming messages relay in the *thalamus* of the upper brainstem on their way to the cerebral hemispheres.

The brainstem is very old, in evolutionary terms, and for lower vertebrates, such as frogs, it encompasses nearly all of the animal's brain. In humans, the brainstem contains the circuits of "higher reflexes" which control breathing, cycles of waking and sleeping, body temperature, hunger, and thirst. The brainstem also contains primitive perceptual centers, like those which control the reflex movements of the eye muscles when something "catches your eye." Other higher reflexes are involved in the mechanisms of the *cerebellum,* the neurological computer which regulates and coordinates the movements of muscles in such activities as walking and standing upright.

The most striking feature of brain evolution in mammals is the growth of the forebrain out of the brainstem; in higher mammals (cats, monkeys, humans), the forebrain is so large as to completely bury the brainstem within. The outer layer of the forebrain hemispheres is a mantle of *cerebral cortex* (cortex means shell). The cortex consists of densely packed cells. It apparently underlies higher cognitive functions. The increase in cortical surface area creates the convolutions which so characteristically wrinkle the hemispheres of the human brain. This folding up of cortex enables more of the tissue to be packed into a skull of a fixed size (fixed by mother's pelvic anatomy).

The cerebral cortex also functions in perception and the control of action. Incoming sensory messages, in the form of nerve signals from the peripheral sense organs, create crisscrossing patterns in space and time. They are eventually relayed to receiving areas on the cortex. For example, there is a cortical area on the upper surface of each temporal lobe which receives

A

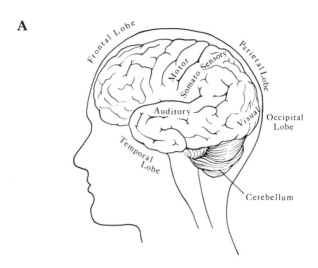

Frontal Lobe

Parietal Lobe

Motor

Somato Sensory

Auditory

Visual

Occipital Lobe

Temporal Lobe

Cerebellum

B

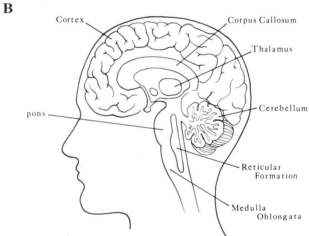

Cortex

Corpus Callosum

Thalamus

pons

Cerebellum

Reticular Formation

Medulla Oblongata

FIGURE 1-4. Two views of the human brain. (a) Side view, revealing the gross anatomy of the left cerebral hemisphere, in relation to the spinal cord and cerebellum. (b) Medial view, showing the inside surface of the right hemisphere and a slice through the cerebellum, brainstem, and spinal cord.

The spinal cord, running through the vertebra of the spine, transmits sensory messages to the brain and motor commands to the muscles. The upper end of the spinal cord forms the brainstem. Behind the brainstem is the cerebellum, which functions in the coordination of movement and posture. The brainstem is enveloped by the hemispheres of the forebrain. The outer surface of the hemispheres are wrinkled by the convolutions of the cerebral cortex (neocortex).

30

neural information originating in the ear. Other cortical areas are known to receive sensory information from the retina of the eye and from the surface of the skin. Still other cortical areas guide fine motor activities and organize muscular contractions into orderly programs of movement.

The main functional elements of the brain are thousands of millions of nerve cells, or *neurons,* which interconnect with each other in unimaginably complicated ways. Neurons are composed of a *cell body* and of fibers—called *axons* and *dendrites*—which project away from the cell body (see Figure 1-5a). Neurons are electrically active, and they continually change their electrical states. One change is the firing off of a brief

FIGURE 1–5. (a) Schematic drawing of a neuron. Incoming stimulation from other neurons and from sensory receptors changes the electrical potential across the membranes of the dendrites and cell body. If the change is large enough, the neuron fires off a spike potential which is propagated down the length of the axon, to modify the activity of other neurons or muscle fibers. (b) A neuron of the forebrain, illustrating the diversity of synaptic endings possible between nerve cells. Synaptic "spines" are found on different structures on the dendrites and cell body. Some synapses are excitatory, others inhibitory. The fine fiber at the bottom is the cell's axon. (From L. H. Hamlyn, "An Electron Microscope Study of Pyramidal Neurons in the Ammon's Horn of the Rabbit," *Journal of Anatomy,* 1963, **97**, pp. 189–201. Reproduced with permission of the publisher.)

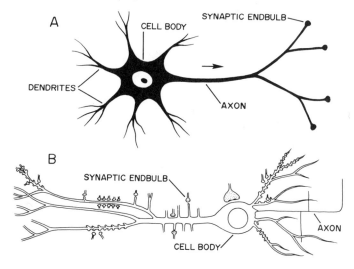

pulse of electrical negativity. The pulse travels rapidly down the axon at speeds of up to 200 m.p.h. This propagation of impulses, or *spike potentials,* as they are called, is the way neurons transmit messages. Sometimes, these messages travel over great distances: axons up to 3 feet long may emanate from cell bodies less than 1/100 inch in diameter. There is a great diversity of neuronal shapes and functions. Many neurons extend less than 1/100 inch, including dendrites and axon.

Another electrical change characterizes the activities of dendrites. Here, incoming axons from other neurons hook up to the cell, and the effects tend to be slower shifts in electrical charge. These charges wax and wane very slowly, compared to the spike potentials of the axons. Also, unlike the axonic impulses, which fire in an all-or-none manner, the electrical changes in dendrites tend to be graded, changing by degrees. If the dendrites and cell body reach a certain threshold of electrical negativity, then a spike potential will be generated at the base of the axon and transmitted —no longer graded—down to the tips of this fiber.

FIGURE 1-6. Three views of a small piece of brain tissue. (a) A portion of one of the folds of the cerebellum, showing a variety of cell types and interconnections. (b) A closer look at one of those cells, the large Purkinje cell. This cell is about $\frac{1}{3}$mm², counting the area of its dendritic tree structure (up to 200,000 branches). (c) A portion of one of the thinnest fiber branches, revealing synaptic spines which connect with passing fibers (in white). (From The Metaphorical Brain by Michael Arbib, New York: John Wiley and Sons, 1972. Reproduced with permission of the publisher.)

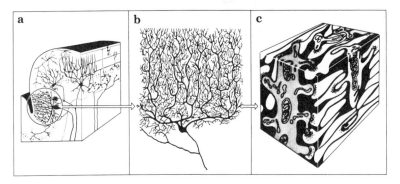

The places where nerve cells hook up are called *synapses*. A synapse transmits electrical information from the end of an axon branchlet to the cell onto which the axon terminates (see Figure 1-5b). The synapse is actually an extremely narrow space or cleft, which is bridged momentarily by chemical substances that are stored in the axon and released when the axon is fired. The chemicals travel across the cleft to electrically excite the receiving cell. In this way, the neurons of the brain form networks, through which the simple electrical messages of dendrites and axons become articulated into complex brain processes—processes which underlie behavior and thought.

Figure 1-6 gives a feel for the complexity of the brain by showing a piece of brain tissue under three different magnifications. In each view, the anatomical "grain" reveals complex interconnections between the building blocks of a tiny section of the brain. Considering that there are 10 billion nerve cells in the brain, the enormous organized complexity can be appreciated. Scientific understanding of this complexity is in its infancy.

Recommended Readings

PHILOSOPHY OF MIND

SHAFFER, J.A. *Philosophy of Mind*. Englewood Cliffs, N.J.: Prentice-Hall, 1968.

MALCOLM, N. *Problems of Mind: Descartes to Wittgenstein*. New York: Harper & Row, 1971.

BORING, E.G. *A History of Experimental Psychology*, 2nd edition. New York: Appleton-Century-Crofts, 1950.

CHAPPELL, V.C. (ed.). *The Philosophy of Mind*. Englewood Cliffs, N.J.: Prentice-Hall, 1962.

ARTIFICIAL INTELLIGENCE

RAPHAEL, B. *The Thinking Computer: Mind Inside Matter*. San Francisco: W.H. Freeman, 1976.

HUNT, E.B. *Artificial Intelligence*. New York: Academic Press, 1976.

THE BRAIN—GENERAL

GARDNER, E. *Fundamentals of Neurology*, 6th ed. Philadelphia: W.B. Saunders, 1975.

THOMPSON, R.F. *Introduction to Physiological Psychology*. New York: Harper & Row, 1975.

QUARTON, G.C., T. MELNECHUK, and F.O. SCHMITT, (eds.). *The Neurosciences: A Study Program*. New York: Rockefeller University Press, 1967.

SCHMITT, F.O. (ed.). *The Neurosciences: Second Study Program*. New York: Rockefeller University Press, 1970.

SCHMITT, F.O. and F.G. WORDEN, (eds.). *The Neurosciences: Third Study Program*. Cambridge, Mass.: M.I.T. Press, 1974.

Seeing

We say that a perceptive person has "insight." When we understand someone, we "see" what he means. To have "vision" means
to predict the future. These common expressions all emphasize
the fact that sight is our most highly developed sense. We
depend on it for information about our world to an extent even

2

greater than hearing, upon which human speech is based. Our most vivid memories are coded visually. We often remark that we saw something clearly in our mind's eye, but rarely that we heard something in our mind's ear.*

Because of its importance to us, more is known about the physiology and psychology of our sense of sight than of any other sense. This chapter will explore what is known and what is speculated about the physical basis of the ability to see. The tour will be selective, and it will center on processes which enable *pattern vision*—the recognition of visual forms in brain tissue and by machines. Much that is known about such things as the physiological basis of color vision and stereoscopic depth perception will not be covered, but what is presented will suffice for our purposes. By studying vision, we will also have a model which can represent the machinery of other kinds of perceptions.

The Visual System

The eye is frequently likened to a camera. Like a camera, it regulates the amount of light entering (with an iris), and it focuses an image (with a lens) onto a photosensitive surface (film, retina). The mosaic of receptor cells on the retina of the eye transforms light energy into electrical energy in nerve tissue. For this reason, perhaps a more modern analogy for the eye would be a TV camera.

In the center of the retina is an area called the *fovea*, which is packed very densely with receptors and provides for the clearest vision. Precise reflexes in the brain control the movements of the eyes so that points of interest can be analyzed by the detailed vision of the fovea. The very fact that the eye actively scans a visual scene means that the eye sends to the brain not a whole picture of what we see, but rather a sequence

*Never that we smelled it in our mind's nose!

of "visual snapshots," created by the abrupt flicks which characterize eye movement. One major problem for neuroscientists is to discover the means by which the brain integrates these loosely related pieces into the coherent visual image we see. Beyond the retina, any analogy of the visual system with a camera breaks down.

The retina is actually a piece of brain. It splits off from the brain relatively late in embryonic development, so it is neurologically complex. Unlike other sense organs, like the basilar membrane of the inner ear, the retina contains several layers of nerve cells, connected in orderly patterns. One function of these nerve networks is to increase the contrast of the retinal image (much like the contrast control circuit on a TV set). Contrast enhancement is an adaptive trait for the visual system to have evolved, because it accentuates edges, and edges are usually the most informative elements of the visual scene. The effects of retinal contrast enhancement can be seen in the familiar *simultaneous contrast illusion* (Figure 2-1). The neural mechanisms of retinal contrast enhancement are reasonably well understood, as a result of recent research findings with the eyes of the horseshoe crab *(Limulus)*.[1] These mechanisms furnish an explanation for certain aspects of seeing.

After relaying at a station deep within the brain, the fibers

FIGURE 2-1. The simultaneous contrast illusion. The small squares are all equal in brightness, yet they are perceived as differing, because their backgrounds differ. This effect is probably due to a retinal mechanism which accentuates contrast at borders.

of the optic tract project back to the visual cortex on the occipital lobe. Figure 2-2 shows that the right halves of each visual field project to the left hemisphere and the left halves to the right hemisphere. The drawing of Figure 2-2 was made in 1899 by the Spanish anatomist Ramón y Cajal, who discovered the nature of these connections. One aspect of this drawing was a guess by Cajal: that individual nerve cells in the cortex receive signals from both eyes. This conjecture has only recently been confirmed with the new techniques of recording the electrical activity from individual cortical cells. These "single-cell recording" techniques have revealed that approximately 80 percent of

FIGURE 2-2. The visual pathways. Fibers from the retinas from the optic nerves, which partially cross at their point of entry to the brain. After a single relay in the middle of the brain, the visual information is projected backward to the visual cortex. The crossing of the optic nerves is such that information from the right half of the visual field, in each eye, projects to the left hemisphere of the brain, and vice versa for the left visual half-field. (Drawing by the Spanish neuro-anatomist, Santiago Ramón y Cajal [1899].)

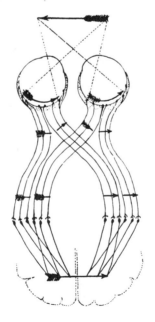

neurons in the primary visual cortex (the area receiving information directly from the eye) are responsive to stimulation from either eye. This anatomical arrangement is probably involved in the stereoscopic perception of depth, where information gathered from the two eyes is fused into a single "cyclopean retina."[2]

The primary visual cortex is also known as the *striate cortex,* because it appears striped in cross section. Beyond the primary cortex, there are neural connections to secondary visual areas surrounding it in the occipital lobe. These secondary areas, called *prestriate cortex,* have important roles in pattern vision discussed later in the chapter. The exact functions of prestriate areas are still unknown. The prestriate areas make connections with areas in many distant parts of the brain. The importance of these connections is also not well understood, and other anatomical connections are still to be discovered.

Each half-retina maps in an orderly fashion onto its primary visual cortex. The mapping preserves the relationships of neighboring points to one another, so that retinal points close to one another stimulate cortical points which are close. This fact has led to a popular misconception that the visual cortex acts as a viewing screen upon which the retina is projected. According to this misconception, the process of visual perception is then thought of as similar to seeing a movie. The idea is naive. What is usually implied in the movie analogy is that there is some tiny man—an "homunculus"—who sits in the brain and views the screen. Otherwise, who is watching the movie? The problem arises when we ask how the homunculus sees. Is there another, tinier homunculus inside his brain? Clearly there is no stopping point to this infinite regress.*

In addition to the visual cortex, there is another area of the brain which receives fibers from the optic nerve. This area is located on the back of the brainstem and is called the *optic*

---

*Some ancient peoples apparently believed in the homunculus theory because if you look closely into someone else's eye, you see a little person staring back at you (try this). As an explanation, it is similar to the position taken by Descartes (Chapter 1), with the soul playing the part of the homunculus.

tectum. In birds and amphibians—animals which have no visual cortex—this region constitutes the whole of their visual brain. In mammals, like us, the optic tectum functions to locate objects in the periphery of the visual field and then to guide head and eye movements toward them. Hamsters with damaged tectal regions fail to notice food objects in their paths. Yet they are quite capable of identifying abstract patterns for a reward, if these designs are placed right in front of their faces. Hamsters without the visual cortex, however, are unable to identify even the simplest of patterns, but they orient their eyes toward moving objects, and so they may appear to be seeing perfectly well.

Gerald Schneider, the physiologist who discovered these facts, concluded that mammals have two independent visual systems. One, the cortical system, enables the organism to see *what* a thing is. The other, the tectal system, alerts him that there is something there in the first place. It tells him where it is, where to look.[3] Precisely how this distinction between the two types of vision applies to human brains is not completely clear, since unlike hamsters, people are totally blind if they lose their visual cortex. Also, the optic tectum is so well buried beneath brain structures that cases of isolated tectal damage in people are unknown.

The Segmentation of Gestalts

At the level of the brain, the next business of seeing (next, at least in a psychological sense) is the segmentation of the visual scene into its component objects. The importance of this process of segmenting objects in the visual field from one another and from the background was pointed out early in this century by the Gestalt psychologists.[4] Figure 2-3 illustrates one aspect of this visual process and points out that the segregation of figure from ground is not so much a property of the visual objects themselves as it is a function performed by our nervous system.

FIGURE 2–3. Figure-ground organization. A goblet or two faces are seen, depending on how your visual brain segments the scene.

In 1932 a German psychologist named von Senden published a monograph which became widely quoted. It was a compilation of all reports in the medical literature of the experiences of blind persons who had undergone new forms of surgery designed to remove cataracts from their eyes. (A cataract is an opacity of the lens of the eye which can completely obscure vision). These patients were born with cataracts, and they were given sight for the first time in adulthood, after spending their earlier years in blindness. When the bandages were removed from their eyes, they typically were unable to understand the visual patterns which fell on their retinas. Although they obviously had new sensations of a visual kind, they could not, until after many weeks of experience with their new sense of sight, identify even the simplest kinds of objects—figures, like triangles or squares, which they had experienced throughout their lives by the sense of touch. Some of the difficulty was attributable to purely optical problems resulting from the surgery and from earlier disuse of the eye muscles. But much of it was not. To distinguish a triangle from a square, for example, patients would laboriously search out and count the corners of the figures. Even after a particular form had been well learned, it might become unrecognizable if it was illuminated by colored light.

Despite the fact that elementary pattern vision was not initially available and had to be exercised or learned, there was an even more primitive ability which was often present from the beginning: the ability to segregate objects in the visual field and distinguish them from background. Even before they could see what the objects were, the cataract patients could see how many there were. If von Senden were writing his monograph today, he might be tempted to hazard the guess that this figure-ground property of visual perception was mediated by tectal vision. In any event, the experience of these patients indicates that the process of segmentation from one another of forms in a visual scene may be separate from the task of identifying the objects themselves.[5]

One approach to understanding how the brain enables us to see is to try to build a machine which "sees," in the sense of correctly identifying objects on the basis of their figural properties. Typically, this involves hooking up an electronic eye, such as a TV camera, to a computer. The task then boils down to programming the computer to translate the visual information, coded as points of differing light intensity, into perceived objects (e.g., "3 chairs and a table in location X").

Computer scientists who work on this problem often find that, analogously to human vision, the first stages must involve some sort of segmenting into unified forms, or Gestalts. One solution to this problem is illustrated in Figure 2-4.

Pattern Recognition

The ability to recognize a face as a face and a tree as a tree is the most fundamental and important of all aspects of human vision. It is a process which is usually so efficient that we take it completely for granted (see Figure 2-5). Pattern recognition is

FIGURE 2-4. Region analysis from a computer program that "perceives." In the first column, the computer has analyzed the TV picture into regions of equal brightness. The second and third columns show steps in the simplification of the scenes into fewer regions, which correspond to meaningful areas in the picture. This process is analogous to the segmentation of Gestalts in human vision. (From The Thinking Computer: Mind Inside Matter by Bertram Raphael. San Francisco: W. H. Freeman and Company, Copyright© 1976.)

at the very crux of the mind–body issue. It is the process of giving meaning to visual sensations. How is it that we can organize the myriad impulses coming upstream from the retina—sensations which have never appeared in that exact configuration, or size, or place, or orientation in the visual field—and correctly see them as a familiar object? Or, more difficult still, how is it that we can visually identify something we have never encountered before, such as a new automobile, or an unusual flower?

Consider a computer-driven robot, like Shakey (see Chap-

FIGURE 2-5. Pattern vision is an interpretive process, an activity. The process becomes apparent when stimulus conditions become degraded, as in this photograph. Once the identification is made, the process runs off quickly and smoothly, so that the figure is immediately seen on subsequent viewings. See the footnote on page 46 to see if you could discover the figure in this picture. (Photo by H. H. Pittman from the National Audubon Society Collection. By permission of Photo Researchers, Inc.)

ter 1), equipped with a TV camera and range-finder for eyes, mechanical hands, and motor-driven wheels. Now, tell this computer to walk into your bedroom and bring back your comb.

If all the previous glimpses of combs had fallen on exactly the same place on the robot's video retina, then there would be no problem. Our computer would "digitize" the retinal image into a grid of zeros or ones, or some other representation of light intensity at points on the TV screen. The internal pattern representing a comb could be simply the list of points making up this configuration (see Figure 2-6a). The digitized TV image would need only to be tested for congruence to the internal pattern.

But consider: to be effective, the robot must be able to recognize the image of the comb no matter where on the screen it happens to fall and at many different possible orientations (Figure 2-6b). Also, as the robot moves about the room, the comb's projected size on the video screen changes enormously, yet the computer must not be confused into thinking that it sees different objects (Figure 2-6c). Finally, our robot must be able to identify any number of actual shapes as instances of the same pattern ("comb"), just as we do—even if some of the teeth are missing, or if it is more elongated than combs the robot has seen before, or if the spine of the comb is fat, or if it's thin, square, or rounded. It is remarkable that the task of finding a comb among all the other objects in a room is a task which we can perform in a few moments.

This hypothetical scheme for pattern recognition is called *template-matching*, because it involves the matching of an incoming stimulus pattern to an internal idealized form, or template. A template-matching process is used by the machines in banks which automatically read account numbers from checks. However, unlike a check's account numbers, a visual stimulus in real-world environments can be of a different size, orientation, or position in the visual field than on the template.

FIGURE 2-6. Hypothetical computer-robot trying to find a comb. In (a), the robot learns the pattern for a comb by recording the configuration as a template. In (b), the robot fails to recognize the comb, because it is oriented differently on the robot's retina. In (c), recognition fails because the robot is standing further away and the projected size of the image is too small. This example illustrates that a simple template-matching process fails as a model for pattern recognition.

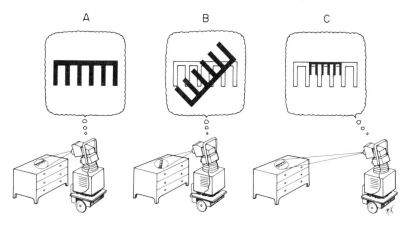

A   B   C

Several attempts have been made with computer programs to counter this problem by introducing another stage prior to template matching. This "preprocessing" stage would normalize every input to a standard position, size, and orientation, based on its geometric properties. However, slight deviations in shape from the template could still produce mismatches. More sophisticated prepocessing stages would complicate the model sufficiently so as to constitute the bulk of the mechanism. That is, most of the intelligence of the pattern recognizer would occur in preprocessing stages, and so it would no longer be a template-matching theory.[6]

As computer technology has developed, the opportunity has arisen for building intelligent robots for such things as unmanned space exploration. This technological opportunity has led to much of the current understanding of the difficulties of pattern recognition. The psychological study of pattern vision in man and animals has benefited from collaboration with computer science, because theoretical formulations of processes for seeing must be made perfectly explicit before they can be implemented by a computer.

Logically, the process of pattern recognition must involve first, what the psychologist Jerome Bruner has called an act of "categorization."[7] The inputs to the system, whether a human (brain) system or a mechanical (computer) system, are diverse instances of the pattern, which are classed together at the output stage as belonging to the same category. "Tree" would be one such category, or perhaps "elm tree." "My dentist Sheldon's face" could be another. By using the term "categorization," Bruner does not mean that the process is verbal or even conscious. Much of it, certainly, is not available to conscious inspection. Probably we are aware of just the output of the process—the identification itself—which we call "seeing." Dogs and other animals must be able to do the same sorts of things in order to perceive in their worlds. And the process must be so

* The figure in photo 2-5 is a camouflaged rifleman.

rapid and efficient as to allow us to recognize the moving object in the corner of our visual field as a lady stepping off the curb, even as we continue to listen to the car's radio.

We probably would want to add that a unique category cannot be retrieved for every form that we perceive. In that case we would never be able to account for seeing something new; our experience would consist entirely of known categories like "the elm tree on Waverly Place." The categories must be *schematic;* that is they must represent such things as abstract or average elm trees. Several relevant schematic categories would be output for every unique visual object input to the system. One could think of a newly seen tree activating schematic categories relevant to individual trees one has seen in the past, to telephone poles (if it is tall and thin), or to hedges (if it is short and fat), etc.

A second logical point about the processes involved in pattern recognition is that they must ultimately involve contact with some representation of visual experience "stored" in some form of memory. At some stage, the current state of the visual system must be matched to previously known states in order for the act of categorization to take place. The most difficult questions for brain theory are "In what form are the objects being matched?" and "How does the visual stimulus get abstracted into that form?"

The Tuning of Visual Neurons

One important line of evidence bearing on these questions has come from laboratory investigations of the electrical activity of individual neurons in the visual systems of animals. This research was aimed at finding out what characteristics of visual stimuli individual nerve cells are sensitive to. It involves the use of extremely fine-tipped *micro-electrodes,* made of metal or glass drawn out so finely that they can be less than 1 micron (1/1000mm) at the tip, so small that they cannot be seen with ordinary light microscopes. With the aid of these electrodes, physiologists were able to pick up the electrical activity emanating from single neurons.

Using a delicate mechanical micro-manipulator, the physiologist sinks a micro-electrode into a mass of living brain tissue, moving it tiny fractions of a millimeter at a time, until a neuron is found. Often there is considerable probing until the electrode is positioned effectively, since the brain's mass contains other kinds of supportive cells separating the neurons. Eventually, the electrode comes close enough to a neuron, and this event is signaled by a burst of static from a loudspeaker connected to the electrode via amplifiers. The static is caused by a train of spike impulses which characterize the activity of nerve cells. By moving spots of light or more complex shapes in front of the experimental animal's eyes, changes are observed in the firing rate of the cell which is being monitored, and it is found by this method that different cells are "tuned" to specific types of stimuli as well as to specific places on the retina.

In 1959 a group of researchers at M.I.T. investigated the visual system of the frog with these techniques, and they came up with a curious finding. All of the neural units going toward the frog's brain from the frog's retina could be classified into a few distinct types:

a.   Type 1 cells, or *contrast detectors,* fire maximally when a boundary between a light and a dark region remains stationary in the proper part of the visual field for that neuron. (Every visual neuron has a particular area on the retina to which it is responsive. Stimulation outside of this area produces no response.)

b.   Type 2 cells are *net-convexity detectors,* which respond maximally to small, dark, convexly curved boundaries of a certain small size (about 2 to 3 degrees of visual angle). Furthermore, the unit responds only if this stimulus moves across its region of the visual field. The response is strongest to small, black spots which move in a jerky motion and it ceases if the object comes to a halt.

c. Type 3 cells, or *moving-edge detectors,* respond to any light-dark boundary (edge) which is in motion across a relatively large region of the visual field.

d. Type 4 cells are *net-dimming detectors*—cells which respond to a sudden dimming of the illumination. Like Type 3 neurons, these units are also sensitive to stimuli of the proper type over a wide area of the visual field.[8]

The curious finding of these experiments is that they showed that the information the frog's eye sends to the frog's brain is already in a very highly coded form. Furthermore, the code makes a great deal of sense in terms of the animal's survival needs. The net-convexity detectors (Type 2) appear to be flying bug perceivers, and Types 3 and 4 seem ideally specialized for signaling the sudden approach of a large predator!

This kind of preprocessing of visual information at the retina would seem well suited to an organism, like the frog, which interacts with its environment in a highly stereotyped manner. The frog has no visual cortex, its main visual brain being the evolutionarily older optic tectum of the brainstem, discussed earlier. Frogs are very skilled at snatching flies out of the air with precise darting movements of their long tongues. They are also moderately capable of eluding the grasp of a human child. Frogs are not very good, however, at adapting their behavior to a changing environment. A frog will starve to death if it is up to its knees in freshly killed but immobile flies. For such an organism, the quick detection of a few critical features seems to have considerable survival value.

Animals with more highly evolved brains can adapt better to changing environmental circumstances by learning to modify their behavior in substantial ways. So, it might be expected that among higher vertebrates the information sent upstream from the eye would be less highly coded or of a more general kind of information, more useful for an adaptable brain to interpret according to changing interests.

This expectation has been confirmed. Similar kinds of experiments carried out on the visual systems of cats and monkeys (mammals, like ourselves) reveal that the information sent up the optic nerves of these animals is information mostly about *place*—locus of stimulation in the visual field—rather than about more abstract properties of the stimulus. The optic nerve of mammals preserves the image falling on the mosaic of retinal receptors, and it is only at a much later stage—at the cortex—that information is extracted from the image.

The place in the visual field from which a particular neural unit responds to stimulation is termed the *receptive field* of that neuron. Receptive fields of a nerve fiber coming from the retina typically look like the one in Figure 2-7a. Cells with such

FIGURE 2-7. (a) Receptive fields of cells of the optic nerve. Light falling within the area marked "+" tends to fire the cell, whereas light falling within the "−" region inhibits it. The first cell responds when its center is stimulated by light; the second when the center is darker than the surround. Neurons with these concentric types of receptive fields signal visual contrasts (borders and edges). (b) Receptive fields of cells in the visual cortex. These cells are also sensitive to contrasts, but because of their elongated shapes, the optimal stimuli are slits, bars, and edges in the proper orientation. In (i), the stimulus is aligned properly, and so excitation exceeds inhibition. In (ii), the stimulus has no effect.

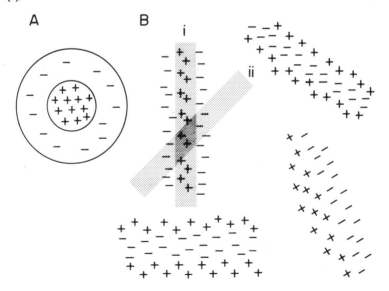

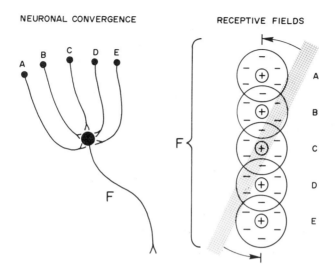

NEURONAL CONVERGENCE   RECEPTIVE FIELDS

FIGURE 2-8. Anatomical convergence of cells from the visual pathway onto cells in the visual cortex. This arrangement, which is believed to characterize projections to the visual cortex, would have all the properties of cortical line detectors. Cells from the optic tract (a–e) converge on cortical neuron f, so that excitation of any one of them will excite f, and excitation of more than one will excite f more strongly. The receptive fields of these cells are illustrated at the right of the figure. The incoming neurons have concentric receptive fields, but their centers are all aligned, so that stimulation anywhere in the broader region will excite cortical cell f.

receptive fields will respond to light falling anywhere within the central area (marked by "+"s) with a diameter of .1 to 1 mm in a particular place on the retina. The retinal cells preserve the features of the retinal image, point by point.

At the visual cortex, however, a transformation occurs. Cortical cells respond best to lines and edges. Typical receptive fields of cells in the striate cortex are shown in Figure 2-7b. Cells at this stage in the visual system are line detectors. They signal information about the occurrence of lines and edges in specific orientations at specific places in the field. A simple type of anatomical convergence, at the cortex, of incoming neurons with adjacent receptive fields would account for the behavior of line detectors (see Figure 2-8).

Beyond the primary visual cortex, and into the secondary, prestriate zone, the receptive fields still respond to lines and edges, but they are more "abstract." That is, these cells respond not to lines in definite places in the field, but rather to lines of the proper orientation anywhere within a larger region.

The discovery of these abstract cells in the cortex suggested a solution to the problem, discussed earlier, of how a pattern could be recognized no matter where on the retina it fell. Prestriate cells detect features of a stimulus abstractly, not tied to a particular place in the field.

The most successful computer schemes for recognizing patterns rely on processes for extracting features. A list of these features constitutes an abstract representation of the pattern. Prestriate cells in the brain may function like the computer's feature detectors. Some of these cells respond only to lines moving in a certain direction. Others have even been observed which respond maximally to corners or angles.[9]

The fact that individual cells of the visual cortex have such precise "tuning characteristics" raises the possibility that there might exist, elsewhere in the brain, cells which are tuned to even more abstract features of a visual stimulus. The process of feature extraction in visual cortex would seem to serve as the first major stage in the neural machinery for pattern vision.

It is tempting to speculate on how far the idea of anatomical convergence can be taken. It is possible to imagine hierarchically organized sets of feature detectors in the brain with greater and greater specificity (in terms of the features they respond to) and greater and greater generality (in terms of the different sizes or orientations of target stimuli they accept). Perhaps some cells would fire only when a yellow object moved horizontally across the field, and perhaps these neurons and other similar ones would converge on a still higher-order cell which responded, for example, only to yellow Volkswagens.[10] But "yellow Volkswagen neurons" seem implausible on a number of grounds.[11]

Pandemonium and Feature Analysis

The first convincing demonstration that a computer could recognize patterns in a sophisticated way was accomplished with a program called "Pandemonium," written in 1959 by Oliver

Selfridge. This program relied on feature detection, and so might be considered similar in operation to the visual cortex. Pandemonium was able to do such things as identify handwritten letters—characters like those shown in Figure 2-9. The program was also capable of learning from its perceptual experience, and it would improve its performance as it went along.

Pandemonium operates on a grid of 32 × 32 picture elements which serves as its retina. A particular object to be recognized is represented to the computer as a pattern of "1"s and "0"s on the grid, depending on whether or not a grid element was covered by the pattern. The computer program operates on this matrix to extract features from the pattern, such as the number of intersections of lines or whether or not there is a downward-pointing angle.

The list of features the program generates for a pattern on its retina would be compared "in parallel" with criterion lists of features for every object the computer had stored in its memory. That criterion list which had the closest fit to the input pattern's list was identified as the answer.

Figure 2-10 shows a fanciful illustration of this parallel process, represented here as a group of "demons," all shouting at once (a "pandemonium"). Demons being very egotistical, each

FIGURE 2-9. Recognizable specimens of hand-printed A's. Though different, these patterns are all identified by "Pandemonium." (After U. Neisser, Cognitive Psychology, New York: Appleton-Century-Crofts, 1967. Reprinted by permission of Prentice-Hall, Inc.)

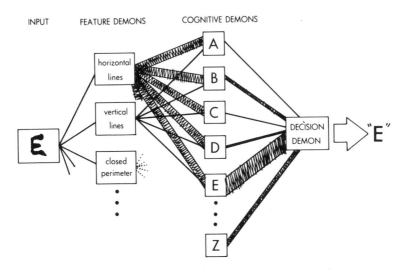

FIGURE 2-10. Pandemonium, a computer program which recognizes patterns. The input image (a hand-printed letter) is analyzed by "feature demons," and each feature demon shouts loudly or softly, depending on the degree to which it finds evidence of itself in the image (demons are very egotistical). Cognitive demons listen to the shouts of the feature demons. A cognitive demon shouts whenever it hears evidence of its own features. The chorus of shouts (the "pandemonium") is heard by the decision demon, who guesses what the pattern is. The decision demon can take into account such external factors as the letter preceding the in-letter being analyzed.

looks for evidence of his representation in the input pattern and shouts very loudly when he finds it. He shouts as loudly as he is certain of having seen himself. Ultimately, a "decision demon" weighs each shout (because, even among demons, some opinions are worth more than others), and comes to a decision. The "cognitive demons" themselves weight the shouts of "feature demons" at the next level down. It is by adjusting the weights at these stages, on the basis of success or error in identifying a pattern, that the program can learn.

The performance of Pademonium on the task of identifying handwritten characters was quite respectable: on one test it made only 10 percent fewer identifications than people did. This program was an early attempt, and subsequently even more sophisticated pattern-recognition devices have appeared. The extraction of features has proved to be a viable procedure for most of these programs, and it is a curious fact that Pandemonium was invented at about the same time as feature detectors were discovered in the visual cortex.[12]

Some recent lines of thought suggest that the feature which the human visual system extracts may be the "spatial frequencies" which comprise an image. Spatial-frequency analysis is similar to methods used by electronic engineers to decompose a complicated wave form (a radio wave or a sound wave) into its component pure sine waves. In the case of vision, we can talk of a pattern's being composed of waves of brightness, waves rising over bright regions and falling over darker ones, and the mathematical decomposition of this complicated wave would result in a list of the individual frequencies (cycles per degree of visual angle) which make up the complex pattern. This list is called a *spatial-frequency spectrum,* and it would serve, in a pattern-recognition scheme, as a list of features. One current theory is that cortical line detectors reflect part of the mechanism for extracting spatial-frequency information from visual patterns.[13]

Figure 2-11 shows a curious visual phenomenon which can be explained by the spatial frequency theory. This block portrait was produced by taking a famous painting and averaging the brightness values within each little block area. The portrait is unrecognizable, until we blur the image (try squinting hard at it through almost closed eyelids, or viewing it from a far distance). This is paradoxical, because blurring actually removes optical information! The paradox is resolved when the picture is analyzed in terms of its spatial frequencies. When this is done, it is found that blurring removes the spatial frequencies produced artificially by the edges, frequencies which act as visual "noise" to mask the frequencies of the face.[14]

Equipotentiality and Neural Holograms

A number of facts about visual perception suggest that the neural circuitry involved in pattern vision is both more complex and more obscure (in terms of present-day knowledge) than

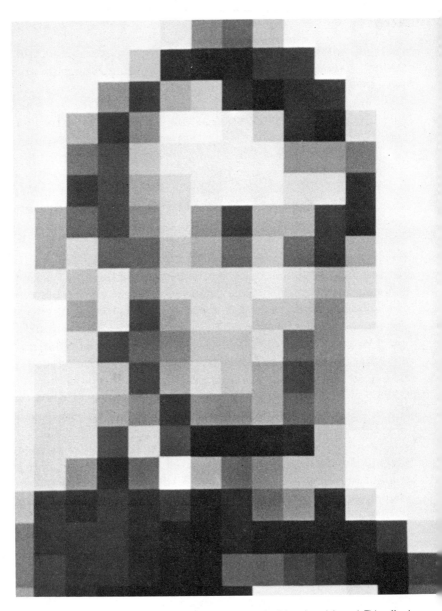

FIGURE 2–11. Block portrait, which becomes recognizable when blurred. This effect is believed to be due to spatial-frequency interactions in the visual cortex. (From L. D. Harmon and B. Julesz, <u>Science</u>, 1973, Vol. 180, no. 4091. Reproduced with permission of the publisher and the authors.)

one might expect from considering the evidence on feature coding. One of these basic facts was uncovered over 30 years ago, in a series of experiments by the neuropsychologist Karl Lashley.

Lashley wanted to find out where in the brain a physical memory record ("engram" was his term for this) was stored. In what particular area was contained the neural representation of a visual experience, a remembered discrimination between patterns? Lashley's technique was to cut out pieces of a rat's brain, after training the animal to jump at one of two doors to get food. Each door was painted with a different geometric design, and a hungry rat learned to discriminate between the two patterns in order to be rewarded with food. Lashley argued that the learning process must involve some modification of brain tissue because that is what memory fundamentally is, in neuronal terms. Lashley's method was systematically to remove different areas of visual cortex in different animals to find out which areas were critical to the memory of the learned visual discrimination. Lashley reasoned that the engram must be in the visual cortex, because total destruction of this area resulted in the rat's being unable to perform a simple visual discrimination, while the destruction of other cortical areas did not seem to be critical.

What Lashley concluded from his experiments was that the engram was in no particular place, and so it must be everywhere! He could remove up to 80 percent of a rat's visual cortex and still not make the animal unable to perform what it had learned. As long as there was some small remnant of visual cortex—and it didn't seem to matter which part of the visual cortex—the rat could perform the discrimination. On the basis of this result, Lashley proposed what he called the principle of *equipotentiality* of cortical tissue, which stated that within a functional region (like visual cortex) any piece of tissue was equal to any other in its ability to mediate the learned behavior. The principle implied that the engram, rather than being localized in a particular set of neurons, was distributed all over the visual cortex.[15]

For Lashley and his followers, the implications of this

finding were not restricted to memory alone. Equipotentiality
was taken to mean that whatever process underlies pattern
vision, it too must be distributed equipotentially over the cortex
and not contained in isolated pathways. This phenomenon was
not only demonstrated in Lashley's experiments, but it seemed
to follow from the facts of stimulus equivalence in pattern
vision. That one can recognize a figure anywhere in the visual
field seemed to Lashley to argue for a neural process which
involves the whole of the cortical tissue. The perception of
patterns must involve neural activities which transcend local
excitation.

Today, we can see that this last argument is unfounded, in
the light of what is known about feature extraction. But, still,
there were compelling visual phenomena in humans which
seemed to Lashley to parallel equipotentiality in rats. These
were the well-known *completion effects*. When a small part of the
visual cortex in man is damaged, either by a wound or by a
stroke, or only temporarily by the constriction of blood vessels
accompanying migraine headaches, the person suffers a blind
spot *(scotoma)* in the visual field. The precise location of a
scotoma can be mapped with small spots of light, and the
location of the scotoma accurately predicts the part of the visual
cortex which is affected. Although mapping the visual field with
spots of light might disclose definite holes in the visual field,
within which nothing can be detected, often people with scotomas do not see these holes, but rather they "complete" or fill in
this area so that it appears continuous with the rest of the field.
Lashley, who himself had attacks of migraine, described such an
experience:

> Talking with a friend, I glanced just to the right of his face,
> whereon his head disappeared. His shoulders and necktie were
> still visible, but the vertical stripes in the wallpaper behind him
> seemed to extend right down to the necktie. Quick mapping
> revealed an area of total blindness covering about 30 degrees. . . .

It was quite impossible to see this as a blank area when projected on the striped wall or other uniformly patterned surface, although any intervening object failed to be seen.[16]

The completion across visual scotoma is so strong as to hide the fact that there is normally a blind spot in everyone's visual field at the *optic disc*. The optic disc is an area on the retina, 15 degrees from the fovea, where the blood vessels which nourish the retina enter and where the ganglion fibers exit to form the optic nerve. Because there are no rods or cones in this region, it is blind. You can observe this fact by closing one eye and fixating a spot on the wall with the other. Holding a pencil at arm's length near the fixation spot, slowly move it toward the outside of the visual field, all the while maintaining fixation on the spot. Soon you will see the tip of the pencil disappear and then reappear again as it emerges toward the periphery of the field. The fact that we are not normally aware of this hole in our vision is but another example of the completion phenomenon.

Lashley's experimental findings and the facts of scotoma completion point to the existence of a distributed visual process—distributed in the sense of not being tied to specific networks of neurons. What this process might be remains a puzzle, but an interesting analogue has now been found in the new technology of holograms.

A *hologram* is an optical system which uses a laser beam to record and reproduce three-dimensional visual images. Holography is like photography in that both methods record visual information on a photographic plate. But whereas an ordinary photograph records the reflected light from one point on the object at only a single point on the film, every point on the hologram records the entire picture. In a sense, the hologram "freezes" the entire unfocused wave front of light reflected from an object. The information is stored in the form of an interference pattern, which is recorded on the photographic plate.

Upon viewing the hologram, which is accomplished by shining a laser beam through the plate, the original wave front is reconstructed.[17] (See Figure 2-12.)

The advantages of holography over conventional photographic methods of image storage are several:

1. The information contained in the hologram is three-dimensional and not confined to one focal plane. A viewer can focus his eyes on any number of planes of depth in the reconstructed image, and to some extent it is even possible to view in depth around the sides of the image.

2. A large number of different images, in the form of interference patterns, can be stored on the same photographic plate. The angle of incidence of the laser beam and its wavelength determine which particular image is retrieved from the hologram.

3. The hologram is resistant to damage. The information contained in it is distributed and reduplicated as an interference pattern over the whole photographic plate, so that any piece of the hologram, no matter how small, will suffice to reconstruct the entire image. Destruction of parts of the hologram affects only the resolution (how much detail can be seen) in the reconstructed image.

The relevance of holograms to the neurophysiology of vision should be obvious. This last property is precisely the mysterious equipotentiality which Lashley found in the visual cortex!

There are other variants on the holographic method described above. In a procedure called *association holography,* the laser reflection from two objects, *A* and *B,* can each serve as the reference wave for the other. That is, rather than having an unperturbed laser as a reference beam for interference with the wave front reflected from an object, two complex wave fronts—one a laser reflection from *A* and one a laser reflection from *B*—interfere with each other to produce a holographic

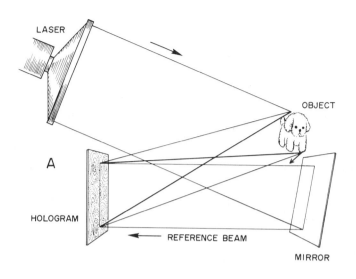

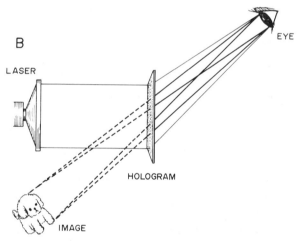

FIGURE 2-12. Holography. (a) Laser light, reflected from the object, interacts with an undisturbed pure laser beam to produce an optical interference pattern, recorded on film as a hologram. (b) The image of the object is reconstructed by shining a laser beam through the hologram, releasing the complex wave front originally recorded. Some theorists believe that there are holographic-like processes in the brain which underlie pattern vision. (After "Photography by Laser" by E. N. Leith and J. Upatnieks, © 1965 by Scientific American, Inc. All rights reserved.)

pattern. With this arrangement, the presence of a wave front from A is necessary to reconstruct from the hologram a ghost image of B.[18]

An association hologram is a compelling model for the brain process underlying vision, because in addition to having equipotentiality, it can also be used as a device for recognizing patterns. With some kinds of association holograms, different instances of the input pattern's reflection of laser light could reconstruct the same output image. In one case, holograms have been constructed which, when illuminated by a laser projection of a human face, respond with an optical image of that person's name. Since many images could be stored on the hologram simultaneously, the system could serve to recognize a large number of patterns.

As a pattern recognizer, an association hologram has translational invariance. That is, it doesn't matter where on the hologram the image falls. It follows from the fact that the information is distributed and reduplicated over the entire hologram that the image can be retrieved from any part of it. However, holograms are not size invariant, except in the reverse sense: changing the frequency of the laser alters the size of the retrieved image.

An associative hologram would also provide a mechanism for the completeness of vision. Earlier, it was pointed out that the eye sends a series of "snapshots" to the visual cortex—a piecewise sampling of the visual world, and not the complete images which we experience. The hologram solves this problem. Under some circumstances, association holograms can be constructed in which parts of an image interfere associatively with one another, so that the whole image will appear when the hologram is illuminated by any part of the input. (The other type of visual completeness, the completion of scotomas on the hologram itself, would of course be a property of all holograms, because they display equipotentiality.)

Holography presents another example of the curious effect technological discovery has on scientific discovery. The laser hologram had not been invented for two years before several brain theories simultaneously saw that it could serve as a model for the wholistic brain process for which Lashley argued.[19] One of these, the neuropsychologist Karl Pribram, believes that hologram-like processes in the brain might form the basis for all of our conscious experiences and set these events apart from the majority of neural occurrences which do not result in awareness.[20] Another of these theorists, the psychologist Bela Julesz, put the matter this way:

> If a few years ago someone had presented us with a black box having a few seemingly ad hoc properties (such as the ability to store several images without interfering with each other; the closer an input image resembled its stored version the sharper the recall; the fact that an input in the form of a segment of a stored image may retrieve the entire memory; the invariance against horizontal and vertical shifts of the input; the insensitivity of this storage against large destruction of the black box, etc.) we would have answered without hesitation that the box contained a piece of cortex of some higher animal. Yet, now a few years later we would not be so certain and would give a somewhat different answer. We would say that the box contained either a peice of cortex *or* a hologram.[21]

The suggestion is not that an optical hologram could be found in brain tissue, but that something *like* a holographic interference process was operating in the cortex. Other waves besides those of light can have complicated interference interactions, and it is well-known that there are waves of electrical potential (brain waves) generated in the cortex. It has also been suggested that even "waves" of nerve pulses could serve as a basis for holography. In fact, Lashley himself, without any dream of a hologram to guide him, suggested many years ago that electrical interference patterns emerging from large populations of neurons could furnish the mechanism that was called for.

A major conceptual problem remains, and that problem is embodied in the question of what is the brain's equivalent of a laser beam? What is the neural analogue to a device which sends out light waves which are "coherent," i.e., all in phase with each other? No electrical phenomena of this sort have ever been discovered in the brain, and besides, brain waves are at frequencies that are too low to carry any significant amount of information for holographic purposes. Some theorists have demonstrated mathematically that networks of neurons could display all the relevant properties of holograms without having the need for a laser beam. But this has not been accomplished with real images nor identified in brains, and it remains only a theoretical possibility.

The reason that the holographic hypothesis has had such a great appeal would seem to be due as much as to its exotic nature as to its ability to explain such things as scotoma completion. The transformation of neural pulses into a visual experience seems to us so mysterious that it cries for a mechanism out of science fiction. For that reason, the neural substrate of pattern vision may turn out to be something as complex and difficult to comprehend as a hologram. Or, as holograms become commonplace and as neurophysiology advances, the analogy may appear as useful and as limited as earlier comparisons of the visual process with cameras and movies.

Visual Agnosia

The mechanisms of pattern vision are strangely illuminated by clinical studies of what happens when people sustain damage to the visual cortex. As discussed earlier in this chapter, lesions to primary visual cortex (straite cortex) produce scotomas, something like holes in the visual field. If the scotoma is large enough to encompass all of the primary visual projection area, total blindness will result. Lesions to prestriate areas immediately surrounding the primary area produce a more curious kind of deficit, known as *visual agnosia.*

Persons with visual agnosia sense visual objects around

them, but they are unable to identify these objects by visual means alone. Their primary visual abilities are judged to be intact, because often no scotoma can be found when the visual field is mapped by spots of light. Visual agnostics usually have no difficulty avoiding objects in their path.

Higher intellectual deficits are usually ruled out because there is no impairment on intelligence tests and because these patients are able to discuss the same things which they cannot identify visually. The ability to identify things by the sense of touch is unimpaired. Earlier terms for this condition were "mind-blindness" or "imperception." The term "visual agnosia" was coined, curiously enough, by Sigmund Freud, who, as a young neurologist, conducted some of the earliest studies of this condition. It was originally thought that these cases were evidence for the separation of cortical functioning into lower "sensory" and higher "perceptive" domains. Visual agnostics were believed to be either unable to organize elementary sensations into coherent forms or unable to give a form its meaning by linking it with a stored memory.

The late Russian neuropsychologist Alexander Luria, who for many years studied the effects of brain lesions in man, believed that the essence of visual agnosia is in the inability to combine individual parts of the image into complete patterns: "A patient with a lesion of the secondary visual zones is not blind; he can still see the individual features, and, sometimes, the individual parts of objects. His defect is that he cannot combine these individual features into complete forms, and is therefore compelled to *deduce* the meaning of the image."[22] Luria illustrated this point with the case of a patient who carefully examines the drawing of a pair of eyeglasses. He becomes confused at this inability to identify the picture, and he starts to guess. "There is a circle . . . and another circle . . . and a stick . . . a cross-bar . . . why, it must be a bicycle!"

For Luria, the paradigm for all cases of visual agnosia is a rare form known as *simultagnosia*. In simultagnosia, one object may be recognized if presented alone, but not if it is introduced with another object in the visual field. According to Luria, all forms of visual agnosia result from a failure to build up or to synthesize an internal model of the visual object from separately perceived parts.

It must be emphasized that the defects of these patients are specific to visual perception. Patients with visual agnosia can recognize objects perfectly well by touch and do well on tests of logical thinking and grammatical understanding. Furthermore, they appear to have the ability to perceive simple sensations in the visual field.

However, the clinical evidence is not in actuality so uncomplicated. There is today considerable controversy over whether the classic symptoms of visual agnosia ever exist independent of subtle primary visual defects or of slight impairments of language which might affect the patient's ability to name objects he actually can see. For example, one common occurrence in agnostic patients is what has been called instances of "negative pseudo-recognitions." Here the patient seems to toy with the correct answer, but then rejects it. On being shown a picture of a mouse the patient might say, "It's not a cat," indicating that some meaning of the visual object is perceived, but that inappropriate verbal associations are made. The question of whether visual agnosia is all of one type, or whether there are separable subtypes further complicates the interpretation of the disability.[23] What the neurological controversy points out above all else is that the exact mechanisms subserved by secondary visual areas in the cortex are still largely unknown.

One of the more curious forms of visual agnosia is a rare specific agnosia for human faces. Termed *prosopagnosia* (from the Greek *prospon* = face), this neurological curiosity is said to result from damage to occipital and posterior temporal cortex in the right hemisphere. The unfortunate patients with this problem are unable to recognize the faces of familiar persons, even though they appear to see other kinds of visual objects normally. This disability can make a person unable to recognize even his or her own reflection in a mirror!

The existence of such a purely dissociable type of agnosia leads to the inference that there is a brain center specialized for the perception of human faces. This is entirely plausible when one considers the tremendous communicative importance the gestures of the face play in human interactions.[24] The face is known to be the first pattern to which human infants respond strongly.[25] Considering that there are hundreds of faces which we must routinely discriminate, despite the fact that faces are all very similar visual objects, it would not be surprising to learn that a special brain system had evolved to make these subtle discriminations.

Evidence for prosopagnosia as a pure type of deficit comes from a study done by Robert Yin, while still a graduate student at M.I.T. Yin tested a large number of brain-damaged patients at a neurology clinic. Half of these patients had brain wounds in the right posterior cortex. The other half had lesions in other cortical areas and were considered a control group. Yin compared these two groups on their abilities to recognize pictures of human faces. Some of the pictures were shown on a previous day and were therefore familiar to the patients. The rest of the pictures in the test were new.

Now, Yin had previously demonstrated that normal people are only slightly poorer at recognizing pictures of houses and other objects presented upside down than if these pictures were presented for recognition in their normal orientation, but that people are especially bad at recognizing upside-down faces. This fact, in itself, might argue for facial recognition as a dissociable ability. But what Yin then demonstrated with the brain-damaged groups was that even though the right-posterior patients performed worse than the control group in recognizing faces, they were actually *better* than the control group in recognizing inverted faces. Yin's explanation was that the right brain-damaged groups were forced to use the ordinary, nonspecialized visual brain for recognizing faces, and since these nonspecialized areas didn't have a strong bias for orientation, they were not impaired at recognizing inverted faces.[26]

The mechanisms taking place in these "higher visual centers" beyond the primary visual cortex can, at the moment, only be speculated upon. The mystery seems to deepen with each new finding. What is clear is that there are probably more than just two visual systems (cortical and tectal), and that the processes by which we see are more numerous, more complex, and more various than the directness of our visual world would make it appear.

Seeing with the Skin

One of the earliest questions philosophers and scientists asked about brain functioning was how sensory *quality* was determined; how is it that stimulation in certain sensory channels resulted in visual sensations, while stimulation in others produced auditory or tactile or olfactory experiences? The modern answer to this question was formulated by the nineteenth-century German physiologist Johannes Müller, who called it the "doctrine of specific nerve energies." Müller's doctrine stated that it was the property of each sensory nerve to give rise to its appropriate sensation (what Müller meant by "energy" was "quality"), and he thought that these differences between sensory nerves might be determined by the particular place in the brain where a sensory nerve terminated.[27]

Müller's doctrine at the time was a thoughtful compilation of the new data on the brain's functions. It was an argument against an ancient philosophical position that the nerves conducted to the brain qualitative copies of the external stimulus. Today his doctrine seems only common sense.

Müller's major line of evidence was that different stimuli affecting the same nerve always give rise to that nerve's particular sensory quality. A blow on the head will "give a person what will make his ears ring" or "what will make his eyes flash fire." You can experience for yourself the effects of mechanically stimulating the optic nerve by closing your eyes in a dark room and pressing on the eyelid above the outer corner of your eye. You will see a spot of light on the very inside corner of your eye. This light, called a *pressure phosphene,* is caused by a mechanical pressure on the neural tissue in the retina which is transmitted through the fluid of the eyeball. The doctrine of specific nerve energies would say that phosphenes occur because no matter what the stimulus which sets off activity in the optic nerve, the result is activity in the visual cortex, where it is decided that what is experienced is visual.

A recent attempt to invent a device which would give sight to the blind raises a possibility which would challenge Müller's doctrine. This technique, known as "vision-substitution," is based on a device which has a matrix of 400 tiny vibrators to translate the signal from a TV camera into a pattern of tactile stimulation on the skin of the back (see Figure 2-13). In tests of the equipment, both blind and sighted persons have been able to identify visual objects with only a little practice. These subjects also show a "looming reaction"—they duck when the tactile image is suddenly increased in size. This is similar to the startle reflex elicited when a retinal image is suddenly enlarged (usually signaling rapid approach). When the subjects were asked to identify objects with the TV camera fixed, they felt the objects to be on their backs. But when they were free to move the camera and scan the visual displays, they perceived the objects to be externally localized in front of them![28]

Although the technology for this kind of visual prosthesis is still in its infancy, it raises the question of whether it can ultimately provide the same quality of experience through the skin of the back as normal vision provides through the retina of the eye. Experiences of persons testing this technique would seem to answer in the affirmative. Since tactile stimulation produces its primary cortical activity in the somatosensory area of the parietal lobe rather than in the occipital cortex, it might be argued that visual experience *can* be generated in nerve

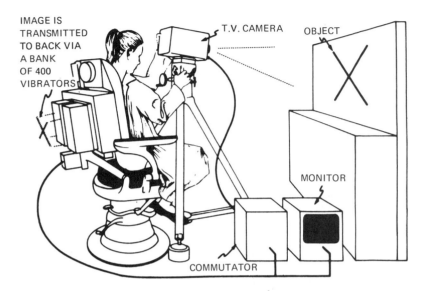

FIGURE 2-13. Vision-substitution system for the blind. A TV image is translated into a vibratory pattern on the back. (From B. W. White *et al.*, "Seeing with the Skin," Perception and Psychophysics, 1970, **7**, p. 23. Reproduced with permission of the publisher and author.)

tissue other than in the visual cortex. This would challenge the doctrine of specific nerve energies. The revised law would state that it is the *manner* in which the information is processed, rather than the locus of stimulation in the brain, which determines that a sensory experience will be visual or auditory or tactile.

Today we would recognize that Müller did not really answer the question he started out to answer; he just redefined it. We might still ask why certain neurons in the brain produce visual sensations while others result in the hearing of a sound. Undoubtedly the answer is complex, and some part of it probably involves the role of past experience. It seems entirely plausible that the brain is able to assign spatial attributes to sensations in the optic nerve because these sensations have been related to *information* about arrays of objects in space. Sensations in the auditory nerve have been related to quite different patterns of information—about modulations of air pressure over time.[29]

Is Seeing a Brain Process?

The topic of this chapter provides an opportunity to try out the language of identity theory—the view, discussed in Chapter 1, that conscious mental experiences and brain processes are one and the same thing. Is seeing a brain process? The development of pattern-recognizing machines should erase all doubt that *vision*—regarded as the successful identification and discrimination of optically presented patterns—can be understood as a material process. But what of the conscious experience of seeing?

More is known about the physiology and psychology of the visual system than about any other cognitive function in the brain. This no doubt derives from the importance of the sense of vision in our conscious experience. But what is there, in all that has been discovered, to indicate where the correspondence lies between visual mechanisms and mind? How can the picture of the world which I see actually be one and the same thing as activity in my brain?

In the examples given in Chapter 1, a cloud and a mass of particles in suspension are said to be identical, because they are observed in the same place under two different conditions: from far away and from up close (or, alternatively with low and with high magnification). For the example of lightning's identity with the motion of charged particles, there are also two conditions of observation: with one's eyes at a distance and with voltmeters and similar measuring devices (the latter measurements being interpreted through theoretical propositions of physics which validate them and give them meaning). To determine that conscious experience was identical to a brain process, we would similarly have to observe this experience under two different conditions. What could these conditions be?

Suppose someone invented a machine which detected activity in your visual brain tissue and decoded this information into a video picture which could be taped. You could subsequently view the videotape and compare it to the visual experience you just had.[30] (Assume for a moment that memory presents no problem, since most of us can faithfully recall great detail from the very recent past.) If you felt that the two-dimensional TV picture so created was a faithful representation of what you had seen a moment ago before your very eyes, would you then be tempted to say that the brain events out of which the picture was synthesized were the same as your visual experience?

It seems to me that you might. But as in the case of lightning, the identity makes sense only through the mediation of a theory which interprets tha machine's measurements. What if the machine recorded its information from the cells in the optic nerve? Here, the accomplishment would not be very impressive, because we know that the retina projects upstream in a point-to-point arrangement. However, if the TV picture was created from electrodes in prestriate cortex, and if the TV image was accompanied by a theory which explained the transformation in terms of the neural elements of pattern recognition, then the statement of identity would be made more plausible.

But once said, "Seeing is a brain process" conveys very little understanding of either seeing or brain processes. It would seem that the identity could establish that particular brain events were manifest in conscious visual awareness while others were not—and this would raise some interesting questions about the function of this particular class of events in the brain. But the theory would already have specified what these brain events were, so the methodology is circular (as it is, one must add, in Newtonian physics, the example *par excellence* of scientific explanation.[31])

Recommended Readings

PERCEPTION

SHIFFMAN, R. *Sensation and Perception.* New York: John Wiley & Sons, 1976.
GREGORY, R.M. *Eye and Brain,* 2nd ed. New York: McGraw-Hill, 1973.
HELD, R., and W. RICHARDS, *Perception: Mechanisms and Models.* San Francisco: W.H. Freeman, 1971.

PATTERN RECOGNITION

DODWELL, P.C. *Visual Pattern Recognition.* New York Holt, Rinehart & Winston, 1970.
NEISSER, U. *Cognitive Psychology.* New York: Appleton-Century-Crofts, 1967.
WINSTON, P.H. *The Psychology of Computer Vision.* New York: McGraw-Hill, 1975

VISUAL AGNOSIA

GARDNER, H. *The Shattered Mind.* New York: Alfred A. Knopf, 1975.
LURIA, A.R. *Higher Cortical Functions in Man.* New York: Basic Books, 1966

Waking
and
Sleeping

We know about consciousness because we know what it is to be unconscious. That constrast forces itself upon us every morning when we awaken from sleep. Recent discoveries about the control centers in the brain for waking and sleeping have demonstrated the possibilities for a physiology of consciousness.

3

Waking

To be "wide awake" is to be alert, to think clearly, and to respond rapidly. When you are wide awake, your brain is at its most efficient. It is able to process sensory messages accurately, to solve problems, make decisions, and control bodily movements quickly and precisely. While mental processes are not completely absent during sleep, they are not directed outward to reach for goals. This much should be obvious.

It also should be obvious that there are *degrees* of waking. The lethargy which follows a heavy meal, which you would still describe as an awake or conscious state, feels much different from the intense vigilance you felt in the midst of a tennis game earlier in the day. Yet, even that lethargy can be instantly dissolved when an old friend surprises you with his appearance at the door.

Many years ago the famous Russian physiologist Ivan Pavlov theorized that there was a brain process which corresponded to these degrees of wakefulness. He believed that it related to variations in the level of "tone" of the cerebral cortex—analogous to variations in the level of muscle tone. The cerebral cortex is the most newly evolved part of the vertebrate brain, and the most characteristic specialization of the human brain. It often has been assumed that it contains the machinery of consciousness.

In 1949, Pavlov's hypothesis was confirmed when two physiologists, Giuseppe Moruzzi, an Italian, and Horace Magoun, an American, announced that they had discovered a brain system which regulated the general activity level of the cortex. This system was not itself part of the cortex, as Pavlov had believed. Rather, it arose from far down in the brainstem to bombard the thalamus and the cortex with a stream of impulses. This stream functioned to maintain vigilance. When it was absent, drowsiness and sleep ensued.

The mechanism was named the *reticular activating system (RAS)*, because it is driven by the *reticular formation*, a finger-sized mass of tissue located along the axis of the brainstem (see Figure 3-1).

What Moruzzi and Magoun had done was to show that electrical stimulation of the reticular formation in sleeping

FIGURE 3–1. Lateral view of the brain, showing the reticular activating system (RAS). The term "reticular" comes from the Latin **reticulum,** meaning "network." Unlike sensory and motor neurons, which have long axons and are specialized for transmitting impulses over long distances, the reticular formation (A) is composed largely of densely intermingled neurons with short dendrites and axons. This neuronal architecture makes the reticular formation well suited for gradually changing its level of activity by degrees, by changes in the slow, graded potentials of the dendrites. The dense intermingling of fibers makes this structure capable of integrating the effects of stimulation from many sources.

The reticular formation receives inputs from sensory pathways (B) on their way upstream to the cortex. As they pass by the brainstem, sensory neurons branch (C), giving off extra axons to the reticular formation. The result is that whenever a specific sensory message, such as a tickle or a sound, travels upstream to its sensory receiving area in the cortex (D), it also stimulates the reticular formation. The reticular formation then relays its own state of activation to the cortex. Unlike the sensory pathways, which travel to specific sensory receiving areas, the reticular formation projects diffusely, to large areas of the cortex. The diffuseness of its projections enables the RAS to work nonspecifically. That is, incoming nerve signals from any source will affect not only a specific receiving area (D), but through the action of RAS, it can activate all other areas of the cortex (E, F, G, H, I).

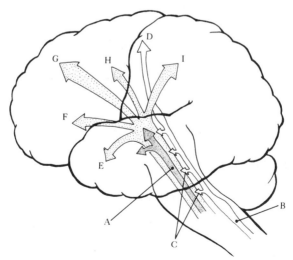

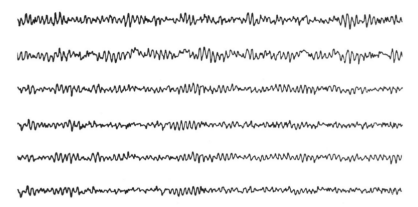

Figure 3-2. Alpha waves come in "trains" or shorter "bursts" in the EEG of wakefulness. Shown here are 10 seconds of EEG taken from six different places over the head of one subject.

laboratory animals produced immediate and long-lasting signs of arousal in the cerebral cortex. These signs were certain patterns of brain waves produced by the cortex and recorded as an *electroencephalogram (EEG)*.

The EEG pattern of a sleeping person is characterized by large, rhythmic slow waves, which are replaced upon awakening by the "desynchronized" brain waves of wakefulness. The rhythmic slow waves seem to reflect the synchronization of millions of neurons, as they wax and wane together in pulsations of excitability. When the cortex is not in this condition—when it is *de*synchronized—the neurons' excitability cycles are not locked to each other in time, and they can perform their functions independently. For this reason (and because it is seen when an animal or human is most alert and attentive), the desynchronized EEG is called an "activation pattern." Even when we are awake, however, synchronized electrical waves, called *alpha waves,* appear in the EEG (see Figures 3-2 and 3-3). Like the synchronized waves of sleep (which are even slower) the alpha waves indicate that the underlying brain tissue is idling. However, unlike the slow waves of sleep, the alpha waves can be instantly replaced by desynchronized, activated cortex. Synchronized alpha waves are *momentary* idling patterns. In EEG's of wakefulness, alpha waves typically come in short bursts.

There are large differences among people in the abundance of alpha waves in their EEG. Children generally have more than adults. Anxious people tend to have less than

FIGURE 3-3. Hypothetical scheme of the micro-activity in the cortex which produces desynchronized, activated EEG versus synchronized EEG slow waves, in this case, the alpha waves of relaxed wakefulness. A population of cortical neurons is governed by an oscillating cycle of excitability, which gives rise to the EEG waves.

In (a), all the neurons are governed by the same oscillator, and they are thus synchronized to be excitable at exactly the same points in time. This group is redundant in terms of the information different neurons can carry.

In (b), different subgroups of neurons can be excited independently. In this state, the system would be able to carry more information, because each subgroup can function at different points in time. The sum of activity from the different excitability cycles would give rise to the desynchronized EEG shown here. (Modified from D. B. Lindsley. In D. Sheer, ed., Electrical Stimulation of the Brain, © 1961 by the Hogg Foundation for Mental Health. Reproduced with permission of the University of Texas Press and the authors.)

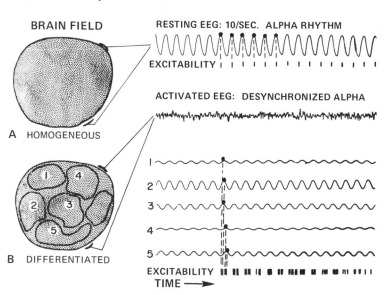

nonanxious people. These differences may reflect important individual differences among people in their "styles" of consciousness.[1]

Following Moruzzi and Magoun's discovery of the functions of the brainstem RAS, other findings on the RAS soon emerged from other laboratories. Making lesions in the RAS produced animals who were stuporous. They could be momentarily aroused, perhaps, by a loud noise or a sharp pain, but the arousal did not last for more than a few seconds, after which the animal would lapse again into a perpetual sleep. If an awake animal was stimulated by electrodes implanted deep into the RAS, it would show signs of alerting, turning its head, and pricking its ears, as if looking around for something which attracted interest. Stimulation of the RAS also increased the brain's sensitivity: during stimulation, animals could detect very faint tones and more easily distinguish tiny differences in pitch.

Also, it was found that a monkey's "knee-jerk" reflex could be enhanced or diminished by stimulating different parts of the reticular formation. What this means is that the RAS controls the brain's level of output as well as its input. Actually, the RAS governs outgoing motor signals of several kinds, including the stream of pulses which maintain muscle tone, and the signals which coordinate fine body movements.

There is a further complication to the story, a very important one. In addition to being alerted by the RAS, parts of the cortex can themselves exert a downstream influence on the reticular formation. The cortex is thus capable of regulating, in part, its own level of activation. The significance of this should be clear to anyone who has rallied his or her flagging powers of concentration through a boring lecture or who has been kept wide awake at night by worrying.[2]

The discovery of the RAS was regarded as a great step forward in understanding the physical basis of consciousness. The existence of this brain system now makes it clear that waking consciousness does not arise from a unitary physiological condition. Rather, it is characterized, at least physiologically, as a graded continuum of intensity. Cortical activation governed by the RAS can change gradually, by degrees, from the excitement of danger or discovery, to the stupor of fatigue.

Some brain researchers, struck by the generality of the RAS's function in alerting the cortex and in coordinating muscle systems, have come to the conclusion that this system is a general regulator or integrator of behavior—a kind of traffic control center for the brain.[3] One reason for this view is that the RAS not only functions in the regulation of overall vigilance, but also appears to govern things more subtly. That is, it seems to govern processes which seem very much like what we call "attention."

Attention and the Orienting Reaction

> We do not notice the ticking of the clock, the noise of the city streets, or the roaring of the brook near the house; and even the din of a foundry or factory will not mingle with the thoughts of its workers, if they have been there long enough.

These lines are from William James' popular turn-of-the-century textbook *The Principles of Psychology*. They point to a familiar insight. In terms of function, James' examples of inattention can be seen as the workings of a mental "economy": attention parcels out resources to important events.

That consciousness is limited is a conclusion drawn from the facts of selective attention, so the theory is somewhat circular. Still, the basic fact is that we can pay attention to only one thing, or at most a few things, at any one time. Psychologists like to use the example of a cocktail party, where you can eavesdrop on any one of a number of simultaneous conversations, picking out the thread of each, but only one at a time. This "paying" of attention—the image is the parceling out of a scarce resource—is made necessary by a bottleneck somewhere in the chain of events between the excitation of sense organs and the execution of a response.

A great deal of research in the field of experimental psychology characterizes the bottleneck as being a limited-capacity "central processing unit"—some kind of sophisticated cognitive system, or brain system, which categorizes, analyzes, and decides how to process uncertain or unknown inputs.[4] This "central processor" idea is an analogy drawn from computers (see Figure 3-4). If its physiological substrate could be found, it might turn out to be the machinery of consciousness itself. As the English scientist Lord Adrian put it, "the signals from the sense organs must be treated differently when we attend to them than when we do not, and if we could decide where and how the divergence arises, we should be nearer to understanding how the level of consciousness is reached."[5]

We pay attention, by and large, to things which have importance to us, and a large measure of what makes up a thing's importance is its novelty or unexpectedness. As in the opening quote from James, we pay attention to things which

FIGURE 3–4. Broadbent's information-processing model of selective attention. The units consist of sensory imput channels and a short-term memory—two initial stages which process information all at once, or in <u>parallel</u>. These units feed into a bottleneck in the system—a stage analogous to the central-processing unit of a digital computer, which operates on information one piece at a time, or <u>serially</u>. Broadbent conceived of the junction between parallel and serial units to be a kind of attentional switch or filter. The model explains such things as people's inability to switch attention back and forth (between, say, different messages in the two ears) beyond a certain rate. It also explains the embarrassing occurrences when we ask someone to repeat a phrase, and then, before the reply can be given, we catch ourselves retrieving the meaning which had eluded us. (The latter is explained by the persistence of sensory information in parallel short-term memory banks.)

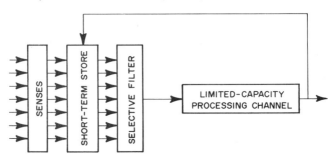

are new to us or uncertain, and we neglect things which are predictable. We don't have to devote much "brain power" to things which have happened before, because a good deal about them is already known. In support of this analysis is the discovery by psychologists of an apparently inborn *need* to attend to the unknown.[6]

Attending to uncertain things is economical, provided that the *expected* events, if they have significance to us, can be dealt with unconsciously by other, less intricate brain resources. In an evolutionary sense, the economy works because uncertain or unexpected things frequently signal danger. Noticing the sound of the rattle might keep you from stepping on the snake. Attention to unpredicted variations in the environment may be adaptive in another way. It might form the basis of discovery. Attention to novelty might lead humans to notice how to make fire, or, perhaps, what cures cancer.

One line of research, conducted largely by Russian scientists, has linked the activities of the RAS to the tuning of attention to novelty. Again, the starting point was Pavlov, who in 1910 introduced the term *orienting reaction,* or *orienting reflex,* to describe the set of physiological changes evoked, in animals and men, by surprising or novel stimuli. Pavlov classified this reaction as one of a group of adaptive reflexes. The group also included the defensive reflexes, such as a startle response to extremely loud noise. The orienting reflex was described as the "what is it?" reflex. It acts to orient eyes, ears, and other receptor organs toward a surprising stimulus.

The components of this reaction include desynchronization of the EEG (described in the previous section), increases in the sensitivity of receptor organs (such as dilation of the pupil of the eye), and adjustments of the skeletal musculature (an arrest of ongoing activity, or the turning of the eyes and head toward the source of stimulation). In addition, there are other changes, such as a momentary pause in breathing, constriction of blood vessels in the limbs, and dilation of blood vessels in the head (see Table 3-1). All these components of the orienting reflex are

Table 3–1.
Some Components of the Orienting Reaction

COMPONENT	FUNCTION
I. Increases in the sensitivity of sense organs.	
a. Dilation of the pupil of the eye	More light reaches the retina.
b. Photochemical changes in the retina.	Visual system more sensitive to light.
c. ??	Auditory system more sensitive to faint sounds.
II. Changes in skeletal muscles which direct sense organs	Receptors "tune in" on the source of the disturbance.
a. Head and eyes turn toward source of sound.	
b. (In animals) ears prick up and point	
c. (In animals) sniffing.	
III. Changes in general skeletal musculature.	
a. Ongoing actions temporarily arrested.	Removes source of distracting stimulation and frees sense organs; also, makes animal less visible.
b. General muscle tonus rises.	Muscles assume a state of readiness for action.
IV. EEG changes: alpha-blocking (desynchronization).	Cerebral cortex assumes a state of readiness for computation.
V. Vegetation changes	
a. vasoconstriction in limbs; vasodilation in head.	Distributes more blood to the alerted brain.
b. Galvanic skin reaction (palmar "sweat" response).	?? One theory is that it facilitates gripping; another is that it increases sensitivity of touch and temperature receptors on the skin.
c. Respiration pause, followed by slower and deeper breathing.	?? Increases smell sensitivity? Removes source of distracting stimulation?
d. Heart rate slows for a couple of beats.	??

understandable as ways to increase the sensitivity of the organism. The dilated pupil lets more light into the eye. Changes in the blood vessels distribute more blood to the brain.

The orienting reaction can be produced artificially by stimulating certain areas of the brainstem RAS so that the level of activation is increased suddenly. Orienting is normally evoked by stimuli which share in the property of being novel or unexpected. Also, it's not an all-or-nothing affair. A strong surprise will arrest any ongoing activity, but mildly surprising things precipitate mild orienting reactions. In most cases, only a few of the components of the reaction can be detected.

When a surprising event becomes repeated and loses its surprisingness, the orienting reaction to it gradually diminishes. This process is called *habituation.* The Russian psychologist E.N. Sokolov, who has been investigating these things for many years, states that habituation of the orienting response depends upon the establishing of a "neuronal model" of the stimulus in the brain. He means by this that there is set up somewhere in the brain a copy of that brain region's original response pattern to an external stimulus. As long as incoming effects of the stimulus continue to match this model, everything is as expected, and no orienting reaction occurs. But when some aspect of the stimulus is changed (its intensity, duration, size, shape, etc.), its incoming neuronal response pattern is mismatched to the model, and an orienting reflex will occur. If your car's engine suddenly emits a slightly different sound, it is likely you will notice the sound of the engine. This is called *dis-habituation.*

Dis-habituation is the reoccurrence of an orienting reaction to a stimulus that had previously been habituated. The experience of habituation as a mental phenomenon is when some slight change in a familiar object forces that thing upon your attention. A common experience is how a friend's face looks to you when he shaves off his moustache.

Sokolov based the theory on his experiments with habituation. He showed that once a person had habituated to a stimulus, such as the beep of a horn, he could be made to give an orienting response again if any parameter of the stimulus was changed: make the horn louder, or softer, or longer, or shorter, or of a different pitch, and the signs of orienting would reoccur. Orienting is not due simply to a general decrease in the brain's sensitivity: softer as well as louder tones will evoke orienting.

The orienting reaction will also occur as a result of the nonappearance of some expected event. Some years ago, when

an elevated section of the New York subway system was disman-
tled, the police started receiving calls from residents of the
apartment buildings next to the tracks. The callers reported
being woken from sleep by mysterious noises, which they
presumed to be burglars or other urban dangers. The whole
affair was very mysterious, until a pattern was discovered. The
awakenings occurred at about the times when the early morning
trains had noisily clattered by the apartment buildings. The
residents were being woken by the *absence* of a noise they had
come to expect, even while they slept![7]

The role of the "neuronal model," according to Sokolov, is
to inhibit the initiation of an orienting response by the RAS. By
this theory, the cortex exerts a suppressive effect on the RAS by
sending inhibitory signals downstream. These inhibitory signals
would be sent to the RAS as long as incoming stimuli continued
to match the neuronal models. When a mismatch occurred, the
inhibition would be lifted, and the RAS would exert its alerting
influence (see Figure 3-5).

Sokolov described neuronal models as being specific to the
physical properties of the stimulus, but some experiments have
shown that *cognitive* properties must also be involved. In one
experiment, subjects were read predictable sequences of numbers, such as "2, 4, 6, 8, 10 . . . ." Occasionally, numbers would
appear which were out of place ("14, 16, 18, 20, *18* . . . "). At
the moments the wrong numbers were spoken, orienting responses would occur.[8] It must be that the neuronal model,
which suppresses orienting to each number in the sequence, can
be a dynamic cognitive operation—it can change its form with
each new element of the sequence.

The concept of a "neuronal model" explains the relationship between a thing's predictability and its importance to us.
We needn't allocate the scarce resources of conscious attention
to things which are predictable, because we already know about
them. To know about something, in this sense, means to have
developed a cognitive structure (a neuronal model, for example)
which contains the information gathered about that thing from
past experience. The neuronal model allows for the perceptual

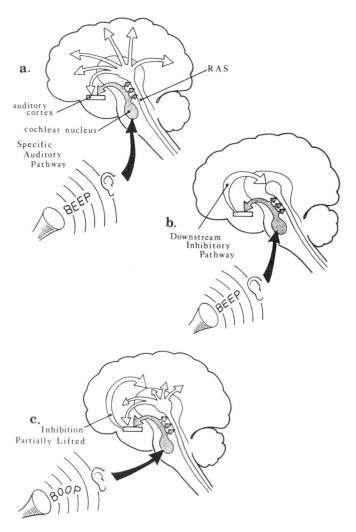

FIGURE 3-5. Sokolov's theory of the orienting reflex. (a) A sudden sound from a car's horn travels to its sensory receiving area (the auditory cortex) via the specific sensory pathway. On the way, it excites the reticular activating system, and the RAS alerts wide areas of cortex. (b) The horn remains on (it's stuck), and the brain habituates to it. This takes place through the action of a neuronal model of the sound, located at or near the auditory cortex. The cortex sends a downstream signal which inhibits the RAS at the level of the thalamus. (c) The car's horn breaks down and changes its pitch. There is a partial mismatch of the auditory signal to the cortical model. The inhibition is weakened, having the effect of alerting the cortex once again. Since the mismatch was slight, the orienting is slight, perhaps localized to auditory cortex.

analysis of a expected event by a match-mismatch process—a process which can be carried out simply, with few of the brain's cognitive resources. Conscious experience, it would seem, is related somehow to the *complexity* of the brain's operation.*

Keep in mind that, in addition to orienting reactions in the EEG (alpha-blocking), there are other kinds of cortical events going on at the same time. These include specific electrical activities, also occurring in sensory cortex, which analyze sights, sounds, and smells. These information-processing activities—for example, the visual mechanisms discussed in Chapter 2—occur in more or less direct response to the same stimulus which evokes an activation response. Even the localized orienting reaction is generalized and nonspecific compared to the specific neural activities related to perceptual information-processing.

The two kinds of cortical events—orienting and information-processing—can occur separately, if certain pathways are surgically interrupted. They also occur separately at other times: during deep sleep and after habituation of the orienting responses. At both of these times, a strong electrical signal (an

---

*Sokolov actually distinguished two different kinds of orienting reaction. One is characterized by a *generalized* activation pattern in the EEG, affecting most or all of the cerebral cortex. It persists (for several minutes or more), and so it is called a "tonic" orienting reaction. The generalized tonic orienting reaction habituates rapidly with the brain's repeated exposure to the stimulus which evoked the reaction. This kind of orienting response can be thought of as bringing about a state of general alertness.

The other form is a *localized* orienting reaction, meaning that it is restricted to the local area of the cortex appropriate for analyzing the particular stimulus which evoked it (e.g., occipital cortex for a visual stimulus). It habituates slowly and can be seen in the EEG in reaction to a stimulus long after the generalized reaction to the stimulus has disappeared. It is "phasic" (as opposed to "tonic") in the sense that it usually doesn't outlast the duration of the stimulus.

The generalized tonic reaction can be thought of as the background level of arousal on which are superimposed the localized phasic orienting reactions. It has been found that the higher the tonic level, the more easily phasic orienting reactions can occur. The generalized reaction involves the brainstem RAS. The localized orienting reactions is thought to be governed by an upper region of the RAS, located in the thalamus.

"evoked response") can be detected in a cortical sensory area, in response to a flashing light, say, or a beeping horn. At the same time, the ongoing EEG reveals a synchronized or deactivated state.[9] In both cases (sleep and habituation), there is also an absense of conscious perception of the stimulus. It would seem that not all cortical activities are reflected in consciousness, perhaps only those related to the desynchronized state.

To return to Sokolov's theory, the physiological embodiment of the neuronal model is most likely located in the cortex rather than in some other part of the brain. Removals of cortex in laboratory animals impair the ability to habituate orienting responses. (Sokolov: "To de-corticate dogs, any stimulus is 'novel!' "[10]) Also, local orienting responses will occur to a previously habituated stimulus if a person is in a drowsy state, when the cortex is at a generally low level of arousal.[11]

Some puzzles remain. For example, how is it that we can be roused from sleep selectively by different stimulus patterns? A new mother will be wakened by the faintest cry from her baby, while the father continues to sleep. Similarly, a sleeper is more easily wakened by the sound of his own name than by other names. These everyday facts seem to imply that some circuits in the cortex can remain vigilant even during sleep.

Automaticity in Perception and Action

After you habituate to a stimulus, it can still be recognized and acted upon in an apparently unconscious or automatic manner. This phenomenon is one aspect of a general tendency toward the unconscious execution of any activity which is performed habitually. Consider the case of a tourist approaching the Golden Gate Bridge for the first time and a commuter viewing it from the same spot, one car behind. What is the difference in their perceptions? They are both looking at the same object in their visual fields, taking mental note of it, categorizing it, identifying it. They would both be able to tell you, for instance, that the color of the bridge is red, that it is suspended from two tall towers by a web of steel cable. Still, there is a sense in which the commuter, who has seeen this bridge twice a day for the last seven years, is not as aware of the bridge. The color of the bridge is less vivid, the towers less imposing and graceful, the web of cables less intricate than when he himself had seen if for the first time.

What the commuter would say about his unawareness is that he knows the route so well that he drives it "automatically." We use the term in everyday speech. It is a common observation, for example, while we are learning some new and complicated physical skill, like hitting a golf ball, that at some point in time the actions become unconscious. Where we once had to pay attention to the coordination of a thousand and one different muscles, now things seem to run off so smoothly that it seems automatic. The term "automatic" refers simply to our lack of mental effort or a lack of awareness. This metaphor is a fortunate one, in terms of what we have called the mental "economy" of attention.

In modern terms, we would say that both tourist and commuter are processing information about the bridge. The tourist is discovering things he did not know before seeing it. He is acquiring considerable amounts of information. The commuter is probably not finding out much new about the bridge itself (unless, of course, it is being repaired or painted). He is, rather, confirming knowledge he already has. He is acquiring less information. What automaticity connotes here is a *reduction in the amount* of information being processed, somewhere in the brain, made possible by the *stereotyping* of the manner in which the information is processed. The stereotyped operation could perhaps indicate that the task of processing the incoming information has been assigned to some other, less flexible brain system than the "limited-capacity central processor" discussed earlier. The match-mismatch process of the "neuronal model" theory is one simple type of stereotyping: it circumscribes, before the fact, the things that can possibly be perceived. In the example of the commuter's complicated perceptual-motor programs which allow him to drive his car more or less automatically, it would seem that something like neuronal models might be involved, but at a higher level of complexity.

The economy of conscious and unconscious processes can be seen most clearly when motor actions become automatized. The symphony conductor Pierre Boulez once described in a TV interview how it was that a person could conduct "five against four," meaning rhythmically moving one's right hand five times while moving four times with the left. This is similar to the task invoked when we challenge a child simultaneously to rub his belly and pat his head. Boulez said that doing "five against four" is simple: one merely had to put one of the hands on "automatic," and then pay attention to the other.

A few years ago I found that an analogous kind of stereotypy occurs in visual perception. When a person looks at a scene over and over again, the eye movements which scan the scene fall into more and more predictable patterns.[12] It is as if the subjects in my experiment had acquired schematic representations of the pictures I showed them, schemas which guided their eyes to those areas of the scene likely to contain something of interest or likely to result in the fastest identification. The usefulness of this process can be appreciated by considering the task of an airline pilot, surrounded by all those meters and dials in the cockpit. No doubt all of our habitual perceptions gain, at least in efficiency, by stereotyped brain programs of this sort.

As in the case with many matters of subjective experience, the psychologist's understanding of automatizing has been anticipated by that of writers and poets. In slightly different language, the notion of automaticity in perception has been a recurrent theme in literature. Romantic poets have dwelt on the lost innocence of childhood, a time when we once perceived things with greater awareness.

> There was a time when meadow, grove and stream,
> The earth and every common sight,

To me did seem
Apparelled in celestial light,
The glory and the freshness of a dream.

(William Wordsworth, 1770–1850,
*"Intimations of Immortality
from Recollections of Early Childhood"*

Henry David Thoreau (1817–1863), associated with the Romantic period in American literature, talked about the trick of bending over to look at the world between his legs. Inverting the visual field in this way produced a curious strangeness to familiar objects. You might try this for yourself (when no one is watching).

All this can be translated into our terms: a child, lacking in experience, has not developed the cognitive structure which would let him process visual information less intensely. And Thoreau, looking between his legs, is carrying out an operation analogous to dis-habituation.[13]

Wakefulness and Consciousness

The RAS furnishes an indisputable substratum for conscious experience. When its activity is lacking, through injury or during sleep, consciousness is diminished.

"Attention" is often taken as a synonym for "consciousness." "Attention," in its broadest sense, refers to the selectivity of perception and thought, and this selectivity no doubt occurs at many different levels in the nervous system. But one particularly important group of attentional mechanisms is intimately related to the workings of the RAS. The "orienting reactions" to novel events, and the related process of habituation to familiar events, point out the link between conscious awareness of things and environmental demands for intense information-processing. Consciousness has something to do with survival, in an evolutionary sense. It is reasonable to suppose that consciousness has evolved along with the brain structures which allow higher organisms to acquire flexible and sophisticated knowledge about their environments.

THE TWO KINDS OF SLEEP

The variations of wakefulness provide some hints about the physical basis of consciousness. The issue is also illuminated by the constrast afforded to us, every night, by periods when awareness is absent or altered. About one-third of our lives is spent in sleep, and for this reason alone the scientific study of sleep is important. Here, we are interested in the possibility that, through finding the physical correlates of mental activity (or inactivity) during sleep, some of the processes involved in waking consciousness may be indirectly revealed.

There has been a great scientific bonanza in the field of sleep research in recent years, and many of the findings have contradicted everyday wisdom about sleep. Modern sleep research began when the development of EEG techniques made it possible to monitor the brain waves of people while they slept. It was then discovered that sleep is not a unitary neurological state, but, rather, it is composed of several distinct EEG stages. These are depicted in Figure 3-6.

Although researchers commonly distinguish several transitional stages in the EEG's of sleep, there are generally acknowledged to be two basic types. One type, *slow-wave sleep* or quiet sleep (stages 2, 3, and 4) is the deepest sleep, at least by the criterion of arousal: it takes an extremely loud sound to waken someone from this state. During this time, surface brain waves are large and roll slowly, indicating that the cortex is resting. Body temperature, breathing, and heart rate all drop to their lowest levels.

The second type of sleep is interspersed in shorter batches throughout the night. It is physiologically a highly active brain state, more like the waking state than slow-wave sleep. The EEG is desynchronized (activated). Also, body temeprature and heart rate go up. But most dramatically, this active sleep state is

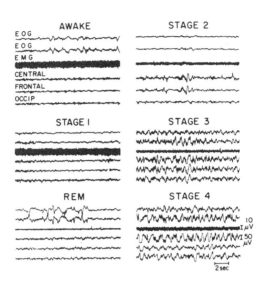

FIGURE 3–6. Stages of sleep as recorded on the electrooculogram (EOG), chin electromyogram (EMG), and electroencephalogram (central, frontal occipital tracings). Note the high EMG and eye movements during wakefulness, compared with the low EMG and rapid eye movements (REM's) during stage REM. The EEG is similar during stage 1 and stage REM, but the EMG is high and REM's are absent in stage 1. Stages 2, 3, and 4 are characterized by slowing of frequency and increase in amplitude of the EEG. (From A. Kales **et al.**, Annals of Internal Medicine, 1968, **68**: 1078. Reproduced with permission of the publisher and author.)

accompanied by rapid flicks of the eyes beneath the closed lids, similar to the movements made by an awake person, whose eyes scan something he is actively seeing. It is these bizarre eye movements— rapid eye movements, or *REM's*—which have given this state its commonly accepted name of *REM sleep*.

During REM sleep, curiously enough, the muscles of the body become flaccid and paralyzed. This is known as *EMG suppression*, because in the laboratory it is seen as a flattening out of the *electromyogram (EMG)*, the electrical activity of the muscles. When physiologists first discovered this state of activated EEG in the midst of deep sleep, they called it "paradoxical sleep"— paradoxical because the cortex appeared awake and yet behaviorally the person was deeply asleep. His muscles exhibited practically no tension, and he was insensitive to outside stimuli.

There is a good deal of regulatity in the alternation of sleep stages. Figure 3-7 shows physiological data from one subject during three successive nights in a sleep laboratory. Typically, the earliest part of sleep is taken up with a descent into the slow-wave sleep of stage 4, the quietest of all sleep stages. After 60–90 minutes the first REM period occurs, usually a brief one. After that, REM periods recur about every 90–100 minutes throughout the night, alternating with slow-wave stages 2, 3, and 4. As the night progresses, REM periods get progressively longer, until the sleeper emerges from the final REM period into wakefulness. In adults, REM comprises about 25 percent of sleeping time.

It is during the REM state that people experience most of

FIGURE 3-7. The sleep stages of a single subject sleeping for three successive nights in the laboratory. Stages are given on the vertical, and hours from the time in bed are on the horizontal. The black bars indicate periods of REM sleep. (From L. E. Abt, and B. P. Riess, eds., Progress in Clinical Psychology, New York: Grune and Stratton, Inc., 1969. Reproduced with permission of the publisher and author.)

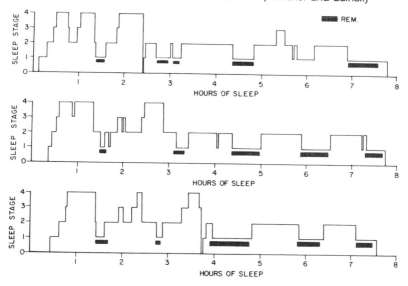

their dreams. If you wake a sleeper while his or her eyes are moving jerkily beneath closed lids, chances are that the person will experience waking from the midst of a vivid dream. The eye movements of REM were tantalizing oddities to their early discoverers, who thought the sleeper was visually scanning the hallucinatory dream—or even that the eye movements might be necessary in order to experience such a strong visual image.[14] However, more recent research indicates that it is difficult to match eye movements with the reported dream content (except in unusual cases, as in a dream of watching a Ping-Pong match),[15] and people can apparently experience vivid visual dreams accompanied by only a few eye movements.[16]

When the cortex is activated during REM sleep, the neurons in the motor cortex are also firing at a relatively high rate. This is the region where a surgeon's electrical probe results in bodily movement. It would seem, therefore, that some inhibitory force is at work, in order to keep these motor impulses from resulting in muscular contractions—otherwise we would be compelled to act out our dreams! The muscular flaccidity of REM sleep apparently serves this function. It is now known that there is a mechanism for this, located in the brainstem right next to the RAS, which is part of the circuitry that initiates REM sleep; this mechanism actively inhibits the outflow of muscle commands from higher brain centers.[17]

EMG suppression is actually one of a group of characteristics of the REM state that are described as *tonic* because they continue throughout the REM period. Other tonic REM characteristics include the EEG activation as well as increases in heart rate, breathing rate, and elevation in temperature. There are also *phasic* characteristics of REM sleep. These are very brief, irregular physiological events, most notably the rapid eye movements themselves. Phasic REM events can be seen in sleeping dogs and cats as fine limb movements and little growls. People have brief muscle twitches, too, but much less than other animals. They occur mostly during REM sleep and are probably the result of strong electrical signals which break through the

EMG blockade. They all might be related to dream content but, as with the eye movements, correlations are difficult to establish. One researcher found that when he awakened his subjects during REM periods, they reported more dreams involving bodily movement if they had shown fine limb movements prior to awakening. There was also some indication that the limbs which moved were more closely related to the movement of the dream than the limbs which didn't move.[18] However, the relationship between limb movements during REM and the content of the dream is not perfect: many times a dreamer will report having a very active dream when no muscle twitches are visible.[19]

The discoverers of the regularity of REM sleep and its relationship to dreaming were William Dement and Nathanial Kleitman at the University of Chicago. Their findings, during the late 1950's, ushered in an era of tremendous interest and research into the nature of sleep. At first, it was thought that dreams and REM periods were perfectly linked, that they were psychological and physiological signs of the very same events. In one study Dement selectively woke sleeping volunteers in different states of sleep. After being woken from a REM episode, about 80 percent of the time they would report that they had been woken from a dream. This compared to only 6 percent of the time after waking from slow-wave sleep.[20] Other sleep researchers, however, have found that this result depends to a great extent on how you define a "dream." If "dream" is taken to mean any mental content whatsoever, including random stray thoughts, then more than 50 percent of slow-wave sleep also contains dreams.

Even so, the dreams of REM sleep and of slow-wave sleep differ drastically. Slow-wave dreams are fragmented, concerned with recent events, and closer to the rational thought of wakefulness. Some examples:

1. (The subject) . . .asked an acquaintance at work for a hammer, so that he could fix something in his apartment.

2.   He was thinking of a point made in his tax class, that you have
     to provide over half of a person's support to claim him as a
     dependent.[21]

The content of REM episodes, on the other hand, tends to be
more bizarre. It is colorful and vivid and composed of many
concrete sensory images. These dreams are often intense experiences, and they tend to be more elaborate and organized
than are slow-wave dreams. The following is an example of a
REM dream:

> I was in the library and I was filing cards, and I came to some
> letter between "a" and "c." I was filing some, I think it was
> Burma, some country, and just as I put that in, there was this
> scene of some woman, who was sent to look for a little girl who
> was lost, and she was sent to Burma. They thought the little girl
> was going there, for some reason. This was sort of like a
> dramatization of what I was doing. I mean I was filing, and then
> it was sort of like you'd imagine it, but I had the feeling it was
> really happening.[22]

Dement believes that the 80 percent dream recall from REM
awakenings underestimates the actual time the REM state is
occupied with dreams. Considering the rapidity with which we
forget dreams upon awakening each morning, Dement thinks
it likely that sometimes forgetting is so rapid that we can lose
dreams immediately upon awakening. If this is true, then
perhaps as much as 100 percent of REM time contains dreams.[23]

     One old myth about dreaming that has been shattered by
recent research is that dreams occur instantaneously in time. A
famous anecdote by an early sleep researcher, the nineteenth-
century French physician André Maury, planted this myth in
the scientific literature. Maury dreamed that he was in Paris
during the "Reign of Terror" following the French Revolution.
In his dream, he was the victim of an elaborate drama involving
his being sentenced to death by guillotine. When the blade of

the guillotine severed his head from his body, he awoke with a start, to find that part of his bed had collapsed and had fallen on the back of his neck, right where the guillotine would have struck! Maury concluded from this that he must have dreamed the whole elaborate sequence of events in a brief interval between the bed's collapse and the time it took him to awake from the blow.[24]

However, several things make it unlikely that dreams are generally so collapsed in time. For one thing, when people are awakened from REM episodes, they can accurately estimate the length of the REM period by how long their dreams seemed to take. Also, the number of words in the dreamer's description of his dream correlates with the objective length of the REM period from which he was woken.

One curiosity of REM sleep is a neurological condition known as *narcolepsy*. A person who has narcolepsy has sleep attacks—episodes of an uncontrollable need to fall asleep in the middle of the day. These attacks can come even in the midst of some absorbing activity. In fact, for some narcoleptics, the attacks are brought on by excitement, so it is not unusual for these unfortunate people to fall abruptly asleep while playing a volleyball game or when laughing at a funny joke.

Though narcolepsy has been known as a clinical entity for many years, it has been discovered only recently that many narcoleptics' sleep attacks begin with sudden onsets of REM in the middle of the day. At night, these narcoleptics enter the REM state almost immediately, whereas in the normal sleep pattern 60–90 minutes of slow-wave sleep precede the first REM episode. This explains why so many narcoleptics experience muscular collapse and paralysis just before their attacks: it is a striking display of the EMG suppression which normally accompanies the REM state. Still another aspect of their REM sleep is reflected in the vivid and sometimes frightening hallucinations which characterize some narcoleptic attacks. Apparently it is possible to experience REM dreams before completely losing consciousness. In these cases, people can be simultaneously conscious of the demands of the outside world and the visions of their dream state.[25]

Why Do We Dream?

Despite the vast amount of research, the biological role of REM sleep is still unknown. The old theory, that dreams are the guardians of sleep, is no longer tenable. According to this theory, dreams occur in response to external disturbances, such as a mosquito bite or a car's horn, which threaten the sleeping state. The dream would be woven about the intruding event in an effort to disguise its true sleep-threatening significance. Sigmund Freud's well-known dream theory was a variant of this view. There are experiments which show that sleepers sometimes *do* incorporate externally occurring events into their dreams. But the sleep-guardian theory is contradicted by the cyclical nature of REM sleep. REM periods recur with regularity, about every 90 minutes during sleep. They therefore appear to be governed by some kind of internal clock, rather than by an external irritation.[26]

One current hypothesis on the function of REM sleep is that these periods play a role in brain maturation, early in life. By this theory, REM sleep in adulthood is a less functional holdover from infancy. It is true that REM occupies a great amount of the sleep of newborn infants (about 50 percent, compared to 25 percent for adults). And since infants sleep a larger portion of the day, about four hours of their day is spent in REM sleep. Physiological signs of the REM state have also been recorded from unborn babies, in the uterus.

An elaboration of the brain-maturation theory states that during REM periods the infant's brain acquires genetically transmitted "programs"—functional connections in the brain which might underlie instinctive behaviors, or other kinds of inherited memories. This position is supported by the fact that

REM sleep is not found in cold-blooded vertebrates (reptiles, amphibians, and fishes), whose behavior patterns seem largely to be determined by permanent, wired-in connections of neurons. Michel Jouvet, the French sleep expert who advanced this theory, reasons that these animals must be governed by programs in the brain that are determined by hard-wired connections, more like an electric garage-door opener circuit than a computer's flexible and more complicated sequences of electronic code. These latter kinds of programs (called "software" in computer terminology) seem to be more descriptive of the brains of mammals and other warm-blooded verebrates. According to Jouvet, it is for transmitting inherited software programs to the developing nervous system that REM sleep evolved.[27]

A less extreme version of this hypothesis states that REM aids in brain development by providing stimulation for the growing brain before birth, at a time when stimulation from external sources is practically nonexistent. The reasoning behind this view rests on well-established findings that early sensory stimulation is necessary for normal brain development. If kittens are raised in an artificial environment without visual patterns, they will grow up to be irreversibly blind.[28]

Another current idea about the function of REM sleep is that it fixes in the brain traces of memories acquired during the previous day. By this theory, the dream reflects the sifting and sorting out—the cognitive reorganization—of current and past memories. Evidence for this view is that the amount of REM sleep often increases following intense or stressful daytime experiences. It also increases following vigorous periods of learning.[29]

Still another theory states that REM periods are the most visible expression of a continous 90-minute physiological clock. According to this view, periods of activity alternate with periods of rest in 90-minute cycles throughout the day, even during waking. This alternation is termed the *"basic rest-and-activity cycle" (BRAC)*. Subtle 90- to 120-minute cycles *have been* detected in wakefulness, for such diverse measurements as stomach contractions, eye-movement activity, EEG rhythms, visual attentiveness, and even daydream occurrence.[30] Further evidence is that the slow-wave sleep state, if induced by continuous stimulation by an electrode implanted in the proper sleep center, can only be maintained for an hour or so, and then the brain must have a REM period before the slow-wave state can recur.

Whatever the function of REM, it appears to be based on a strong internal need. If people are selectively deprived of REM sleep by being wakened at the onset of every REM period, they will have larger amounts of REM during subsequent nights.[31] This "REM rebound" effect seems to imply that people need to get a certain amount of REM sleep each night, and if they don't, they will try to make up for it on succeeding nights.

Curiously enough, some people do not show the REM rebound effect, and these people appear to be having more dreams during slow-wave sleep.[32] Another curiosity: actively hallucinating schizophrenics also show no REM rebound.[33] Maybe there is some kind of need for fantasy—or for some physiological substrate of fantasy experiences—and perhaps under some conditions the fantasies of REM dreams overflow into slow-wave sleep or even into wakefulness.[34]

This type of theory is the most compelling and persistent notion of the function of dreams. Basically, the theory says that we must get our share of fantasy experiences every day—fantasies usually involving intense pleasures and appetites, such as sex or aggression. These theories stress the importance of nighttime fantasy to emotional balance during the daytime. Dreams act as a kind of safety valve for our darker instincts and drives. If these needs are not discharged at night, according to some versions of the theory, bizarre or pathological thought or behavior may occur during the daytime.

Despite its intuitive appeal, the fantasy-need theory of dreams has resisted direct attempts to prove it. For one thing, depriving people of REM by selectively waking them at the start of every REM period does not make them obviously psychotic.

Still, alterations in REM time may have profound effects on a person's mood. An interesting review of what happens when people get too little or too much REM sleep is provided by Cartwright.[35]

Drowsy States

The classification of consciousness into waking and sleeping states blurs the transitions between them. Very little is known about these transitions, but they figure prominently in the mental lives of many of us. Sleep onset has been described as a time rich in visual imagery; many people report having an intense succession of images during this time.[36] These *hypnagogic images* are unconnected by a narrative or story line, and in this regard they are different from REM dreams.

Many creative thinkers have used this state as a source of inspiration. A well-known surrealistic painter is said to have trained himself to fall asleep in a chair with his chin resting on a spoon. The spoon, in turn, was held in one hand, propped by the elbow which rested on a table. As he would fall asleep, his muscles relaxed and his chin would fall, waking him. It was then that he could sketch the images which came to him at the onset of sleep and which would otherwise have been forgotten.

When people relax deeply, the EEG tends to be dominated by alpha waves (8 to 13 cycles per second) over large areas of the cortex. The alpha waves are gradually replaced by a rhythm in the range of 4 to 8 cycles per second, called *theta waves*. Theta waves are faster than the *delta* of deepest slow-wave sleep (which are 0.5 to 3 cycles per second) but they nonetheless appear to be a sign of sleep: during theta, people are relatively unresponsive to signals in their environment. In fact, even during wakefulness, if we are fatigued or bored, the brain can emit bursts of theta. In these cases, it appears that drowsy people have brief interludes of sleep, several seconds at a time. In most cases, people will have several of these "microsleeps," as they are called, and yet be totally unaware of having slept.[37]

Each of the major brain states—waking, slow-wave sleep, and REM sleep—vary from moment to moment in complicated ways. Transient wave forms come and go during each of these states, and the dominant waves are often modulated by smaller waves of different frequencies. The current understanding of waking and sleeping, in terms of these major states, will almost certainly be replaced by a more complex one.

Waking, Sleeping and the Mind–Brain Relationship

Laboratory studies of the mental accompaniments of REM and slow-wave periods of sleep suggest that they involve two different types of mental experience. It is not clear whether dream states reveal subsystems of mind that are obscured by the light of daytime consciousness, or whether they are only reflecting "noise" among deactivated neurons. Whatever the significance of dreaming, it is important to note that consciousness—in the sense of mental experience—is not completely abolished even during the deepest stages of sleep.

We get the impression that our nights are largely devoid of conscious experience because we don't easily remember our dreams. Even the dreams which seem so clear upon awakening are usually forgotten within an hour. What this shows is that persistence in *memory* is an important attribute of what we think of as our conscious experiences. By reports of wakened sleepers, and by most physiological criteria, the REM state appears to be a time of intense mental and brain activity. Yet sleep often seems to us a mental void, simply because we don't recall our dreams.

Slow-wave sleep comes closest to being a state of unconsciousness, but even here we are not completely empty of experience, at least part of the time, because people will report having dream thoughts if awoken from this state. Are there

isolated pieces of cortex which might have been active, though
undetected by conventional EEG methods? Is activated cortex
not really necessary for conscious experience.

The only living state of the human brain which appears
completely devoid of mental activity is *coma,* a continuous sleep
caused by damage to the activation system of the brainstem. In
a state of coma, the cerebral cortex generates slow waves,
resembling the slow waves of deep sleep.

Are there any hard facts here for understanding the
physical basis of consciousness? For one thing, it seems that
there might be a close relationship between activity in the cortex
and conscious experience. The cortical slow waves of non-REM
sleep occur at a period when mental content is at its lowest by
reports of wakened sleepers. At these times, the individual
cortical neurons fire in patterns of bursts and pauses, rather
than more evenly, as they do when we're awake. This pattern
means that there must be many brief intervals every second
when individual neurons are unexcitable and at rest—unlike in
the activated waking state, where they are excitable most of the
time.

Cortical slow waves also occur during wakefulness. The
synchronized alpha waves are similar to the slow waves of sleep,
in that they are both generated by synchronous oscillation of
large populations of neural cells. The electrical oscillations
detected by the EEG electrodes reflect the waxing and waning
of excitatory charges in vast networks of cell dendrites (see
Chapter 1).[38] Both types of EEG appear to signal an idling or
resting state of the cortex. From all this we should be able to say
that we can localize conscious processes in the cortex, but since
cortical activation is regulated by mechanisms of the reticular
formation, the evidence just as easily argues for the involvement
of these structures in producing conscious experience. The
brain lesions which most dramatically abolish consciousness are
lesions not to the cortex, but to the arousal system of the
brainstem. We will again take up this question of cortical versus
brainstem contributions to consciousness in Chapter 6.

Altered States of Consciousness:
The Case of Hypnosis

One of the enduring interests of psychologists has been the study of "altered states of consciousness," by which is meant such things as drug-induced and psychotic visionary experiences, meditative states, states of religious ecstasy, and hypnotic trance. It is an avenue of inquiry into the most exotic and also the most inaccessible of human experiences. For if "ordinary" or waking consciousness is itself difficult to study—because we cannot directly examine another person's mind—how much more difficult it must be to study conscious states which are experienced only occasionally and only by a few.

For brain theory, the study of altered states of consciousness is worthwhile, because variations to "ordinary" consciousness may provide contrasts which elucidate dimensions or components of mind, and this has certainly proven to be true of sleep research. But unlike sleep states, the scientific study of these other "altered states" has been extremely difficult. The controversy surrounding the nature of *hypnotic trance* illustrates the problems. Readers interested in a more general introduction to the psychology of altered states of consciousness are referred to the book edited by Charles Tart, listed in the bibliography for this chapter.

By everyday wisdom, hypnosis is said to be an alteration of consciousness characterized by extreme suggestibility and involving changes in willful control of actions. The hypnotized person is subservient in thought and action to the will of the hypnotist. Common forms are such things as *hyperesthesia* (increased sensitivity): at the suggestion of the hypnotist, the hypnotized person might, for example, be able to feel tiny variations in the texture of surfaces, or experience colors as being more vivid than usual. Or, just the opposite, the hypnotist might suggest an undersensitivity, such as not being able to feel something which is ordinarily painful *(analgesia)* like pricking of the hand with a pin. Hypnotically suggested *hallucinations* are also common experiences. People report seeing things not actually there, or not seeing things which are, after these suggestions were made under hypnosis.

There are variations in the degree to which different people are hypnotizable. Those who can be "deeply" hypnotized feel very much different in that state than when normally awake, and so they are tempted to say that their state of consciousness was altered, or that they were in a "trance." Those who are not as susceptible to hypnosis report only minimal changes, usually feelings of drowsiness or relatation.

The procedures for inducing a hypnotic trance generally involves suggestions—overt or tacit—of relaxation or drowsiness. Most procedures also involve a focus of concentration, ultimately on the hypnotist's voice. Once hypnotized, the subject is given explicit questions, suggestions, or commands, to which he responds cooperatively. Hypnotic suggestions can include those described above and also can entail such things as feats of great strength, detailed recall or acting out of scenes from early childhood (*hypnotic age regression*), and acts of unusual control over parts of the body. Examples of the latter are hypnotically induced labor contractions, and speeding up or lowering of the heartbeat, and there are some documented cases of warts being cured by hypnotic suggestion.[39]

As a medical tool, hypnosis has been in and out of repute many times in its long history. During the fifteenth century in Europe, practitioners were said to cure various ailments by passing magnets over the bodies of sufferers, in order to induce a curative trance. This technique was later abandoned in favor of the hypnotist's own "animal magnetism."[40] In more recent times, it has been convincingly demonstrated that people can be made to withstand painful stimulation when this has been suggested to them under hypnosis.[41] The wider acceptance of hypnosis as a medical anesthetic was apparently halted by the fortuitous discovery of ether anesthesia in 1846.

Scientific questions about hypnosis, at least the hard-nosed questions, would seem to concern the physical basis for this state. What physiological or behavioral signs distinguish it from ordinary waking consciousness or from known states of sleep? Unfortunately, finding answers to this question has been difficult. It was formerly believed that hypnosis was a state of partial sleep; in fact, this is the derivation of the modern term (from *Hypnos,* the Greek god of sleep). This view is no longer held, since it is now known that the EEG of a hypnotized person does not resemble the brain waves of sleep. For the most part, the EEG of a hypnotized person is indistinguishable from that of relaxed wakefulness.[42]

What, then, defines the state of hypnosis? There is a curious lack of agreement among scientific investigators. In practice, most researchers seem to judge the depth of hypnotic trance by how easily their subjects respond to suggestions—from how convincingly they hallucinate or regress in age. Yet according to a prominent critic of "trance" explanations of hypnosis, the criterion of hypersuggestibility "gives rise to circular reasoning: The hypnotic trance state is inferred from the high level of response to suggestions, and, vice versa, the hypnotic trance state is used to account for the high level of response to suggestions from which it is inferred."[43]

Critics also point out that most people are ordinarily quite suggestible. If you are standing upright with your eyes closed, and someone repeatedly tells you that you are swaying back and forth, you are likely to sway, if only a little. By this technique, some people are found to be more suggestible than others, and, interestingly, those people who sway the most are usually the ones who respond the best to hypnotic induction procedures.[44] For many years, the "sway technique" served researchers as an instrument for measuring hypnotic susceptibility.

Another way to demonstrate that people are normally suggestible is to have someone clench his hands together very tightly, fingers interlocked. After some time, in which the subject is exhorted to squeeze his hands together very tightly, the suggestion is made to him that he will be unable to pull them apart. Most people will have some difficulty in separating their hands.

Even in terms of hallucinatory experience, the suggestibility criterion doesn't distinguish hypnotized from nonhypnotized people. This was nicely demonstrated in an experiment conducted by Joseph Juhasz and Theodore Sarbin. They had their subjects—unhypnotized, wide-awake college students—participate in what was billed as an experiment in sensory psychology. The students were to taste samples of water, which they believed contained differing concentrations of salt in solution, and they were to respond for each "salt" or "no salt," depending on whether or not it tasted salty. Most subjects tasted salt about 25 percent of the time, and 12 of the 28 maintained they would testify at a murder trial that they had tasted salt in the solutions that day. The samples actually contained nothing but pure water!

This experiment illustrates the difficulty in using suggestibility as the criterion for distinguishing hypnotic from waking states. It also points out the degree to which internally generated imagery operates in perception. In Chapter 2 this point entered into the discussion of theories of pattern recognition. Ulric Neisser, in his extremely influential book, *Cognitive Psychology*, documented the wealth of evidence pointing to the conclusion that "perceptions" and thought "images" are best conceived of as end points of a continuum. There are cases, like the Juhasz and Sarbin experiment, where the dividing line is not clear.

A classic experiment, published in 1910 by the psychologist C.W. Perky, provides another example. Perky instructed her subjects to observe a small spot in the center of a smoky window, and to imagine different objects (such as a face, or a bowl of fruit) to be at that spot. Unknown to the subjects, very faint pictures of the objects they were to imagine were projected from behind the window. It was clear from their descriptions of their imaginings that they incorporated the projections into their images, and yet most subjects firmly held to the belief that what they saw was the product of their imaginations.[45]

Neisser argues that we do something like "construct" our perceptions. The Perky experiment seems to suggest, further, that we "see" our images. Perceptions and images partake of common mental machinery. The perceptual suggestibility of hypnotic subjects is understandable in this light. What these experiments show, however, is that perceptual suggestibility is not unique to hypnosis.

Some scientific psychologists are skeptical about accepting hypnosis as a trance or an altered state, because no one has been able to show any consistent objective indicators that it is. This "skeptical" school treats the hypnotized person as a player of a *role*—the role of one who is hypnotized.[46] The reasoning is that we all grow up with certain enculturated ideas about hypnosis, including how a hypnotized person is supposed to act. Movies such as *The Manchurian Candidate* or *Sybil,* and even the TV cartoons watched by children, readily give out the information that one who is hypnotized stares blankly into space, talks in a sluggish and mechanical fashion, and doesn't do anything unless he is specifically commanded to do it by the hypnotist. This script, so the skeptical argument goes, is sufficient to establish, in the minds of someone growing up in our culture, the appropriate rules for hypnotic behavior, and the role is willingly, if unconsciously, engaged in by those who are motivated bo become hypnotized. The reasons for wanting to play this role would involve, perhaps, reaping some therapeutic benefit, or simply acquiescing to the strong social demands of the hypnotist's setting.

A well-known demonstration by Martin Orne supports this point of view. In two introductory psychology classes Orne gave lectures on the nature of hypnosis. During the lecture in the first class, a confederate was hypnotized to serve as a demonstration to the class. What the class did not know was that the confederate had previously been hypnotized by Orne and at that time given the specific suggestion that henceforth, whenever he was again hypnotized, he would acquire "catalepsy" of his dominant hand—that is, the hand would remain rigidly in the pose in which it was placed, and unless this pose was changed by someone else, it would not move.

The second psychology class received the same lecture and

demonstration, except in this case the hypnotic subject had not previously been given the suggestion of "catalepsy," and hence he did not manifest this condition. Later, when students from the two classes were themselves hypnotized as volunteers for a research project, members of the first class tended to exhibit "dominant hand catalepsy," while those from the second class did not. Orne concluded that when a person is hypnotized, he behaves in accordance with his perception of what the role entails.[47]

The characterization of the hypnotic state as a role does not mean that a hypnotized person in consciously faking, any more than a judge, in his black robes, is merely feigning an air of authority. We often react to the stylized demands placed on our social behaviors by other people's expectations—expectations of what a student is like when he talks to a teacher, or a lawyer when he or she talks to a client, or a father when he talks to his child. What the role-playing explanation says is that, for one who is motivated to become hypnotized, the situation is rich in demands and cues to proper hypnotic behavior. And since subjective experiences are ineffable kinds of things, hard to remember or describe, it is possible to convince oneself that one is in a trance, an altered state of consciousness.

But how does the skeptical point of view explain hypnotic feats such as acts of great strength, pain analgesia, or the recall of forgotten memories of childhood? The psychologist Theodore X. Barber has spent many years documenting the feats attributed to the hypnotic state. In many cases, he has found the claims to be exaggerations. In others, he has shown them to be instances of unusual abilities, well within the repertoire of normally awake people—at least if they are strongly motivated. An example is the "human plank" trick, a favorite of stage hypnotists. Under hypnosis, the hypnotic subject's body is made so rigid that he can support himself with his head on one chair and his ankles on another. Actually, this turns out to be well within the abilities of almost any man who can be induced simply to try it.

As for the reduction of pain under hypnosis, Barber's research and that of others have shown similar analgesic effects (including the reduction of galvanic skin responses which normally accompany painful stimulation) following instructions simply to relax and concentrate on something else. One particularly interesting technique involves regarding the pain merely as an interesting sensation, to be attended to no differently than any ordinary sound or tickle.

The recall of early childhood memories during hypnotic age regression might be explained either as fanciful reconstructions or as benefits to memory which ordinarily accompany deep relaxation and concentration.

The feats which constitute the most compelling evidence for an "altered state" interpretation are those in which hypnotized people perform surprising acts of control over their body's physiology. For example, hypnotic subjects have been reported to raise blisters on an area of skin where a hallucinated match inflicted a hallucinated burn. Barber has shown that in many cases, it is possible to demonstrate that the subjects who respond to these hypnotic suggestions are people who already have highly "suggestible" aspects to their physiology. In the cases of blistering, it appears that these subjects had past histories of dermatological reactions to emotional situations.[48]

There have been several reports of hypnotists' curing warts by suggestion. In one such study, two Scottish investigators gave their patients the hypnotic suggestion that their warts would disappear on one side of the body only. After several months, 9 of the 14 patients had the warts disappear on the "treated" side, but not on the other.[49] This study, remarkable though it may be, is less evidence for the reality of hypnosis than it is for the precise control people can sometimes exert over so-called "involuntary" physiological functions. Other studies have shown that warts can be cured by the application of *placebos* (inert medicines), such as painting the warts with blue vegetable coloring and telling the patient it is an effective treatment.[50] There is, in the field of "psychosomatic medicine," documentation of a wide variety of known placebo effects. These range from the simple vegetable-dye cure for warts (and the more famous and perhaps equally effective one of swinging a cat around your head), to severe cases of cancer which were apparently cured by belief in the efficacy of a physiologically inert medicine.[51]

There has been increasing recognition in recent years that people possess previously unsuspected abilities to control aspects of their physiology which are traditionally regarded as "involuntary." The new medical technology known as "biofeedback" rests on this assumption, and scores of laboratory experiments have demonstrated that conscious control can be acquired over such things as blood pressure, muscle tension, skin temperature, swallowing reflexes, and heart rate.[52] What is impressive about hypnotic techniques, biofeedback research, and placebo effects in medicine is that they all demonstrate the tremendous potential for "conscious" or "mental" control over bodily processes of many kinds. If people can do strange things under hypnosis, it also appears that they can do the same things on their own!

In Barber's thorough review of the published experiments on hypnosis, he concludes that the evidence for a "state" explanation is lacking;

> It has been assumed that the hypnotic-trance state is real—that there is some reliable way to tell whether a person is hypnotized or not, some simply physiological measure—brain waves, eye movements, pulse rate or galvanic skin responses, for example—that would clearly distinguish a hypnotized person from a normally awake person. Unfortunately, there is no such test.[53]

REM sleep is described as an "altered state" of consciousness by the "presence of one or more attributes that are absent at all other times, or absent in a specific constellation."[54] Thus do two leading investigators justify the use of the term "state." The frozen state of water can be characterized by its rigidity and solidity. REM is a state of consciousness characterized by dream thoughts and by its physiological concomitants (EEG activation, EMG suppression, and a lot of phasic "twitches" of the nervous system). The dream thoughts themselves are intangible, and we do not comprehend them well enough—Wittgenstein might say we do not have the language to comprehend them—to distinguish them, objectively, from such phenomena as daydreams or hypnagogic fantasies. It is the consistency, orderliness, and objectivity of the *physical* descriptors which compel us to apply the term "state." Unlike REM sleep, there are no known objective signs which characterize hypnosis.

What the dispute between the skeptical and credulous views of hypnosis shows is what the Behaviorists used to argue so vehemently: that mental events are slippery, intangible sorts of things, hard to describe and impossible to view from the outside. How we regard them seems to be strongly influenced by preconceptions, limitations of the language, and probably by the act of introspection itself.

Some of the same difficulties in pinning down hypnosis as a state are shared by meditation. Although meditation practices undoubtedly involved alterations in perception, feeling and thought—sometimes quite profound—their physiological basis is elusive.[55] Despite the claims of partisans,[56] it turns out to be very difficult to distinguish a meditator from someone who is merely relaxed and drowsy. One recent report suggested that practitioners of a popular form of Yogic meditation (transcendental meditation) actually appear to be taking brief naps.[57]

An interesting exception to this generalization was provided in a 1965 report by the Japanese psychiatrists Akira Kasamatsu and Tomio Hirai. In their studies of a Zen master, Kasamatsu and Hirai observed that the EEG of their subject in meditation was characterized by large amounts of alpha-wave activity. This in itself did not distinguish this EEG from that of many other meditators, nor from that of ordinary people who are completely relaxed. But when the experimenters tried to evoke orienting reactions in their subject's EEG by presenting a series of audible clicks at unpredictable times, a unique pattern emerged. The Zen masters didn't habituate! Unlike normal subjects, for whom the first few clicks would produce alpha-blocking but later clicks would show hardly any effect, these Zen masters showed no tendency to cease reacting to the stimuli, even after many trials.[58]

Now, one of the descriptions commonly given of Zen practice is that the meditator learns to "open up" —to become simultaneously aware of everything around him. Also, the meditator becomes able to make his mind like a "mirror" —reflecting things that go by the window of consciousness but not grasping at any one of them.[59] This description could be applied to the EEG data. The click stimulus is reacted to on the twentieth trial just as on the first. It seems as if the meditator's awareness of the things around him was not confined, as it is normally, by the focus of selective attention. Here, possibly, is a physiological analogue of the idea of "expanding" one's consciousness.

William James remarked that consciousness was properly described as a "stream" composed of many intermingling tributaries and currents.[60] This still appears to be a better metaphor than "states." Nevertheless, several major states can be distinguished on the basis of gross brain wave characteristics: the alternation of desynchronized EEG with alpha, in wakefulness; the large, rolling slow waves of deep sleep; and the neural excitability coupled with muscular flaccidity in REM. Perhaps a sophisticated brain science of the future can discover the hidden signs which chacterize other, subtler states of consciousness.

Recommended Readings

WAKING, ATTENTION, AND ORIENTING

Magoun, H.W. *The Waking Brain.* Springfield, Ill.: Charles C Thomas, 1963.
Norman, D.A. *Memory and Attention.* New York: John Wiley & Sons, 1976.

POSNER, M.I. "The Psychobiology of Attention." In M.S. Gazzaniga and C. Blakemore (eds.), *Handbook of Psychobiology.* New York: Academic Press, 1975.

LYNN, R. *Attention, Arousal and the Orientation Reaction.* Oxford: Pergamon Press, 1966.

SLEEPING AND DREAMING

DEMENT, W.C. *Some Must Watch While Some Must Sleep.* San Francisco: W.H. Freeman, 1974.

WEBB, W.B. *Sleep: The Gentle Tyrant.* Englewood Cliffs, N.J.: Prentice-Hall, 1975.

OSWALD, I. *Sleep,* 3rd ed. Middlesex, England: Penguin Books, 1974.

ALTERED STATES OF CONSCIOUSNESS

TART, C.T. (ed.). *Altered States of Consciousness.* New York: John Wiley & Sons, 1969.

SHOR, R., and M. ORNE, (eds.). *The Nature of Hypnosis: Selected Basic Readings.* New York: Holt, Rinehart, and Winston, 1965.

ORNSTEIN, R.E. *The Psychology of Consciousness.* San Francisco: W.H. Freeman, 1972.

Thinking I:
Words
and Other
Images

In this chapter and the next, we take up questions dealing with the physical basis of "thinking." This is a term we apply to many different kinds of mental events: inner speech and visual imaginings, logical reasoning and sudden inspirations. Since all these things depend upon past experience—the meanings of words,

4

the image of someone's face—memory also comes into the consideration of human thought. In the other direction, we must also consider mental links to the future, through plans and intentions. Human thought and behavior are ordinarily organized and directed to the accomplishment of long-term, socially initated goals, reflecting an ability unique in animal evolution. The brain mechanisms underlying this ability to plan represent important neurological embodiments of thought.

It is not exactly clear how the evolution of the human brain allowed for human intelligence. The brains of man and chimpanzee appear quite similar, both in size and structure. Perhaps in the human brain some critical mass was surmounted, maybe in the added memory capacity necessary for language. Certainly, there are precursors of human thought in the capabilities of other animals, particularly the great apes. Genuine acts of invention can be seen in their behavior. The psychologist Wolfgang Köhler, stationed on the island of Tenerife during World War I, observed the mental capacities of a captive ape named Sultan. Sultan was presented with the problem of trying to get a banana just out of reach, beyond the bars of his cage. Köhler observed that Sultan solved this problem in an apparently insightful manner, by assembling a long pole from two shorter sticks and using this pole to retrieve the banana.[1] The "manufacture" of tools has also been observed among wild chimpanzees. Figure 4–1 shows a chimp "fishing" in a termite mound with a long blade of grass it has broken off and prepared for this purpose.[2] It is tempting to view human thinking as having evolved from these rudimentary beginnings. Insight and foresight in animals are familiar forms of mentality, and they argue against any view of human intelligence which sets man apart from the rest of nature.

In discussing the processes of human thought, we are largely dealing with the capabilities of the cerebral cortex, the great folded outer shell of the forebrain which is man's most notable evolutionary achievement. It is the further increase in thickness and area of this part of the brain which has distin-

FIGURE 4–1. Chimpanzee "fishing" for termites with a blade of grass. (Photo by Baron Hugo van Lawick, © National Geographic Society.)

guished the brain of man from his apelike ancestors. This increased mass of cortex has apparently enabled humans to invent automobiles (as well as engines of destruction), to build cities, and to fathom the workings of much of the rest of creation.

No doubt the increase in the size and complexity of the cerebral cortex, which is the main thrust of primate brain evolution, provides the basis for the intelligence of apes as well as man. Figure 4–2 depicts a series of brains of mammals, from which it can be seen that the most striking change is in the amount of cortex not specifically committed to sensory or motor functions. This *"uncommitted cortex,"* largely in the parietal and frontal regions, has no direct connections to the muscles or sense organs.[3] Its neurons speak only to other cortical neurons.

It is not the absolute size of the brain, nor the total number of cortical cells, which explains the cognitive capabilities of

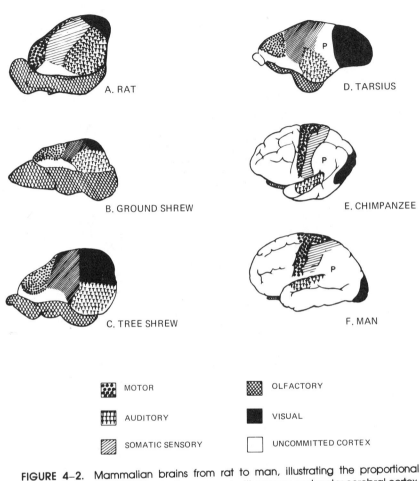

	MOTOR		OLFACTORY
	AUDITORY		VISUAL
	SOMATIC SENSORY		UNCOMMITTED CORTEX

FIGURE 4-2. Mammalian brains from rat to man, illustrating the proportional increase of "uncommitted cortex" compared with sensory and motor cerebral cortex. (Figures not drawn to the same scale.) (From W. Penfield in J. C. Eccles, ed., _Brain and Conscious Experience_, New York: Springer-Verlag, Inc., 1966. Reproduced with permission of the publisher.)

humans. An elephant's brain is much larger, a dolphin's brain is more convoluted, and a whale's brain contains more cells than man's. More likely, it is the complexity of the interconnections of the new "uncommited" cortex which enables man to outstrip other animals in intelligence.[4]

Our knowledge about the workings of the "uncommitted cortex" in man comes largely from studies of the effects of localized brain damage in these areas. Although ethical considerations prohibit making experimental lesions in human brains, accidental "experiments" are seen daily in the neurology clinic as a result of strokes, tumors, and missile wounds.[5] Though the precise location of the lesion may not be known, the types of symptoms which result may provide a catalog of underlying regularities from which the brain scientist can infer the structure of thought.

Making inferences from data on brain lesions is a primitive and probably limited scientific method. It presupposes that the processes observed are discretely and locally organized in the brain—an assumption which is regarded as highly doubtful. As the psychologist Richard Gregory remarked, just because your radio emits a howl when you remove a transistor, you are not justified in calling the removed part a "howl-squelching center."[6]

Keeping these difficulties in mind, we will approach the evidence from brain damage to see what can be learned about the structural basis of thought. By considering the regularities associated with local disruptions and disconnections of brain functioning, we might be able to view in isolation some of the components of mind.

The Nature of Human Language

There is at least one profound discontinuity in the evolution of thinking. People use inventive language and animals don't. The human brain contains highly developed capabilities for manipulating abstract language symbols, symbols which form the basis for particularly human and particularly strong methods of remembering things past, envisioning things yet to come, and directing the stream of consciousness into controlled channels.

Human language is primarily a system for communication, but it differs from other kinds of animal communication in important ways. Apes and monkeys make gestures of threat and appeasement, charging, howling, shaking tree branches. These and other displays serve to mark off physical and psychic territories. These organized systems of communication function largely to avoid fighting within the species and to regulate smooth social interaction.[7] Some gestural systems are quite sophisticated, as in the waggle dance of the honeybee, which signals to co-workers in the hive the direction and distance of a food source (see Figure 4–3).[8]

Many animals communicate by a sense of smell. For example, the female silkworm secretes chemical odors when she is sexually receptive. Like a guided missile, the male silkworm homes in on the increasing concentration of this chemical, centered at the tip of the female's abdomen.[9]

All these kinds of animal communication differ from human language by being limited in the number of different messages possible to produce or understand. For example, bands of gibbon monkeys use a dozen or so distinct vocal calls, each one bearing a separate message.

The symbols of human language, however, can be recombined endlessly. The sound units of the language (phonemes) can be combined into a very large number of words, and these words, in turn, can be combined by a system of rules (called *grammar* or *syntax*) into a potentially endless variety of sentences. The total number of meaningful statements possible for a speaker of human language to say or understand is indefinitely large.[10] The other side of this coin is that humans *invent* new utterances when using language. This essential quality of human language is called *propositionality* (a sensible message is called a proposition).[11]

Why didn't propositional language evolve in other species? Are any other animals, particularly our closest evolutionary cousins, capable of comprehending language? A small group of skeptical scientists are currently challenging the conventional belief that apes lack the brain capacity for complex language. A few earlier attempts to teach language to chimpanzees had failed, but now these scientists are trying to teach chimps the

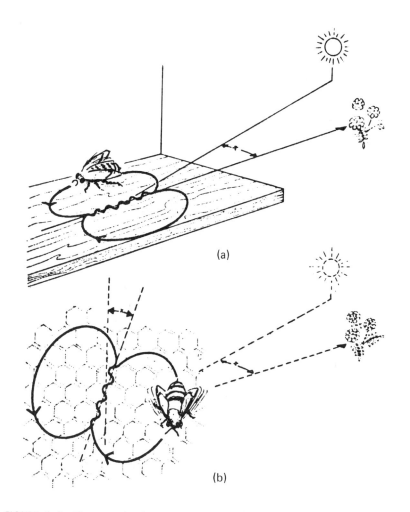

(a)

(b)

FIGURE 4-3. The waggle dance of the honeybee. The returning scout communicates the direction and distance of a food source to co-workers in the hive with a dance in the form of a figure eight. In the middle section of the dance, the bee wags its hindquarters vigorously. The orientation of the bee in the middle section of the dance signals the angle from the hive (with respect to the sun) along which the food source is to be located. Distance from the hive is signaled by the rate of the bee's dancing.

In (a), the bee performs the dance outside the hive, and the straight run of the dance points directly to the food source. If the dance is performed inside the hive (b), the bee orients herself by gravity, with the point directly overhead taking the place of the sun. (From H. Curtis, New York: Worth Publishers, <u>Biology,</u> 1975, p. 411. Based on von Frisch. Reproduced with permission of the publisher.)

use of a sign language, reasoning that the limitation on language in apes might be in the inadequate control over the vocal apparatus, rather than in the cognitive machinery of their brains.

Psychologists Allen and Beatrice Gardner, at the University of Nevada, have been raising chimpanzees from an early age in an environment where the chimps continually interact with humans. The chimps and humans talk to each other in a language of hand gestures called Ameslan, the American Sign Language for the deaf. The animals are rewarded with food or approval for correct performances.

Their first chimp, Washoe, had a vocabulary of nearly 200 words by the time she was five. By itself this might not have been any different, in principle, than training a dog to stand on its hind legs. What was remarkable was the animal's spontaneous combination of words to produce new utterances. For example, Washoe named watermelon a "drink-fruit." She even invented what might be called rudimentary sentences—for example, "more tickle" when she wanted to continue a pleasant game.[12]

Washoe and her chimp colleagues have managed to use Ameslan in ways which challenge preconceptions. The main issue in deciding whether they are truly using language revolves around whether the chimps use a system of rules of word order (a syntax) to construct their sentences, or whether their sentences are really more primitive combinations of words.[13] The chimps do distinguish between different word orders, and have even been observed to understand relationships based on them. The request "Lucy tickle Roger" was correctly understood the first time, even though Lucy had been familiar only with the phrase involving herself as object ("Roger tickle Lucy").[14] The seeds of human language competence may indeed be present in the brains of other animals.

Despite the debate over whether Washoe's language is truly propositional, or truly human in other respects,[15] it seems safe to say that whatever chimpanzee language capabilities turn out to be, their performance will probably fall far short of the abilities of even a five-year-old human. In considering why monkeys and apes don't use language as we do, we raise questions which get to the essence of human nature. The answers revolve around the capabilities of the human brain to learn and to use language. This is the domain of a new discipline known as *neurolinguistics*. We turn now to some fundamental considerations of neurolinguistics.

Human language is, first of all, an auditory code. It is primarily spoken and heard, and only later, in human history and child development, is it extended to a written, visual medium.[16] This primacy of the sense of hearing can be seen in the brain's anatomical organization for language. The cortical region for the perception of speech, *Wernicke's area,* lies next to the area on the temporal lobe which receives and analyzes auditory information (see Figure 4–4).

Some insights into the nature of language are afforded by considerations of brain anatomy. Wernicke's area is not merely an appendage of the auditory cortex. Even though it is most intimately related to audition, this region also has important neural connections with other sensory systems, most notably the visual cortex in the occipital lobe and the somato-sensory cortex of the parietal lobe (the sensory cortex which represents the

FIGURE 4–4.   Left cerebral cortex, showing regions related to speech and language.

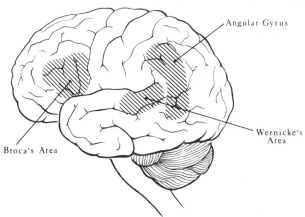

body's surfaces). These overlapping, multi-sensory connections are characteristic of the newly evolved "uncommitted cortex."[17]

One speculation on the origin of language is that the multi-sensory nature of this new cortex provided the basis for naming objects. According to this view, *naming* is the original form of abstract thought and the most basic act of human language.[18] Naming involves the abstracting out of experience certain stimulus qualities over others, as when a number of distinctly different objects are categorized together as "tree." This ability may rely on the making of cross-sensory associations. For example, in order to know the name for a pencil, the sound \'pen(t)-səl\ must be associated with the sight and feel, perhaps even the smell, of a pencil. Brain damage to a part of the cortex near Wernicke's area, at a place which connects language systems to the different sensory regions, sometimes causes an isolated inability to name objects *(anomia)*, even when other language functions are spared. The cortical area involved in most cases of anomia is called the *angular gyrus*. It lies at the intersection of the temporal, occipital, and parietal lobes, at the place where information from auditory, visual, and somato-sensory systems comes together (see Figure 4–4).[19]

Wernicke's area and the other cortical regions which participate in spoken and written language are located in the left cerebral hemisphere in most adults. This asymmetry is known as *lateralization*. Although there are exceptions and complications to this rule, the first basic fact of neurolinguistics is that in about 95 percent of all cases where brain damage produces some loss of language competence, the damage involves the left side.*

---

*The few exceptions are mostly left-handers (6%–12% of the population, depending upon one's definition of sinistrality). Among sinistrals, about half are lateralized for language, although the roles of the right and left hemispheres may be reversed. In general, left-handers are less strongly lateralized than right-handers. A sizeable proportion of sinistrals appear to have language functions about equally distributed in both hemispheres. The evidence for this is that one-sided brain damage is less likely to eliminate language capabilities for left-handers. "Lefties" also tend to be more ambidextrous than "righties,"

The asymmetry of the the human brain for language functioning is a striking exception to the general plan of bilateral symmetry found in other vertebrates. Human brain asymmetry also shows itself in the usually greater dexterity of one hand over the other (the word "dexterity" comes from the Latin for "right"). While other animals will show paw preferences, these preferences are not nearly so strong as in man, nor as consistent from one animal to another within a species. The structural asymmetry of the human brain in the vicinity of Wernicke's area, though slight, is visible to the naked eye and is present at birth.[20]

Interestingly enough, in most people the same side of the brain (the left) both controls the preferred hand and contains the centers which mediate language.* The relationship between language dominance and right-handedness, both apparently inherited and both based in the left hemisphere, is currently a subject of great scientific curiosity. Does language somehow determine hand dominance? Or did man's superior manual dexterity, having evolved for the manipulation of tools, somehow prepare the left hemisphere for accommodating language? Or is there a common third factor underlying both evolutionary achievements? This question will be discussed later, when we look into the specialized functions of each cerebral hemisphere.

The key to understanding human language competence

---

another indication of weaker brain lateralization for people who prefer their left hand.

Left-handers, as a group, comprise a greater variety of kinds of lateral brain organization and include people with strong, weak, and mixed patterns of hemispheric dominance. For this reason, it is hard to make generalizations, but some types of lefties, at least, are thought to differ in subtle but important ways from right-handers in their usual modes of thinking and problem-solving. (See Dimond, S. J., and J. G. Beaumont, (eds.), *Hemisphere Function in the Human Brain.* New York: Wiley, 1974.)

---

*Recall that the left side of the brain receives information from and controls the movements of the right side of the body. Such neural relationships are referred to as *contralateral.*

lies in the workings of the left-sided suprasensory cortex (refer again to Figure 4–4). From electrically stimulating the brains of monkeys, it has been found that vocalizations, of the type these monkeys use in communicating with one another, is produced by stimulating the parts of the older subcortical brain, linked to the neural control of emotional states.[21] This is an interesting finding in view of the fact that the vocalizations of these primates occur mostly in emotionally charged situations, situations related to threat, aggression, fear, or separation. In man, however, the areas of the brain which produce effects on speech when stimulated are in the new cortex, centered on Wernicke's area.[22] This difference suggests that while animal communications arise as expressions of emotional needs, human language evolved as a qualitatively different and separate function.[23]

The most challenging task facing neurolinguists is to understand the organization of the left hemisphere and the neural processes which mediate language. Modern linguistics has shown that the production and understanding of language is not based on simple associations between strings of words and the things they denote.[24] Rather, language competence seems to be based on a complicated system of logic, called a *generative grammar*. According to this view, sentences are created out of underlying, abstract, proto-linguistic statements called *deep structures*. Deep structures are the unconscious kernels of language. They are transformed by the generative grammar into actual spoken language (called *surface structures*). For example, the surface structure "A wise man is honest" breaks down into a deep structure which includes the components "A man is wise" and "A man is honest." The processes of transformation by a generative grammar give human languages a potentially infinite number of different grammatical sentences which could be spoken or comprehended. This is because grammatical units can be compounded indefinitely, as in "The dog who chased the cat who ate the rat who ate the malt. . . ."[25] Something like a generative grammar mechanism in the brain seems necessary in order to explain the propositionality of human languages.

Noam Chomsky, the M.I.T. linguist who proposed this view of language, asserts that it is possible to analyze all human languages—languages that are as seemingly different as English and Chinese—and show that their deep structures are basically identical.[26] If this is so, then it also might be true, as Chomsky believes, that this "universal grammar"—the fundamental ground-plan of human language—is genetically pre-wired into the brain. The strongest evidence for this is the fact that children from different backgrounds and different cultures seem to pick up language in about the same sequence of stages and at about the same age in their development. They all acquire language without any special training program, just as they learn to walk without being taught how. That is, children seem to learn the grammatical structure of language by some kind of *resonance*—like the ringing of a tuning fork by another sound of its own pitch. In this case, the resonance would be the resonance of a ripening internal brain mechanism with the language patterns it hears.[27]

Whether or not there is a universal grammar wired into the brains of all humans at birth, the challenge of neurolinguistics is to discover and decode the mechanisms which underlie the understanding and production of language. Although the task is well beyond the reach of current brain science, a few important facts have been uncovered—uncovered in the neurology clinic through observation of the ways in which people lose their language competence following brain injury.

Aphasia

Much of what is known about the organization of language in the brain comes from studies of patients with brains damaged by the accidents of man (bullet wounds) or of nature (strokes). *Aphasia* is the name given to this variety of language disturbance resulting from brain damage. There are many different types of aphasia. Some involve only difficulties in the naming of things (*anomia*), with language comprehension remaining relatively intact. Some involve only an inability to read (*alexia*). Some unfortunate people are found to be unable to understand or produce any form of language, either spoken or written (*global aphasia*). Descriptions of a few types of aphasia are given in Table 4–1.

The earliest discovery made about the aphasias was that they could be broken down into two main subtypes. People with

Table 4–1.
Some Forms of Aphasia

	SYMPTOMS	LESION SITE
Global aphasia	Comprehension and production of speech faulty or absent.	Widespread left-hemisphere damage affecting both Broca's and Wernicke's areas.
Broca's aphasia	Comprehension intact, but absent or extremely labored speech; omission of small grammatical words; writing comparably disordered.	Motor speech area in left frontal lobe (Broca's area).
Wernicke's aphasia	Outward form of speech preserved, but speech mostly meaningless; comprehension of spoken and written speech extremely faulty; writing also impaired; paraphasic utterances.	Auditory speech area in left temporal lobe (Wernicke's area).
Conduction aphasia	Spoken and written language output same as for Wernicke's aphasia, but comprehension and reading appear intact; inability to repeat words.	Disconnection of fiber tract in parietal lobe which connects Wernicke's area to Broca's area.
Pure word deafness	Comprehension normal for written language, but impaired for spoken language, despite normal hearing. Verbal and written expression normal.	Deep temporal lobe lesion, disconnecting Wernicke's area from auditory inputs.
Anomia (amnestic aphasia)	Severe difficulties in the naming of objects, with normal grammar, articulation, and comprehension.	Lesion to angular gyrus (near Wernicke's area): disruption of multi-sensory associations.

receptive aphasias have trouble with the comprehension of speech, but they go through the motions of speaking anyway. They don't understand too well what they or other people say, and they usually produce speech which is largely "word salad." For example, a doctor who suffered a stroke told his own physician, "I'm a male demaploze on my own. I still know my tubaboys what for I have that's gone hell and some them go."[28]

The other main type of aphasia includes people whose comprehension of language is intact but who have difficulty getting out what they want to say. This second category of aphasic patients have what are called *expressive* disorders.

The brain lesions associated with expressive disorders tend to be near a region in the left frontal cortex, known as *Broca's area*. Lesions associated with receptive disorders tend to be located further back, in the vicinity of *Wernicke's area*. These two regions are shown in Figure 4–4.

A person with *Broca's aphasia* speaks very little. When he is questioned, his answers will be extremely halting, and he will appear to have difficulties in getting the words out. The speech of Broca's aphasia has been characterized as "telegraphese"—similar to messages sent in telegrams. There is an absence of the small grammatical parts of speech ("or," "and," "the," "with"), and verbs are given in the simplest, uninflected form ("Me go now"; "He drive car"). The following is an interview with a Broca's aphasic, as reported by the neuropsychologist Howard Gardner.†

> *Doctor:* (I asked Mr. Ford about his work before he entered the hospital.)
> *Patient:* I'm a sig...no...man...uh, well,...again. (These words emitted slowly, and with great effort...)
> *Doctor:* Let me help you (I interjected). You were a signal...
> *Patient:* A sig-nal man...right.
> *Doctor:* Were you in the Coast Guard?

†From *The Shattered Mind* by Howard Gardner. New York: Alfred A. Knopf, 1975. Reprinted with permission.

Patient: No, . . . er, . . . yes, . . . yes . . . ship . . .
Massachu . . . chusetts . . . Coastguard . . . years.
(He raised his hands twice, indicating the
number "nineteen".)

Doctor: Oh, you were in the Coast Guard for nineteen years.

Patient: Oh . . .boy . . .right . . .right.

Doctor: Why are you in the hospital, Mr. Ford?

Patient: (He pointed to his paralyzed arm and said, "Arm no
good," then to his mouth and said, "Speech . . .can't
say . . .talk, you see.")

Doctor: What happened to make you lose your speech?

Patient: Head, fall, Jesus Christ, me no good, str, str . . .oh
Jesus . . .stroke.[29]

Since people with this condition usually understand written and spoken speech quite well, Broca's aphasia seems to be a problem with the motor end of the speech apparatus. This connection can be seen by observing that Broca's area lies adjacent to the piece of motor cortex controlling the muscles of the face, mouth, and throat. Broca's aphasics can usually repeat back sentences or words which they have difficulty emitting spontaneously. This shows that the condition is not due to simple paralysis or disruption of the motor mechanism itself. The difficulty appears, rather, more in the nature of damage to an area which generates the *programs* to operate the speech muscles in a coordinated sequence.

Wernicke's aphasics present a very different condition. The speech of a person who has Wernicke's aphasia may be rapid and fluent, containing all the little grammatical words and maintaining the correct rhythm and melody of normal speech, but all the while it makes little or no sense. Below is a segment from Gardner's interview with a Wernicke's aphasic.†

†From *The Shattered Mind* by Howard Gardner. New York: Alfred A. Knopf, 1975. Reprinted with permission.

Doctor: What brings you to the hospital?
Patient: Boy, I'm sweating, I'm awfully nervous, you know, once
            in a while I get caught up, I can't mention the tarripoi,
            a month ago, quite a little, I've done a lot well, I impose
            a lot, while, on the other hand, you know what I mean,
            I have to run around, look it over, trebbin and all that
            sort of stuff.
Doctor: (I attempted several times to break in, but was unable
            to do so against this relentlessly steady and rapid outflow.
            Finally, I put up my hand, rested it on Gorgan's shoul-
            der, and was able to gain a moment's reprieve.)
            Thank you, Mr. Gorgan. I want to ask you a few . . .
Patient: Oh sure, go ahead, any old think you want. If I could
            I would. Oh, I'm taking the word the wrong way to say,
            all of the barbers here whenever they stopy you it's
            going around and around, if you know what I mean,
            that is tying and tying for repucer, repuceration, well,
            we were trying the best that we could while another
            time it was with the beds over there the same thing . . .[30]

Noticeable in this patient's speech is the presence of several
paraphasias, the substitution of inappropriate or nonsensical
words which might sound like the intended word (e.g., the
neologism "repuceration"). Often the paraphasic substitution is
more obvious (e.g., "tying" for "trying").[31] Wernicke's aphasics
tend to write with the same disordered output found in their
spoken utterances.

Carl Wernicke was a German neurologist who, in 1874,
published the classic work first describing this link between
anatomy and symptom type. Wernicke's explanation has served
as the basis for most modern attempts to explain the various
aphasias. Wernicke's theory was that the comprehension of the
meaning of language involves the arousal of auditory images in
the temporal speech area. In order for language to become
articulated into spoken utterances, these auditory images must
be relayed to the frontal speech area, there to be transduced

into a programmed pattern of impulses—a sort of musical score for the keyboard of the motor cortex.

Wernicke's area, lying close to the cortical pattern analyzers for the sense of hearing, is involved in perceiving and understanding speech. Damage to this area impairs the ability to say meaningful things, so verbal thinking may also involve perceiving one's own inner speech. The fluent "word salad" of a Wernicke's aphasic apparently comes from a speech generator released from the control of a system which analyzes meaning. Since reading and writing are learned by reference to spoken language and depend upon the understanding of language meanings, these functions should be impaired in Wernicke's aphasia, but spared in Broca's aphasia. This is usually so.

Difficulty in naming things is central to the problems of someone with temporal-lobe (receptive) aphasia. It is becoming clear that in many of these cases, the word-finding problem is not simply due to a disconnection between the acoustic representation of a word and its memory image. Rather, there is a more general disruption in the whole network of associations between words, and it is this network of associations which constitutes a word's meaning. For example, the meaning of "tree" is bound up with its associations to "green," "bark," "leaves," "soil," "wood," "tall," etc. Often a Wernicke's aphasic will not be able to name an object pointed to, but will instead retrieve another name in the same category (e.g., "bowl" for "glass"), indicating that part of the associative network is still intact and operative.[32]

The associative network which gives a word its meaning underlies what linguists call the "semantic" aspect of language, as opposed to the "syntactic" or grammatical processes which are involved in the production and decoding of word order in sentences. Although it's difficult to disentangle these two processes in normal speech, it is beginning to appear that frontal language areas are more involved with syntax, and that the posterior language region is more closely tied to semantics or meaning. Frontal lesions result in speech which is agrammatic, but meaningful. Posterior lesions disrupt the understanding of the meanings of words and result in speech which is grammatical, but vacuous.

The complete separation of auditory and motor speech processes implied by Wernicke's theory is probably somewhat artificial, since normally the two most likely act in some sort of synchrony.[33] Most people will describe their "inner speech" as somewhere between an auditory and a kinesthetic experience, related both to a sound image and to a feeling in the mouth and throat. Also, there is good reason to believe that articulatory, motor processes of the brain are intimately involved when we perceive other people's speech and when we formulate verbal thoughts of our own.[34] A third point comes from some recent studies which show that Broca's aphasics can be shown to have difficulties in comprehending sentences, especially if the meaning of the sentence is embedded in a complex grammatical construction, such as, "The lion that the tiger is chasing is fat."[35]

Broca's and Wernicke's aphasia are not always seen in pure form, although this fact may reflect nothing more than the randomness of brain damage. Many experts today reject Wernicke's theory as overly simplistic. But the fact is that it has served as the best explanatory model to date for certain forms of aphasia. One of these is a rare disorder known as *pure alexia without agraphia*. In this condition, a person is unable to comprehend written speech, but all other language functions are essentially intact, including the ability to copy words which are nevertheless not recognized or understood. Such a person may be able to write sentences which he later cannot read! The lesion which produces this condition is one which destroys the left visual cortex and the interhemispheric connections from the right visual cortex to the speech regions in the left hemisphere. Visual input does not reach the speech area; hence reading is impaired. But the right visual cortex can analyze the purely visual information needed for copying words, without being able to understand them.[36]

One of the curiosities of aphasia is the amazing resiliency

shown by the brains of young children, who recover from damage which would permanently devastate an adult. Most children who are rendered aphasic recover fully, especially if they are young enough at the time of the injury and if the right hemisphere is spared. The lateralization of language functions to the left hemisphere is probably not complete until after age 12 or so. Although the left hemisphere is specialized for language, there is the potential for the right hemisphere to acquire these functions in the growing brain. In children, the right hemisphere can relearn lost abilities if the left is damaged.

In general, children also appear to have greater right-hemisphere participation in language than adults. Another difference is that there are no fluent, Wernicke's type aphasics among children; when a child becomes aphasic, he tends to be mute.[37] The organization of language in the brain changes considerably during early development.

After age 12 to 14, when lateralization of language is almost completed, the effects of aphasia tend to be more permanent.[38] This is also the age when people with normal brains find it more difficult to learn a new language. A person who learns a second language after age 12 usually speaks with a foreign accent.[39]

The changes which occur in the organization of language in a child's brain may be just the most visible form of changes which occur throughout life. There are differences in aphasic symptoms typically shown by a 30-year-old and those shown by a 50-year-old.[40] Perhaps we continue to rearrange our neural furniture to accommodate changing cognitive needs.

In Chapter 1 we saw that philosophers and psychologists have been concerned with the question of the relationship of language to thought. Does language mirror some more fundamental operations of human thought, some basic capability for "abstract" thinking? Conversely, might the casts of language mold all varieties of human thinking, as Whorf believed?[41]

The evidence from aphasia is mixed. A person can be

severely aphasic and still be able to solve difficult nonverbal problems. On the other hand, it's also true that Wernicke's aphasics are often impaired on nonverbal tests of intelligence.

It does sometimes seem as if we are pursued by inner voices, but for most of us this is just one component of intelligent thought. Anticipating what a juicy orange tastes like does not necessarily involve talking to oneself.

The next section describes how recent discoveries about the brain have separated out a fundamental division in the structure of human thinking. The division is between thinking based on language processes and thinking based on the manipulation of nonverbal images. This frontier of research promises some answers to the age-old question of the relationship of language to thought, but what is even more important, it bears strongly on the issue of the relationship of body to mind.

Dividing the Mind

Since damage to the right hemisphere of the brain does not produce the thought disorders characteristic of aphasia, it was believed until only recently that the right hemisphere was like a spare tire—that it was capable of taking over the functions of language if the left side were damaged in childhood, but basically it had no specialized functions of its own. All higher mental activities were viewed as the province of the left. The right side was designated the "nondominant" or "minor" hemisphere.

This view has changed considerably, and the discovery of the specialized functions of the right hemisphere ranks as one of the important scientific achievements of this century. The discovery came about, in large part, through observation of the bizarre consequences which followed the surgical separation of the two hemispheres. This separation was accomplished in what was called a *split-brain operation* (commissurotomy), performed on a small number of patients during the 1960's as an experimental treatment for severe epilepsy. The operation involved the severing of all direct connections between the two hemispheres of the brain.*

The most important of these connections is a giant flattened cable of nerve fibers, the *corpus callosum*, which connects corresponding parts of cortex on the right and the left. The corpus callosum normally functions to transmit information between the hemispheres and to coordinate their activities. It is composed of some 200 million nerve fibers, representing as many nerve cells as in all sensory and motor pathways combined.

In most cases, the split-brain operation was a success. Patients returned home to resume their lives, no longer plagued by the frequent seizures which had previously tormented them. Side effects were barely noticeable. A casual interaction with one of these people would not reveal that he or she differed from the rest of humanity by virtue of the separation of the two halves of his or her brain.

Yet, strange behaviors could be revealed in the laboratory by the use of special tests. In one of these tests, the patient is asked to place her hand behind a curtain, where, unseen by her eyes, a key is placed in the hand. A short time later she is asked to pick out, from a group of objects, the one previously held in her hand, using only the sense of touch. This presents no problem, if the same hand is used as before. But if the hands are switched—if, say the right hand first felt the key and the examiner requires that the left does the searching—then the patient's performance is no better than chance. Quite literally, one hand does not know what the other is doing!

*Epileptic seizures come about as a result of a propagating "electrical storm" in the brain. Usually this condition is controllable by drugs, but in certain severe cases, where drugs are not effective, removing diseased or damaged areas in the brain eliminates the trigger for the attacks. In severe, life-threatening cases, where no precise trigger area can be located, a radical surgery such as the split-brain operation is resorted to as a last hope. The surgical separation of the two hemispheres was intended to keep the seizures, which start in one hemisphere, from spreading to the other one, thus leaving the spared hemisphere capable of continued functioning during an attack.

The explanation is that the tactile information originally gathered about the key was projected, as it is normally, to the somato-sensory cortex on the opposite, or *contralateral*, side of the brain (see Figure 4–5). There it was analyzed and registered. But since the connections between the two sensory areas were cut, there was no way for the cortex which controlled the other hand to know about what was felt.*

In a variation of this test, the patient is asked to describe verbally an object felt behind the curtain. If the right hand does the feeling, there is no problem. The patient says, "I felt the key," just as you or I would do in that situation. However, if the key is placed in the left hand, the patient denies feeling anything, or says that her left hand felt numb. Sensory information from the left hand is not directly connected to the hemisphere with language capability. The left hemisphere, which was doing the talking, could not say what the left hand grasped, even when the patient could correctly pick out the key with her left hand (right hemisphere).

This unusual state of affairs was brought about because the tests *lateralized* the input, i.e., they restricted the sensory information to one hemisphere only. In everyday life sensory information is sent simultaneously to both sides of the brain. Although each half of the visual field projects to only one hemisphere, the eyes scan visual objects, and this ensures that both hemispheres see pretty much the same thing. Rarely do these patients have to identify something on the basis of touch alone, but even then, both hands can do the feeling.

Occasionally, split-brain patients report experiences which mirror the duality of their minds. One patient reported finding himself pulling his pants up with one hand and down with the

---

*This is a bit of an oversimplification. There are actually some direct, or *ipsilateral*, somato-sensory and motor connections between the right hemisphere and the right half of the body, and between the left and the left. However, these pathways are less well developed and possibly not used very much. Under some circumstances, discussed later, ipsilateral motor control can be inferred in split-brain patients.

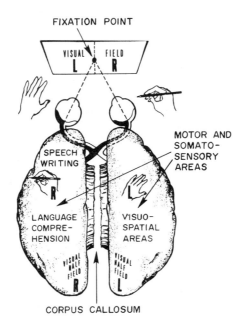

FIXATION POINT

VISUAL FIELD
L   R

MOTOR AND
SOMATO-
SENSORY
AREAS

SPEECH
WRITING

LANGUAGE
COMPRE-
HENSION

VISUO-
SPATIAL
AREAS

VISUAL
HALF
FIELD
R

VISUAL
HALF
FIELD
L

CORPUS CALLOSUM

FIGURE 4–5. Schematic outline of brain organization related to split-brain experiments. Note that sensation from the left half of the body and motor control over that half of the body project to the right hemisphere, and vice versa for the right side of the body. This relationship also holds for projections of the left and right sides of the visual field. These projections are referred to as **contralateral**. (After R. W. Sperry, "Hemisphere Deconnection and Unity in Conscious Awareness," <u>American Psychologist</u>, 1968, **23**, pp. 723–733. Copyright© 1968 by the American Psychological Association. Reproduced with permission.)

other. Another patient, during an argument with his wife, grabbed her with his left hand and shook her violently, while at the same time the right hand attempted to come to her aid and restrain the aggressing left.[42]

Results similar to those found with lateralized tactile information were found by lateralizing visual input. Since each half of visual field of each eye projects to the opposite occipital cortex, then by the preventing of eye movements, the visual cortex of each hemisphere could be separately stimulated (see

Figure 4–5). To get around the problem of eye movement, a picture is flashed, to the right or left of a fixation point, using a device called a tachistoscope. With this technique, split-brain patients behave as if there is a doubling of the visual world, even though they aren't aware of any duality in perception. An object that was flashed in one visual half-field is recognized only if it appears again in the same half-field. If it is later presented to the other side, the patient responds as if she had never seen it before. Two completely different visual inputs can even be flashed simultaneously to each side of the fixation point, and what is "seen" in this situation depends upon which hemisphere is interrogated.

When sensory information was lateralized in those ways it was as if two separate persons, two independent minds, existed within the same body! Although the right hemisphere was mute, it understood enough spoken language to point, upon interrogation, and identify objects it had felt or seen. It thus seemed to have the capability for being independently conscious.

Roger Sperry, of the California Institute of Technology, one of the pioneers in this strange byway of the mind, summarized his observations as follows: "Instead of the normally unified single stream of consciousness, these patients behave in many ways as if they have two independent streams of conscious awareness, one in each hemisphere, each of which is cut off from and out of contact with the mental experiences of the other."[43]

Sperry's conclusion is supported by observations of the few rare cases where a whole cerebral hemisphere is removed by surgery, for treatment of a large brain tumor. The removal of the whole dominant left hemisphere, despite devastating loss of language capability, can nonetheless leave a person appearing alert, responsive, and intelligent.[44]

Clearly, the right hemisphere is more than a spare tire. It seems to have the capacity for supporting conscious awareness even in the absence of its talkative partner.

The Intelligence of the Right Hemisphere

The split-brain operation permitted a rare glimpse into the separate cognitive capabilities of each hemisphere. By completely lateralizing stimulation—restricting information to one hemisphere or the other—it was possible to question each hemisphere separately to see what each could do. Even though the right hemisphere could not answer by means of speech, it could respond by means of the choices made with the left hand.[45]

Though mute, the right hemisphere was found able to understand some spoken language. For example, when asked to pick out with the left hand "an object that makes things bigger," one split-brain patient responded by retrieving a magnifying glass.[46] However, there are doubts as to whether the silent hemisphere normally has this much verbal understanding, since other patients do not show as much comprehension on the right.[47] It is generally believed that the right hemisphere understands speech at about the level of a 2- or 3-year-old child.[48]

The right hemisphere is also capable of some very limited types of verbal expression, not true propositional speech, but rather such things as occasional swear words, emotional outbursts, or overlearned expressions ("yes," "no," "I don't know"). This kind of speech has been described as "automatic," to distinguish it from the propositional ability of the left—the ability to construct novel speech utterances.[49]

Given that the right hemisphere is for the most part mute, it is surprising to find that it sings better than the left. The right hemisphere excels in both the perception and expression of music. People who become aphasic as a result of left-hemisphere damage may even be able to sing entire songs, although they are not able to speak the same words without music. Indeed, an often helpful treatment for aphasics is to get them to sing their conversation. One patient, who had the entire left hemisphere removed for treatment of a brain tumor, was asked to define the word "spangled." She placed her hand over her heart and sang the song "God Bless America" it its entirety.[50] Damage to the right hemisphere will often result in flat and monotonous speaking, speech devoid of its melodic components. There is a complication, however. People who are trained musicians seem to have a greater amount of left-hemisphere participation in the perception of music, indicating, perhaps, a more analytical style of musical comprehension.[51]

The supreme achievement of the right hemisphere is not music, however, but *visuo-spatial thinking*. To see what is meant by this term, try the exercise of contemplating how you would get to the nearest grocery.

Your thoughts were probably not a list of verbal propositions, but more likely they could be described as a sequence of visual images, or perhaps a map, albeit a fuzzy one. These thoughts involve, primarily, the spatial relationships between different objects and landmarks in your neighborhood. Or, consider another problem, that of dividing a pie into 4 equal pieces. To solve this problem, most people would not think of dividing 360 degrees by 4 and then measuring off 90-degree slices with a compass. Rather, a direct solution usually presents itself, in the form of an image of a pie with two perpendicular cuts. Figure 4–6 shows more examples of this kind of thinking.

People with right-hemisphere brain damage tend to have difficulties with visuo-spatial thinking. Their drawings of objects are distorted and disorganized. They may have trouble finding the way home. Or they may have difficulty in comprehending the space articulated by their own bodies. For example, in dressing themselves, they may get horribly mixed up, inserting limbs into the wrong holes, or getting a shirt on upside down.[52]

In Chapter 2 we saw that there appears to be an area in the cortex specialized for the visual perception of human faces. The evidence points to this region's lying somewhere in the posterior part of the right hemisphere. Split-brain patients have an extremely difficult time learning to associate names and faces, and this may come about because the region for facial perception has been disconnected from left-hemisphere proc-

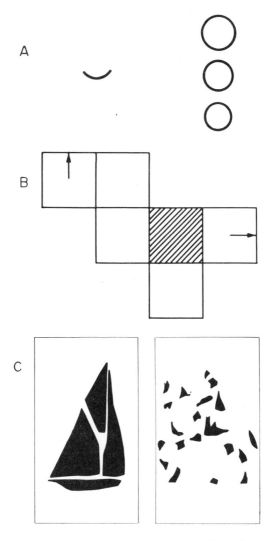

FIGURE 4-6. Some examples of visuo-spatial thinking. The right hemisphere of the brain is specialized for comprehending relationships between objects in space, including abilities for visualization. (a) Part-whole problem. Pick out the circle on the right which contains the segment shown on the left. (After R. D. Nebes, **Cortex**, 1971, **7**, pp. 333–349.) (b) Cube-folding. Mentally fold the figure into a cube, using the striped side as the base, and decide whether or not the two arrows meet. (From C.J. Furst, **Nature**, 1976, **260**, pp. 254–255, after Shepard and Feng.) (c) Gestalt-completion. What do these figures depict? (From R. F. Street, A Gestalt Completion Test, Contributions to Education No. 481, New York: Teachers College Press, 1931.)

esses underlying naming. These patients have been known to resort to elaborate verbal strategies to overcome this difficulty, such as remembering the formula, "Fred has a mustache and a mole on his cheek."

Split-brain patients also have great trouble in assembling colored blocks to make a pattern, if they are required to use the dominant right hand. The left hand has no trouble with this task, because it is controlled by the right hemisphere, which excels in this type of visuo-spatial ability. In a film made by Roger Sperry of one of these testing sessions, it can be seen that the patient becomes frustrated as his right hand, his better hand, fails miserably at the block assembly task. His frustration is especially understandable in view of the fact that he had previously succeeded when allowed to use his left hand. As his frustration mounts, the left hand, somewhat eerily, approaches the blocks and takes over the task of assembling them. Even after this renegade left hand is forcibly removed by the experimenter, it can be seen tentatively inching up again toward the blocks!

The findings on hemispheric specialization that have come from studying cases of brain damage have been verified in normal people also, by means of special tests. Most right-handed people recognize words better and faster if they are flashed tachistoscopically to the right visual half-field. Conversely, most of us recognize pictures of shapes or faces better and faster in the left half-field.[53] This is understandable if we assume that, although the information in the normal brain is eventually accessible to both hemispheres, visual information from the left visual half-field is transmitted more faithfully to visuo-spatial analyzers in the right hemisphere, and information from the right half-field is transmitted more faithfully to language analyzers in the left.

The right-hemisphere regions implicated in many kinds of visuo-spatial thought disorders are the newly evolved "uncommitted" areas of the parietal and temporal cortex. They include regions which on the other side of the brain are devoted to the understanding of spoken and written speech (Wernicke's area). Visuo-spatial thinking is not restricted to vision. People with right-hemisphere brain damage also have trouble recognizing things by their sense of touch. It is as if the new cortical areas which border on the sensory areas for vision and touch operate to construct a representation of the world which is more abstract than that given by either sensory modality alone. This suprasensory spatial ability may arise from cognitive machinery as powerful and advanced, perhaps as specifically human, as the suprasensory language system of the left hemisphere.

It is now pretty well accepted that our hominid ancestors were apes who had come down from the trees with a very poor sense of smell. Their ecological niche required them to range broadly over large territories. Without a good sense of smell, they were without the devices that other land-dwelling mammals, such as wolves, use to map their range. Perhaps the evolution of a sophisticated mental-mapping ability was a response to this environmental pressure.[54]

Hemispheric Specialization

The converging evidence from many sources is that the two cerebral hemispheres of the human brain are specialized for different kinds of knowing. Why do humans differ in this way from other animals? Part of the answer comes from trying to consider the fundamental nature of the specialization.

Sperry and his colleagues see the specialized operations of the two hemispheres as arising from a basic incompatibility between the two modes of thought. Verbal, logical, analytical thinking is the domain of the left hemisphere, and it excels in such things as human speech, abstract conceptualizations, logic, and mathematics. In these operations of thought, things are coded in a linear sequence, one symbol at a time. The other mode of cognition—the domain of the right hemisphere—is what has been described as visuo-spatial or pictorial. The right hemisphere is involved with configurations in space, where relationships occur simultaneously, all at once.

A split-brain patient makes drawings with his right hand (left hemisphere) in which the details are all present but the relationships of the parts to one another are incorrect. That is, the drawings are correct in their analysis, but not in their synthesis. The right hemisphere excels at synthesizing the relationships of objects into unified wholes. The left is specialized for dissecting things into pieces or properties, with the aid of the symbols of language.

The dichotomy suggested by Sperry and co-workers as the key to understanding the two modes of thought is "analytic" versus "synthetic."[55] The reason for the anatomical separation of the two spheres of thinking would lie in a fundamental incompatibility between their modes of operation.

The psychologist Robert Ornstein gives a forceful example of this incompatibility. Ask someone to describe a spiral staircase. In most cases, the answer will be abstract, roundabout, and not very helpful if you've never seen such a staircase and don't know what "spiral" designates. Also, in most cases, the person describing the staircase will make a hand motion indicating the form of the object, as if to overcome the impossibility of verbally describing it with the simplicity of a gesture. This illustrates the ease with which an inherently visuo-spatial or synthetic concept can be communicated using the proper mode.[56]

On the other hand (more precisely, in the other hemisphere), it is difficult to code abstract thoughts in a concrete, synthetic manner. Consider drawing, or communicating by a charade, the proposition "Truth is the best vindication against slander."

Despite the analytic/synthetic characterization of left and right specialization, the exact nature of the difference, in terms of brain mechanisms or processes of manipulating information, is still not understood.

One clue, however, comes from the finding that the left hemisphere is much better than the right in making fine discriminations in time, as in the task of deciding which of two successive audible clicks came first.[57] Perhaps this advantage is what allows the left hemisphere to analyze speech, which, as was pointed out earlier, is a temporal code—a code in time. Researchers at the Haskins Laboratories in Connecticut have experimented with speech sounds artificially produced by a computer. They found that the ability to perceive the sounds of speech rests on the decoding of extremely rapid changes in voice patterns. These subtle changes are what distinguish speech consonant sounds from one another.[58] The left hemisphere plays a dominant role in the perception of these rapid consonant phonemes ("ba," "da"), but vowel sounds, which are acoustically simpler and don't contain rapid sound transitions, are perceived equally well by both hemispheres.[59] It is the consonant pho-nemes which carry most of the information in human speech. THE TRETH EF THES ESSERSHEN SHED BE KLER FREM E BREF DEMENSTRESHEN.

Related to this idea is an explanation of hemispheric specialization based on the relation of language to handedness. Josephine Semmes, of the National Institute of Mental Health, believes that both language and the dominant hand require a basic specialized brain organization which provides for fine, articulatory, muscular control. In the case of language, the muscular control would be in the muscles of the chest, throat, and mouth in the production of speech.

Semmes reviewed a large number of cases of one-sided brain damage and concluded that the left hemisphere is more *focally* organized than the right. In the left, small circumscribed lesions produced deficits in cognition and in movement, whereas in the right hemisphere, it seemed that the lesion had to be more extensive to show effects. Semmes feels that these differ-ences underlie the separate abilities of the hemispheres. The right, being more diffusely organized, would be better able to coordinate information from separated regions and hence would be better at performing spatial syntheses. The focal organization of the left hemisphere would give it the ability to control precise muscular movements, both the fine articulatory movements of the dominant hand and those of the vocal apparatus.[60] Focal organization implies short distances between nerve cells, so this form of brain organization would also account for the left hemisphere's superiority in making fine time discriminations, since nerve impulses could traverse neural circuits faster if the circuits were packed more closely.

Whatever the exact mechanisms, it seems clear that there are two different kinds of brain codes operating to give each hemisphere its characteristic mode of thought. One code is a sequential or "serial" process, based on elements which change over time, as do the sounds of speech. The other is a simultaneous or "parallel" process, a code which operates over space, all at once. One is primarily an outgrowth of the sense of hearing; the other is more related to the sense of seeing.

It seems that human brains evolved lateral specialization because this would effectively double the brain's cognitive capacity, given a constant overall brain size. Our primitive ancestors were defenseless creatures, unprotected by fangs or claws, and impossibly slow. They would have been easy prey for other large animals, except for their main evolutionary advantage: the intelligence to outwit predators. The newly evolved areas of the cortex gave these ancestors the capabilities to use tools for defense, food, and shelter. To accommodate the vastly increased cortex in a small skull cavity, the cerebral cortex was folded up into the many convolutions which wrinkle the surface of the primate brain. In man, it is likely that lateral specialization furthered a similar end.

Laterality and Cognitive Style

In the search for common ground, writers have resurrected older dualities of thought to characterize the differences between the two hemispheres. Table 4–2 gives some of these

Table 4-2.
Proposed Dualities of Thought*

AUTHORS	DUALITIES	
Assagioli	intellect	intuition
Bateson & Jackson	digital	analogic
Blackburn	intellectual	sensuous
Bruner	rational	metaphoric
Freud	secondary process	primary process
Goldstein	abstract	concrete
Guilford	convergent	divergent
Humphrey & Zangwill	propositional	imaginative
James	differential	existential
Kagan & Moss	analytic	relational
Lee	lineal	nonlineal
Maslow	rational	intuitive
Neisser	sequential	parallel
Polanyi	explicit	tacit
Sechnov	successive	simultaneous

*Adapted from J. E. Bogen, "Some Educational Aspects of Hemispheric Specialization." UCLA Educator, 1975, 17, 24–32. Reprinted with permission.

dichotomies and shows that, independent of the recent neurological discoveries, psychologists and others have tended to divide the mind in two.

For example, "rational" thought versus "intuitive" thought is one of these dualities. Much has been written about the way in which the rational and the intuitive create an interplay of ideas.[61] Even cold, scientific thinking is often described as involving inspiration by flashes of insight, arising out of dark recesses of the mind. Could it be that the unspoken visuo-spatial intelligence of the right hemisphere underlies what previously had been called "intuition"?

A famous example of intuitive insight in science is the discovery of the chemical structure of benzene. The chemist Friedrich Kekula had been struggling with this problem for some time. Then, late one night on the way home from his laboratory, Kekula started to doze off on the bus. In a semiconscious dream state, there appeared a visual image of a bunch of snakes, each of which grasped the tail of another. They formed a ring, and Kekula woke to the realization that here was the cyclic chemical structure he had been searching for. It is significant in this regard that split-brain patients often say that they don't dream, even though they may have enjoyed normal dream lives before their operation.[62] Apparently dreams are related to right-hemisphere functioning, and the surgical disconnection prevents dream processes, which may still be going on, from reaching the side of the brain which speaks.

A related finding is that people who can be described as "convergent" or left-hemisphere thinkers tend to recall fewer dreams than those whose thought processes might be more characteristic of the right hemisphere. This was true even though there were no differences in the number of REM periods observed for the two groups of people.[63] There is also some evidence that the right hemisphere becomes relatively more active during REM than during slow-wave sleep.[64] Aristotle was convinced that we are always dreaming but that during the daytime it is obscured by noise from the outside world. Today, we might be tempted to say that the activity of the dominant left hemisphere prevents us from being aware of our daytime dreams.

One of the most interesting speculations on hemispheric specialization is that people may differ in the degree to which they rely on right- or left-hemisphere thinking. That is, some people may tend to approach problems using the verbal, analytic machinery of the left hemisphere, while others may rely more on holistic, right-hemisphere visual thinking. This is an interesting possibility, because it suggests a means of understanding personality differences based on principles of brain organization.

Do artists use their right hemispheres more than lawyers? The evidence for this and related questions is not entirely clear. Some evidence is afforded by the way people move their eyes. When someone asks you a difficult question, you will tend to avert your eyes while thinking of the answer. Researchers have found that the direction in which you move your eyes is related to the type of question asked. If it is a verbal or mathematical question, ("divide 144 by 6" or "define the word economics"), then you will tend to move your eyes to the right before answering. If it is a visuo-spatial question ("which way does the profile of George Washington face on a quarter?"), your eyes will tend to move left.[65] The reason for this difference in *lateral eye movements (LEM's)* is probably the selective activation of one hemisphere over the other while solving the problem. Certain areas in the left hemisphere control orientation of the head and eyes to the right, whereas the reverse movements are controlled by the right hemisphere.[66]

Paul Bakan, a psychologist at Simon Fraser University, has found that people differ in their overall tendencies toward left- or right-LEM's. Among Bakan's undergraduate subjects, those who had more left-LEM's were more likely to be majoring in literature or the humanities. Those who were right-movers were more likely to be science or engineering majors. Left-movers are described as being more inner-focused and also more easily hypnotized than right-movers.[67]

Other researchers have tested the idea of hemispheric cognitive styles by looking for differences in analytic versus visuo-spatial abilities between cultures. The reasoning is that as a child grows up within a particular culture, the demands for culturally valued modes of thinking will shape this child's reliance on right- or left-hemisphere skills. Tests reflecting verbal-analytic cognition and visuo-spatial-synthetic cognition were administered to a group of rural Hopi Indians and to a group of urban whites. It was found that the Hopis, whose traditional culture places less reliance on literacy and mathematical education, did relatively poorer than the whites on the left-hemisphere test. However, they were much better than the city-dwelling whites on the test of visuo-spatial ability.[68]

Despite Bakan's findings, there have been some notable failures to find differences in LEM's and other measures of laterality between groups differing on the basis of occupation,[69] and in general, the differences found between groups of people on the basis of right- and left-hemisphere cognition are not large. However, this should not be surprising because psychologists have generally found that people do not seem to fit easily into neat personality categories, reflecting the fact that human thoughts and behaviors are very flexible and are determined more by the demands of a situation than by underlying predispositions.[70]

It is also probably a mistake to stress the differences between linguistic and visuo-spatial thinking without also stating that normally the two kinds of thought interact with each other. Try the problem shown in Figure 4–7. Most likely you will find yourself doing a combination of verbal, logical analysis, together with thinking of a more spatial kind.[71]

The normal operation of the brain probably creates a complex interplay between right- and left-hemisphere thinking.[72] The list in Table 4–2 may indicate no more than the fact that dichotomies arise as a first step in building a theory. Dividing things in two is a primitive but useful form of conceptualizing, which usually gives way to more complex, multifaceted theories.[73] No doubt, an advanced neuropsychology of the future will come to recognize a multiplicity rather than a duality of thought.[74]

The Unity of Consciousness

In trying to understand what split-brain experiments reveal about the nature of consciousness, the first step is to decide whether conscious awareness is actually doubled in these patients. Sperry comes down very forcefully for dual consciousness:

> Everything we have seen so far indicates that the surgery has left these people with two separate minds, that is, two separate spheres of consciousness. What is experienced in the right hemisphere seems to lie entirely outside the realm of awareness

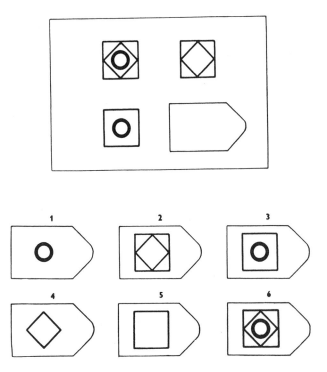

FIGURE 4-7. Verbal and visuo-spatial thinking interact. Pick out the piece from the group at the bottom which best completes the figure at the top. (From J. C. Raven, <u>Standard Progressive Matrices</u>, H. K. Lewis and Company, London. Reproduced with permission.)

of the left hemisphere. This mental division has been demonstrated in regard to perception, cognition, volition, learning, and memory.[75]

To this list of mental attributes, he might also add the capability for emotion. Sperry reports that split-brain patients will show a look of displeasure during testing when " . . .the minor hemisphere, knowing the correct answer but unable to speak, hears the major hemisphere making obvious verbal mistakes."[76]

Sperry goes on to speculate that it is entirely possible that even within a normal, intact brain, dualities of consciousness may exist. If split-brain patients have an illusory feeling of mental unity, then perhaps it is an illusion for us too. A sense of mental unity is preserved for the patients, because two radically different experiences arise in either half-brain only in the laboratory, under very special conditions. Usually, the right and left hemispheres for these persons have different but closely parallel experiences, so that the split is not noticed. For us this is also true, but in addition, the two hemispheres are normally in close communication, via the corpus callosum. They have access to each other's computations and memories.[77]

The implications of Sperry's suggestion are difficult to fathom. What might it mean to say that his patients (or we) ordinarily have two co-existing minds? Do they simply alternate in conscious awareness? Or do we need to revise our fundamental assumptions about personal identity?

Descartes concluded centuries ago that the seat of consciousness must be the pineal gland at the base of the brain, because this was the only structure he could find which was not doubled. This was important to Descartes, since the mind, or soul, appeared to be a single, unified entity. The split-brain demonstrations, and the conclusion that it is possible, with a surgeon's knife, to divide consciousness into two related but relatively independent sub-parts, have caused a great deal of concern among theologically minded scientists, who could not reconcile this conclusion with traditional religious beliefs about the unity of the soul.[78] As a result, it has been suggested, quite irrationally it would seem, that only one side of the split-brain is really conscious (the side which talks) and that the other is merely a clever automaton. This is what we might call a "language-accessibility theory" of consciousness: what becomes conscious are the products of brain processes relating to language, things comprehensible by the constructs of language.

What seems more likely is that conscious experience arises normally from the integral product of the two sides of the brain working in concert. The fact that a surgeon can divide one person into two is startling, but it seems unthinkable only because we have been led to believe that souls are created by God. That a split-brain patient appears to herself and to us to be one person, while Siamese twins appear as two, reflects our feeling that the greatest intimacy of all occurs within the skull.

There are other questions about the unity of mind which seem more amenable to scientific investigation. One curious aspect of brain damage is a condition known as *unilateral spatial neglect*, where damage to occipital and parietal regions of one side (usually the right) leads to a condition in which the patient will not notice what is in the opposite visual half-field, and furthermore, he will not be aware that part of the visual field is missing.

Unilateral spatial neglect arises when the occipital cortex on one side is destroyed. As we saw in Chapter 2, there will be a blindness in the opposite half of the visual field. If the damage is in the left occipital cortex, there will be blindness in the right visual half-field, and vice versa. A person with this kind of disability will make compensating eye movements in order to scan around the region of blindness. However, it is frequently found that with *right-hemisphere* lesions of this type, there are no such compensating eye movements, and there is also a tendency to deny that the left visual field is missing. In these cases, errors of perception are attributed by the patient to defects in the stimulus, rather than to defects in himself.[79]

Spatial neglect extends to tactual space as well, often resulting in a complete unawareness of the left side of the body. Such patients, confronted with paralysis of the left hand, may deny ownership of the paralyzed limb or may joke that it "must have gone to sleep on me."[80] Patients with unilateral neglect have been known to shave only half of their faces, or to eat only the contents of the right side of the plate!

What are we to make of this asymmetry of awareness? Does it mean that the intact left hemisphere is more egotistical than the right, assuming that what it sees encompasses everything there is? Or, perhaps this condition reflects only that, in the absence of the spatially adept right hemisphere, the left does a poor job of comprehending space.[81] Discovering the correct explanation for unilateral neglect may have great consequence for the understanding of consciousness and the brain. Another group of answerable questions revolves around the issue of control: how is it decided which side controls the body's actions at any one time? One theory is that they alternate with one another, one hemisphere taking the reins of the motor system while the other retreats in deference.[82] This state of affairs could be brought about if the hemispheres were connected so that they reciprocally inhibited each other. In this way, activity in one hemisphere would automatically suppress activity in the other. Similar kinds of neural hookups are known to exist in the spinal-cord neurons which balance the movements of opposing muscle groups.

But what decides which hemisphere should take precedence at any given moment? A clever experiment devised by split-brain researchers indicates that what happens is that the hemisphere best suited to do the job of the moment simply takes control. These experiments were based on a "chimeric" stimulus technique, which allows the two hemispheres to be simultaneously shown different half pictures (see Figure 4–8). When the patient was asked to identify, out of a group of similar pictures, which picture was shown, the choice was found to depend on the requirements of the task.

If the patient was told to *point* to the picture she had seen, the choice was determined by the right hemisphere, because the right deals better with the perception and memory of faces. This was true even if the patient was required to point with the right hand! (There appears to be some degree possible of ipsilateral motor control—control of the right hand by the right hemisphere.) If the task was changed, to *naming* the face, the response was determined by what the left hemisphere saw.[83] It is as if each hemisphere decides whether or not to take control, or rather, control may be decided by whichever hemisphere is momentarily the busier. The means of taking control might involve recruiting activation from lower brainstem systems de-

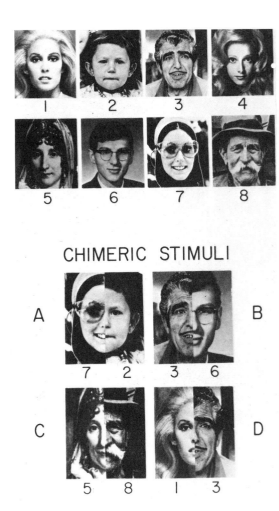

FIGURE 4–8. "Chimeric" stimuli used in tests with split-brain patients (named after "Chimera," a mythical monster made up of parts from different animals).

The subject is told she will see a picture (one of the 8 shown in the upper left). A composite picture is then flashed briefly while the subject fixates the center, and then the subject must choose the picture seen, either verbally, or by pointing with one or the other hand. The choices tend to be determined by the hemisphere best equipped to respond.

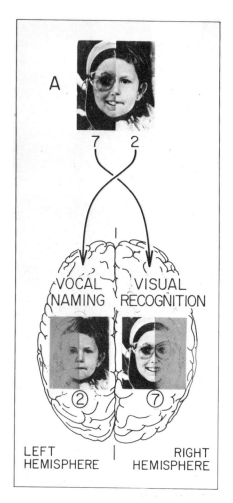

The right half of the figure illustrates what each hemisphere sees. Split-brain patients were unaware that the chimeric stimuli were incomplete or conflicting. They insisted that they saw an entire picture exactly like the one they chose on each trial. It seems that there is a tendency for each hemisphere to fill-in its half picture, and to construct a complete symmetrical image. (From J. Levy, C. Trevarthen, and R. W. Sperry, "Perception of Bilateral Chimeric Figures Following Hemisphere Deconnection," Brain, 1972, 95, pp. 61–78. Photo courtesy of the author, and reproduced with permission of the publisher and authors.)

scribed in the last chapter. Competition could then be minimized by a mechanism, like the one discussed, where the hemispheres reciprocally inhibit one another.

Of all the speculations about the nature of consciousness to come out of split-brain research, perhaps the most titillating to psychologists is David Galin's hypothesis that these findings provide a neurological validation for Freud's notion of an unconscious mind. Sperry reports an incident which occurred while pictures were being flashed to one hemisphere or the other. At one point in a series of geometrical forms, a picture of a nude pinup was shown to the left visual field (right hemisphere) of a split-brain patient. The woman patient blushed and giggled, but when asked what she saw, replied that she had seen nothing, just a flash of light. When asked why she was laughing, the patient at first seemed confused about what to say, and then replied with another laugh, "Dr. Sperry, you have some machine!"[84] Galin points out that if this story were told about someone with an intact brain, the Freudian explanation would be that the embarrassing perception was kept from consciousness by an active process of "repression."[85]

For Freud, the unconscious was an independent realm of mental activity, the reservoir for ideas which spring from primitive wishes and drives. Freud considered the unconscious to be the "true psychic reality," because its urges were not censored by the civilized concerns which govern conscious thought.[86] The unconscious could be glimpsed only indirectly, through everyday slips-of-the-tongue or in dreams, where, for example, a woman's repressed desire to make love with her father might be symbolically transformed into the dream of riding a horse with him.

Galin points out that the right hemisphere's mode of thought is similar to Freud's description of the unconscious, as revealed by the logic of dreams. Freud regarded dreams as a peek into the workings of the unconscious, the "royal road to the unconscious."[87]

By Galin's hypothesis, the normally conscious mind would arise from the integrated operation of the two hemispheres, except at certain times, when, for some reason, they would become functionally blocked from communicating with each other. At that point, what we call conscious experience would arise from the operation of the verbal left hemisphere, and the right would act as an independent reservoir of inaccessible cognition—thoughts which might nevertheless exert their own influence on behavior. Sperry and his co-workers report that, for the most part, the behavior of split-brain patients appears to be guided by the left hemisphere, except in cases where the right has a specific superiority, as in visuo-spatial tasks.

Galin's speculation amounts to what we termed earlier a "language-accessibility theory" of consciousness. This type of theory states that the brain events we experience as conscious are those events which are fathomable by the language systems of the brain. Do "the limits of my language mean the limits of my world"?[88] What, then, of consciousness in young children? What about awareness by the right hemisphere when the left is removed?

At this point, we are well beyond what is actually known about the brain and into a land bordering on neuro-fantasy. Split-brain research has opened a new frontier of scientific investigation into the physical basis of consciousness. The vistas which lie beyond this frontier will perhaps revolutionize our traditional ways of understanding the human mind.

Recommended Readings

LANGUAGE AND THE BRAIN

LENNEBERG, E. H. *Biological Foundations of Language.* New York: John Wiley & Sons, 1967.

GOODGLASS, H., and N. GESCHWIND, "Language Disorders." In E. C. Carterette and M.P. Friedman, (eds.), *Handbook of Perception*, Volume 7. New York: Academic Press, 1976.

HARNAD, S., H. D. STEKLIS, and J. LANCASTER (eds.), "Origins and Evolution of Language and Speech." *Annals of the New York Academy of Sciences,* 1976, Volume 280.

HEMISPHERIC SPECIALIZATION

GAZZANIGA, M.S. *The Bisected Brain.* Englewood Cliffs, N.J.: Prentice-Hall, 1970.

DIMOND, S. J., and J. G. BEAUMONT (eds.). *Hemisphere Function in the Human Brain.* New York: John Wiley & Sons, 1974.

HARNAD, S., R.W. DOTY, L. GOLDSTEIN, J. HAYNES, and G. KRAUTHAMER, (eds.). *Lateralization in the Nervous System.* New York: Academic Press, 1977.

Thinking II: Memories and Plans

Thinking integrates our experience over time. Human thought draws upon experiences which occurred in the past, and it prepares for anticipated futures. The brain systems which enable the overcoming of the here-and-now represent powerful embodiments of mind, and they figure prominently in the

5

organization of human behavior. This chapter deals with mechanisms which are believed to underlie these abilities.

The Physical Basis of Memory

When you look up a new telephone number, it is not difficult to hold the number in mind long enough to dial it. If the line is busy, however, you may need to look up the number again. Similarly, cramming for a test can improve one's grade, but rarely does it result in any lasting memory for the material.

These facts suggest that the large part of things which enter a person's memory are not permanently stored there. Researchers interested in the physical basis of human memory have tried to come to grips with the differences between recent fragile memories (like the telephone number) and the memories which survive to leave an indelible trace on the brain. The most widely accepted explanation is that recent memories and older memories are based upon two different kinds of brain processes. One is like a *short-term storage device,* which accepts indiscriminately and for a short time any detail which one attends to. This short-term memory acts as a kind of self-erasing scratch pad of conscious experience. The other kind, the *long-term-store,* preserves those things which seem important.

The Canadian psychologist Donald Hebb advanced the most influential modern theory. Hebb's formulation is that short-term and long-term memories correspond to different stages in the brain's acquisition of memories.[1] Short-term memory is merely persisting neural activity, set into reverberation by sounds or sights or thoughts. This *dynamic* or active type of memory could be based on something like a closed loop of neurons (see Figure 5–1), in which excitation in the loop would be self-sustaining. The reverberating, dynamic traces would be the brain's scratch pad, preserving an instant of the continuously receding present, fixing it for a moment so that it can be worked upon.

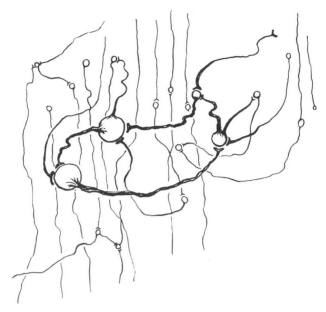

FIGURE 5-1. Reverberating neural circuit of the type proposed by Hebb to explain dynamic short-term memory. Each individual cell might participate in more than one such circuit, so that this memory would share parts of the path. Anatomists have discovered closed loops of this type in brain tissue, and physiologists have observed reverberating neural activity.[2]

Dynamic traces would gradually die out, by Hebb's theory, if a more permanent, *structural* imprint were not made on the active neurons. This structural memory trace is sometimes referred to as an *engram.*

The distinction between dynamic and structural traces parallels the distinction between short-term and long-term memories. Dynamic traces would be like rivulets of water running down a hillside. When the water stops, the pattern of rivulets disappears. But if the water runs long enough, then the rivulets cut channels and wear the pattern into the hillside, so that a permanent "memory" of it has been formed. This analogy further suggests that long-term memories are created out of short-term memories which remain active long enough, an intuitively appealing aspect of the theory, considering that memory improves with repetition and practice.

But why couldn't all memories be based on dynamic traces? After all, the brain is always electrically active, even in sleep. Why postulate structural engrams at all? Research with laboratory animals has decided the issue. If you train a hamster to turn right rather than left in a simple maze in order to get food, the hamster could be said to have acquired a new memory. If that memory is totally embodied in the matrix of ongoing electrical brain activity, then by stopping the activity, you should be able to eradicate the memory.

Now, with hamsters this is a relatively simple matter, because as hibernating creatures, their body temperatures can be lowered to a point where all detectable brain activity ceases, and afterwards they can be revived again. What happens is that reheated hamsters are not forgetful.[3] A structural engram must exist!

The nature of the structural change (the engram) has not yet been discovered, but there are some interesting speculations. The most widely accepted idea is that long-term memory is some kind of change in "synaptic resistance."[4] Some particular group of neurons which all fire simultaneously (or at least very closely in time) become a functional network. This network is the brain's physical representation of a specific memory. When it is activated, you might, for example, recall a certain telephone number in your mind's ear.

Memories are not always active in consciousness (you can recall a phone number, even though you do not constantly think of it); they exist most of the time as potentialities which could become activated under the right circumstances. The "synaptic resistance" hypothesis says that while the network is active, the synapses between the neurons in the network change permanently, so that future activity in one neuron will tend to evoke activity in the next neuron in the chain. Once the recurrent dynamic activity dies down, the network still exists, as potentiality, in the lowered resistance between the neurons. The memory exists in the tendency for the network as a whole to become activated when one or two of the constituent neurons become active.

The synaptic resistance hypothesis can be viewed as a physiological embodiment of the old psychological notion of "association"—by which are explained such things as the word "cow" triggering in your mind the word "milk." "Association" forms the basis for many ancient and modern theories of memory and learning. The "pieces" of a memory become associated by lowered synaptic resistance. Presumably, individual memories could also form associative bonds, whereby one memory evokes another, through a similar mechanism.*

When something we perceive is closely matched to a memory, we say that we recognize it. This feeling of recognition

---

*One frequently discussed possibility underlying these hypothesized changes in synaptic resistance is that the mechanism is regulated by a change in RNA molecules inside individual neurons. RNA are large complex organic molecules in living cells; one of the things they do is control the production of biochemical substances which, in turn, enable the cell to perform its functions. The memory molecules would, in some unknown manner, carry the memory code and use it to regulate the transmission of impulses from one neuron to another (see Landauer, T. K. *Psychological Review,* 1969, 76, 92–96).

Holger Hydén, a Swedish biochemist, has shown that brain cells change their RNA structure as a specific result of learning experiences, and that the cells which change are located in the brain regions related to the learning. For example, right-pawed cats were taught to take food with their left paws, and RNA extracted from the right sensorimotor cortex (which controls the left paw) showed the RNA changes, while RNA from sensorimotor cortex on the other side of the brain did not. Although this discovery, and a few others like it, have created some excitement about a possible biochemical basis for memory, it is premature to reach this conclusion.

One problem with this idea is that almost all the neuron's RNA is found in the cell body, far distant from the synaptic areas of the cell. Besides, the RNA changes Hydén observed could just as easily be a nonspecific indicator of increased neural activity—a by-product of engram formation in the localized region of the brain—without actually carrying the information stored during the learning.

Readers interested in RNA and other theories of engram formation are referred to Entingh, D., *et al.* In Gazzaniga, M. S., and C. Blakemore, *Handbook of Psychobiology.* New York: Academic Press, 1975.

appears to be added on, as a kind of elaboration to the information-processing operations which match an incoming stimulus to a memory trace. The proof of this is that the feeling of recognition can sometimes occur alone, without the actual cognitive recognition.

This is the mysterious feeling of *déjà vu*—the feeling of familiarity, divorced from any obvious memory. This is an experience which almost everyone has, when one feels that the present moment, in all its exact details, has been lived before.[5] The Montreal neurosurgeon Wilder Penfield reported that it is possible to elicit *déjà vu* by electrically stimulating parts of the right temporal lobe of his patients during surgery. They would say at these times that they feel as if they previously experienced the same operating room, the same people, the same conversation.[6] Penfield's electrode may have tapped a separable component of the brain's machinery for remembering, and the brain's occasional misfiring may explain the common experience of *déjà vu*.

It is still unknown where engrams are laid down, in terms of major subdivisions of the brain. Is human memory, as in the case of a computer, restricted to an enclosed box, organized like so many library shelves? Is there a memory organ?

Probably not. The research of E. Roy John at New York University has shown that electrical signs of a specific sensory stimulus can be seen over extensive regions of the brain, both cortical and subcortical, after the stimulus is learned.[7] However, this result is for a very special kind of memory (conditioning in animals). It may well be that human cognitive memories are organized quite differently.

It is frequently assumed that cognitive memory traces are laid down in *cortical* tissue, because the capacity for learning and remembering increases in a manner roughly parallel to the growth of cortex in vertebrate evolution. This is exactly the same reasoning that lies behind the view, discussed earlier, that the cortex is the seat of consciousness.

The link of cortex to memory is inferred from a general

trend in animal evolution known as *encephalization,* which refers to the progressive increase in brain size relative to body size. This trend culminates in the development of the forebrain, particularly the cerebral cortex (see Figure 5–2.) Animals with well-developed cortices are animals with the greatest plasticity or modifiability to their behavior. The behaviors of these animals—dogs, horses, humans—are finely tailored by their experiences, compared to "lower" vertebrates, like frogs and fish, whose behavior is largely pre-wired and less adaptable.[8]

In Chapter 2 we saw that the visual system of the frog is pre-wired and relatively inflexible (a frog will starve in a roomful of dead flies). By this reasoning, the cortex would seem to be the organ of memory, since increased behavioral plasticity requires more and more memory storage space. Cortex is what is added by recent evolution.

The experiments by Lashley on removal of cortex in rats, discussed earlier, showed that cortical memories are not localized in any one particular part of the cortex.[9] Rather, Lashley concluded, the information contained in a single memory is distributed *equipotentially* in cortical tissue, so that small pieces of cortex can independently and equally serve as the site for storage of the same engram. The modern version of this scheme is the hologram theory, discussed in Chapter 2.[10]

The objective definition of memory is that it is a change in behavior as a result of past experience. By this broader definition, isolated pieces of nervous tissue from even peripheral parts of the nervous system are capable of memory.[11] But conscious remembering (remembering as a subjective experience) is probably related to very highly organized and complicated brain events, involving, for the most part, perceptual and linguistic processes which are known to be functions of the cerebral cortex.[12]

Specific kinds of memories *are* lost, in humans, following damage to parts of the "uncommitted cortex." These *specific amnesias* include, for example, the loss of the ability to name colors or to recognize faces. But since the damage is to areas

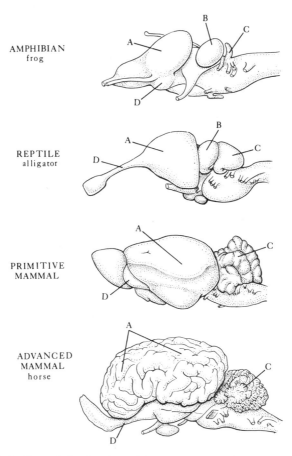

AMPHIBIAN
frog

REPTILE
alligator

PRIMITIVE
MAMMAL

ADVANCED
MAMMAL
horse

FIGURE 5-2. Encephalization in vertebrate evolution. Comparison of brains of different vertebrates to show the growth of the cerebrum in recent evolution. (a) cerebrum; (b) optic tectum (obscured from view in the two mammalian brains by overlying cerebral hemispheres); (c) cerebellum; (d) olfactory lobe. For higher mammals, like the horse, this increase in the cerebral hemispheres is so great that the surface is wrinkled to accommodate the cortex within the skull. The cerebrum evolved as an offshoot of the olfactory system (optic lobe, or "smell brain"), apparently as a structure to coordinate information from different senses. In mammals, the optic center in the brainstem is supplemented by visual cortex, which dominates higher visual functions. The increase in brain size and the control of function by newer structures of the cerebrum is an evolutionary trend known as encephalization. (After A. S. Romer, <u>The Vertebrate Body</u>, 4th ed., Philadelphia: W. B. Saunders, 1970.)

known to be involved in complex information-processing activities, it may be more fruitful to regard specific amnesias as failures of computational machinery rather than problems with the retrieval of memory contents. Nevertheless, the encephalization argument seems difficult to refute. A cortical storage site for human cognitive memory seems likely. However, it also seems likely that older parts of the brain contain the traces of experiences relevant to their own functioning, whether or not these memories ever become conscious.

Certain unusual cases of memory loss, discussed in the next section, point to the conclusion that there are different kinds of memory systems in the brain, some of which can be cut off from conscious access. It may be wrong to imagine that all the parts of a particular memory are stored in any single subdivision of the brain.

The Consolidation of Memories

If you get hit on the head and lose consciousness, there will be a gap of time just before your mishap that you won't remember. This is known as *retrograde amnesia*—"retrograde" because it involves the period of time before the trauma. Gradually, memory for the events of a few hours earlier will return, and eventually you will be able to recall other things that happened, except for one permanent lacuna in your history: the seconds or minutes just before the blow which knocked you unconscious. Something must have happened to these memories; they must have been in an especially vulnerable state.

Like the new telephone number which rapidly disappears from your mind, these memories existed in short-term storage only. Why were no permanent traces made? Why were the young memories so vulnerable to disruption? According to Hebb's theory, mentioned earlier, there is a period of time, a *consolidation period,* during which memories exist only in a dynamic electrical or electrochemical form. During this period, the memories must remain undisturbed in order to hatch as permanent structural engrams. If a dynamic memory trace is disrupted during the consolidation period, by a neuronal shock wave, say, from a blow on the head, it is gone forever.

Consolidation might be an active process of fixing only certain dynamic memories and not others; or it might simply be the passive fate of especially persistent dynamic memories. In this latter eventuality (Hebb's position), the selection of memories for consolidation is determined by all the factors which make a memory persist in dynamic form. This might be the reason why conscious rehearsal is so effective in stamping in such elusive memories as telephone numbers. Sleep following a period of learning is also effective in improving retention, for a related reason: it may prevent the disruption of the dynamic trace by interfering activity.[13]

The time course of memory consolidation has been studied extensively in man, because retrograde amnesia is also produced by a psychiatric treatment known as *electroconvulsive shock (ECS).* In ECS, a strong current is passed across the brain, causing brief convulsions and loss of consciousness. This strange treatment seems to help seriously depressed psychiatric patients, although just how it works is unknown. It is in common enough clinical use that it has provided a large amount of data on memory consolidation.

In ECS amnesia, older memories are generally recovered first, followed by more recent ones. Furthermore, there is a period, from several seconds to a minute or so before the ECS, from which memories never recover.[14] These facts are taken to be evidence for Hebb's consolidation hypothesis.

The disturbances brought to the brain by head trauma or ECS are too diffuse to tell us just what brain structures are affected. Other clues, however, point to a structure known as the *hippocampus.* The hippocampus is part of the *limbic system,* an interconnected group of nerve centers at the border (or "limbus") of the brainstem and the cerebral hemispheres (see Figure 5–3). The few unfortunate people who sustain injury to this area of the brain on both sides are in a bizarre state. They become almost completely unable to learn or remember anything new.

One of these was the famous case of H. M. (his initials), a 27-year-old man who underwent an experimental form of surgical treatment for his epileptic attacks. The attacks had become frequent and uncontrollable despite medication, and surgery was prescribed. Because the hippocampus acted as a trigger for his attacks, the operation involved the removal of the hippocampus from inside of both temporal lobes. The surgery was successful, at least in terms of the epilepsy. H. M.

FIGURE 5–3. Cutaway view of the forebrain to show the hippocampus and related structures of the limbic system. (From Jacques Barbizet, Human Memory and Its Pathology, San Francisco: W. H. Freeman and Company, 1970. Reproduced with permission of the author.)

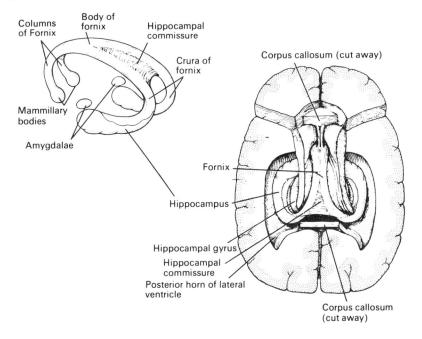

appeared intelligent and alert after the operation: his I.Q. test scores even improved somewhat, probably a result of his not having frequent small seizures during testing. His immediate memory was intact: he could repeat a string of 7 or 8 digits without error.

However, an unfortunate side effect of H. M.'s surgery was that he was, from the day of his operation, totally unable to remember persons and events he encountered. He did not recognize hospital personnel, even though he may have talked with them many times a day. He could not learn the way home to his new house, to which his family moved after the operation, even after living there for many years. If left to his own devices, he would usually return to his old house.

H. M. would read the same magazines and solve the same puzzles over and over, forgetting that he had seen them before. Every time he was reminded of the death of a favorite uncle, an event which occurred some time after H. M.'s surgery, he would act surprised and become emotionally upset over the news!

What made H. M.'s case so remarkable was that all of his other intellectual faculties were apparently spared, including his memories for things in the deep past, before the surgery. He could read normally, solve complicated problems, and remember the details of things in his short-term memory long enough to carry on a sensible conversation. But as soon as his attention was distracted—if a visitor left the room, for instance—he would have no recollection of the visit.

Since H. M.'s earlier memories were intact, his difficulty seemed purely a problem of consolidation. H. M. was frozen in time. He could not form new, permanent engrams.[15]

Although it first appeared that H. M. was incapable of any learning, it was later discovered that his capabilities for *motor learning* were unaffected: he could learn to trace skillfully the outlines of a 5-pointed star while viewing a reversed image of the writing hand and target in a mirror.[16] This is a laboratory analogue of learning to swing a golf club or steer a car. (See Figure 5–4.) At the start of each new session, H. M's perform-

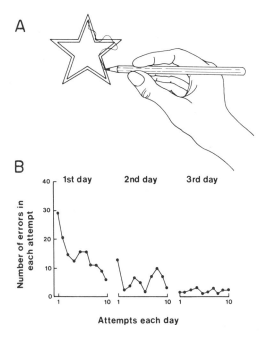

A

B

FIGURE 5-4. Motor learning without conscious memory. (a) The mirror-tracing task, in which the subject must follow the outline of the star figure, viewed reversed in a mirror. (b) The patient, H. M., shows objective improvement in the mirror-tracing task over several days' practice, even though he could not consciously remember the task at the start of each new session. (From <u>Mechanics of the Mind</u> by Colin Blakemore, New York: Cambridge University Press, 1977. Reproduced with permission of the publisher.)

ance showed clearly that he acquired some skill from the days before, but he did not consciously remember having even seen the task previously!

This is a curious *dissociation* of two kinds of memory. What was missing—what we would call a "conscious" memory in this situation—is a perceptual image of the mirror task, or something else which could mediate visual recognition. Some part of H. M. "remembered," but he was not conscious of the memory. A similar case was recently reported of a man who contracted a rare viral infection which attacked his brain. Afterwards, he was incapable of remembering new material on a conscious cognitive level, but he could easily learn new piano pieces. On the days after learning a new piece, he would forget, or, more precisely, he would deny verbally that he knew the piece. But he could still play it without difficulty if someone supplied the opening bars.[17]

Why is motor learning spared by hippocampal lesions, while more cognitive or conscious types of memory are not? It may be that there is more than one kind of memory, mediated by different brain structures. Motor learning may be a more primitive kind of memory, close to the memory capabilities of most animals. An argument in favor of this idea is the fact that destroying the hippocampi in lower animals does not result in the kind of consolidation problem shown by H. M.[18]

There are several interesting speculations about what the hippocampus does in man. One possibility is that it creates an artificial arousal state. Brain arousal appears to be necessary for remembering something,[19] and this would insure that memory selects out what is important. What the hippocampus might do is create a cognitively controlled arousal state which mimics the arousal caused by emotion or surprise. In this way, the human brain can deal with the abstract material of human cognitive learning—material which is dull in terms of immediate reward and punishment.[20] Related to this idea are some current theories which regard the hippocampus as an attention-focuser.[21] Tantalizing here is the fact that the hippocampus is anatomically very close to other limbic structures, which function to mediate drive, emotion, and reward in the brain.[22] When brain surgeons stimulate these areas their patients report experiences of intense pleasure or pain.[23]

Dissociated Memory

The pathologies of memory can reveal mechanisms normally hidden. One interesting class of amnesias known to clinical psychologists are amnesias encountered under conditions of severe emotional stress. They result in the separation, or *disso-ciation,* of certain memories from conscious access: memories relating to emotionally painful experiences may become selectively blocked from consciousness. These memories are not merely forgotten, for they can often be retrieved at a later time, during the course of therapy or under hypnosis.

The most dramatic of these *dissociative amnesias* are cases of "multiple personality." Here is one such case:†

> A 28-year-old married woman was admitted to a hospital, depressed and retarded, after a suicidal attempt. Several days later she became angry and assaultive, claimed that it was "her" fault that she was depressed. She then stated that "Mary" was the depressed person: she was Cynthia. As Cynthia she reported frequently leaving home, picking up sailors and lesbians, and acting in a loose and lascivious manner. As Mary she acted as a dutiful, quiet, submissive housewife and mother, angry and depressed over her husband's poor relationship to her. Periodically she abruptly assumed the character of Cynthia and became loud, boisterous, and uninhibited. In the depressed state she . . . repressed the rage toward her husband, and dutifully attempted to assume her responsibilities as a housewife, as Mary. When overwhelmed by rage, she expressed her rage through defiance and acted her aggressive and sexual urges as Cynthia.[24]

Cynthia knew about the actions of Mary, but Mary appeared completely out of touch with any memory of Cynthia.[25]

Another dissociative amnesia is known as *fugue.* Fugue states are states of mental confusion accompanying flight from a stressful situation, often in the form of aimless wandering. They are typically preceded by some psychological or physical shock, and during the fugue there is a period of time, days or even years, when the victim becomes unable to remember his past life. Sometime later, past memories may return, usually

†From Kolb, L.C., *Noyes's Modern Clinical Psychiatry,* 7th ed. Philadelphia: W.B. Saunders and Co., 1968. Reprinted with permission.

with the curious exception of memories of the fugue period itself.[26] A famous case was reported by William James:

> A clergyman, the Rev. Ansell Bourne, disappeared from his home in Providence, Rhode Island. Two weeks later, under the name of A.J. Brown, he rented a confectioner's shop in Norristown, Pennsylvania and for six weeks maintained it as a business establishment. At this point, he "came to," and asked where he was, insisting that he was a clergyman named Bourne and that he knew nothing of A.J. Brown. His relatives, including his wife, corroborated his identity as a minister, but he remained terrified by his experience and able to give only the vaguest account of its rationale, though the A.J. Brown identity could be recovered under hypnosis.[27]

Psychiatric interpretations of dissociative amnesia tend to be in terms of Freud's theory of the unconscious. By this view, multiple personalities or the confused mental state of fugue represent attempts to cope with unconscious personality conflicts. There is a memory laid down of the workings of the unrecalled selves, but this store of memories is actively blocked or repressed and becomes inaccessible to normal consciousness.

Dissociative amnesias are usually described as "psychogenic" or "affective," because there is no known physical, organic basis to them. They are presumed to operate at a level best understood by talking about feelings and desires, rather than neurons. The distinction most commonly made between organic amnesias (like the hippocampal amnesia) and affective amnesias is a distinction between "hardware" (the memory machine) and "software" (the actual memory content). However, affective amnesias are sufficiently similar to organically based memory dissociations (e.g., dissociations between motor learning and conscious recall in the case of H. M., or between the two halves of a split brain) that it is tempting to speculate that an organic basis for them may ultimately be found.

Memory dissociations also bear strong resemblance to a phenomenon known to drug researchers as *state-dependent* memory. If you train a rat to turn left in a maze to avoid an electric shock, and this training is done while the animal is under the influence of a psycho-active drug (e.g., pentobarbital), the rat may be unable to perform correctly in the maze the next day, after the effects of the drug have worn off. People report similar difficulties remembering the events which transpired during a heavy bout of drinking. For the rats, at least, the original learning recovers when the animal is again under the influence of the drug. This is state-dependent memory: recall is specific to the altered brain state in which the memory was acquired. It is also possible to create a double dissociation: the rat can be trained to turn left when drugged and right when sober.[28]

Jason Brown, a neurologist at New York University, believes that affective memory dissociations are instances of regression to more primitive levels of brain organization, a temporary lapse in the machinery of higher cortical functioning, throwing the control of behavior and thought back to the way the brain was organized in childhood or infancy.[29] As such, affective amnesias may be cases of state-dependent memory.

By Brown's theory, this is the same reason why our memories are not good regarding the events of childhood, or regarding dreams. Somehow, higher levels of brain organization and control do not have access to the memories formed by lower levels. The state-dependency is revealed by the common observation that events of childhood can become vividly recalled in old age, when higher cognitive capabilities lapse somewhat. Also, the repressed memories of fugue and multiple personality are often retrievable by certain drugs (e.g., sodium pentothal) or by hypnosis—operations presumed to block or suspend higher cognitive functions.

According to Brown, we are conscious at any moment by virtue of the highest mental organization we can achieve at that time. Behavior might still be controlled, unconsciously, by lower forms of brain organization, as in H. M.'s mirror drawing, but there is no direct access to consciousness of the workings of lower levels. Brown's theory has important consequences for understanding the physical basis of consciousness. It will be taken up again in the final chapter.

Above all else, cases of memory dissociation point to the fact that what we regard as our enduring, personal conscious identity, or self, is strongly tied to a body of past memories. Memory binds one's past to one's present and so gives us a sense of identity. Memory links waking consciousness in the morning to the consciousness which was extinguished the night before. The etymology of the word "mind" embellishes the point. In Middle English, "mynd" meant something like "remembering."

Just as through memory, your present is linked with your past, so through planning, your present is linked to the future. Many people would ascribe consciousness to an ape but not to a Venus flytrap (the carnivorous plant which closes up on its insect prey), reflecting the fact that human mental experience is strongly bound up with notions of purpose and intention. A purely reflex activity, like that of the plant, would not be considered evidence for the presence of consciousness. However, the goal-oriented strivings of an ape who is trying to reach a banana outside of his cage is a familiar form of mentality.

The long-term organization of most human behavior reflects a very recent advance in brain evolution, the large mass of *frontal cortex* in man and apes. The neurological disturbances of organized and planned behavior provide a glimpse into the physical basis of what we call "foresight."

Phineas Gage and Other Mysteries of the Frontal Lobe

In 1848 an explosion sent a 3-foot iron rod cleanly through the skull and left frontal lobe of a Vermont railroad foreman named Phineas P. Gage. Gage walked away from the accident and recovered, miraculously, after a long convalescence. His intellectual capacities were diminished somewhat, but he was not totally enfeebled. The most severe change was to his personality. His physician described him as becoming "fitful, irreverent, indulging at times in the grossest profanity, . . . manifesting but little deference for his fellows, impatient of restraint or advice when it conflicts with his desires." From the soft-spoken, steady, and alert workman he was before the accident, he became an unreliable adventurer, showing little sense of purpose and taken to wandering aimlessly about the country. He exhibited his head and the iron rod for an admission fee. (His skull and the rod are still on view, at the Harvard Medical School; see Figure 5–5.) On Gage's death, an autopsy revealed extensive damage to anterior portions of his left frontal lobe.[30]

Gage became a famous medical case, because up until that time, the frontal lobes of the brain were considered to be the seat of the highest intellectual faculties. Yet, here was a man with extensive damage to this part of the brain, and who was, for most of the functions of intellect, pretty much intact.

The reason that the frontal lobes were originally considered so important to intelligence was based primarily on anatomy. The dramatic increase in this area during recent brain evolution culminates in the great proliferation of frontal cortex in man, where the frontal lobes account for as much as 25 percent of the brain's weight.[31]

This striking anatomical feature of the human brain led to all sorts of higher intellectual functions being ascribed to it. A popular nineteenth-century authority on "phrenology" (the now discredited science of reading head shapes to discern intelligence and character) localized reflective and reasoning faculties there, such as the mental ability to "perceive causality." (See Figure 5–6.)

Even into the first third of this century, neurologists ascribed to the frontal lobes all of the highest conceivable functions—such things as "synthesis," "ethical thinking," and "awareness of self."[32] Despite advances in understanding the effects of frontal brain damage, its functions are, by and large, still poorly understood.

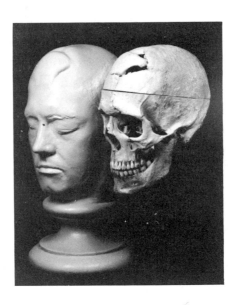

Figure 5-5. (a) The skull and life-mask of Phineas Gage, showing the scars of his injury. (b) The iron rod which was propelled through Gage's left frontal lobe by the explosion. Both skull and rod are on display at the Museum of the Harvard Medical School. (Reprinted with permission of Warren Anatomical Museum, Harvard Medical School, 25 Shattuck St., Boston, MA 02115.)

Frontal Intelligence

Despite the phrenologists' guess, the frontal lobes did not turn out to be the seat of intelligence, at least intelligence of the type measured by mathematical problems or I.Q. tests. From an

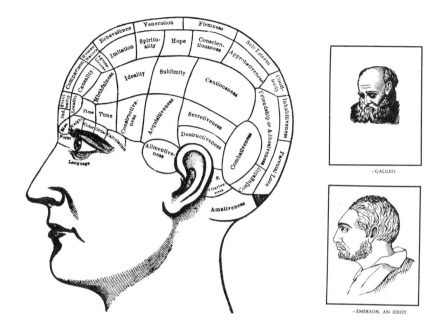

FIGURE 5-6. Phrenology and the frontal lobes. (a) A phrenological chart of the skull (c. 1887), showing the alleged functions of underlying cortical areas. Note the assignment of higher faculties of thought to the frontal parts of the head. (b) Phrenological "evidence" on frontal functions. (From Fowler's <u>Phrenology,</u> 1887.)

Phrenology was originally advanced as a serious attempt to localize psychological faculties to different areas of the brain. The phrenologists believed that a person's character and intellectual capacities could be read from the shape of the skull, with bumps in different regions indicating a well-developed brain "organ' for those faculties. The science of phrenology was soon discredited. Nevertheless, phrenology gained great popularity in the nineteenth century as a means of divining character, like handwriting analysis. The logic of phrenology is not different from the position of many reputable brain scientists of today, namely that certain higher brain functions can be localized to certain regions.

The problem with phrenology is simply that its other assumptions are wrong. For one thing, variations in the shape of the brain, except in rare cases, are not mirrored in the shape of the skull. For another, the sheer size or weight of the brain, or of a particular brain area, does not distinguish between a genius and someone with average mentality, despite the carefully selected examples of phrenologists, such as in Figure (b). The brain of Anatole France was found to be some 1,000 mls at autopsy, and the brain of Turgenev was over 2,000 mls—yet both brains were the seat of great intellectual capacity.

analysis of the deficits suffered by neurology patients with damage to prefrontal cortex, a puzzling and inconsistent picture emerges. Some cases show severe intellectual deficits, while others, like Phineas Gage, show little or none.

Despite these contradictions, certain effects recur. Past memories and skills are usually undisturbed. Performance on intelligence tests is usually only slightly lower: sometimes I.Q. test scores can be higher. The most dramatic changes are in such aspects as tendencies toward capriciousness, diminished initiative, lack of ability to concentrate, and difficulties in apprehending the social context of one's actions.

During the 1930's attempts were made to unravel the knot of frontal functioning by experimenting with frontal lesions in apes. Carlysle Jacobsen at Yale University found that his chimpanzees, after surgery, were particularly impaired in their ability to integrate a sequence of behaviors over an interval of time. Jacobsen used a "delayed reaction" task, in which the chimpanzee is shown a peanut being placed beneath one of two cups. If a delay is introduced between seeing the placement of the peanut and having a chance to retrieve it, normal chimps have no difficulty in finding the peanut. Chimps without frontal lobes can solve this problem immediately after the peanut is placed but fail when delays are introduced.

A chance observation of Jacobsen's had a profound social impact. Jacobsen reported that one particular chimp, before surgery, tended to become emotionally upset by any frustration in the testing situation. This animal would exhibit violent temper tantrums which made the testing all but impossible. However, after recovery from surgery, which damaged both frontal lobes, the chimp became docile, friendly, and cooperative. And even though she continued to make mistakes on the tasks, the mistakes just didn't seem to bother her! "It was as if the animal had joined a 'happiness cult' . . . and had placed its burdens on the Lord."[33]

In 1935 a Portugese physician named Egaz Moniz heard a report of Jacobsen's work at a neurological conference in London. Moniz decided that here might be the key to the problems of the deranged mental patients he had been seeing. Their obsessions and terrors might be the products of faulty frontal-lobe functioning, symptoms of too much frontal control. Moniz reasoned that surgically separating this area from the rest of the brain might be the cure.

In 1936 Moniz performed the first frontal *lobotomy*—the severing of the nerve fibers running between the frontal cortex and lower brain centers. By isolating the frontal cortex, Moniz hoped to cure the suffering of his patients. He optimistically reported that out of 20 such cases, 7 were completely cured by the operation, and 8 showed improvement.

By 1950 the operation was in common practice in European and American mental institutions. In the decade after World War II, 50,000 lobotomies were performed in the United States alone. The ease and low risk of the operation made it possible to lobotomize 10 or more patients a day under local anesthesia in the surgeon's office.[34] Many cases reported at the time did indeed sound like cures. One man, a 54-year-old tool designer, was lobotomized after a long history of extreme anxiety and obsessive physical tics. The operation resulted in his torments being replaced by a "vacuous euphoria." He slowly resumed his normal activities, and a year after the operation he invented and patented a new machine tool.[35] Why lobotomy should have produced such little mental impairment in some cases, when missile wounds and tumors in the frontal lobes can produce so much change, was perhaps due to the incompleteness of the surgical disconnection.

In recent years, lobotomy has become a rare practice, largely because of the discovery that certain intellectual impairments *could* be observed in frontal patients if the correct tests were used.[36] The dramatic changes seen in severe frontal brain damage could also be seen, but more subtly, in lobotomy patients.[37]

The tests which revealed the difficulty were those which required the patient to abstractly organize thought and action. For example, the Card-Sorting Test requires the matching of stimuli on the basis of abstract categories (see Figure 5–7).

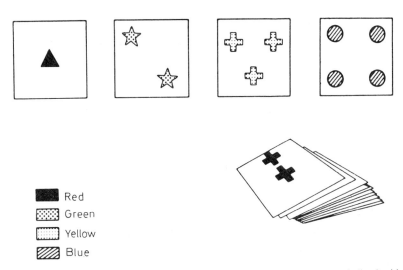

Red
Green
Yellow
Blue

FIGURE 5-7. Card-Sorting Test. The subject is shown four stimulus cards (top) which differ in color, form, and number. A deck of cards (bottom) is to be sorted according to a category designated by the examiner. If the category is number, then the top card in the deck (two red crosses) is to be placed in front of the stimulus card containing two stars. Later, the category for sorting is changed, say, to color—in which case the top card in the deck is correctly placed in front of the stimulus card containing the red triangle. Frontal patients tend to persevere in their use of sorting strategies when these are no longer appropriate. (From B. Milner, <u>Archives of Neurology</u>, 1963, **9**, pp. 90–100. Copyright 1963 by the American Medical Association. Reproduced with permission of the author and publisher.)

Patients with damaged frontal lobes do especially poorly on this test. They are unable to switch the strategies used for sorting. When asked to sort on the basis of color after just having sorted on the basis of form, these patients tend to persevere with the previous rule.[38]

Plans, Intentions, and the Expectancy Wave

Like Jacobsen's chimpanzee, humans with frontal-lobe damage have difficulty in correctly sequencing their actions over time, in integrating their behavior. Sometimes this appears as a problem in shifting to a new plan of action when required; sometimes the problem is in maintaining a plan once it is initiated. The change in Phineas Gage's personality was consistent with this observation. Gage was described as "capricious and vacillating, devising many plans for future operation which are no sooner arranged than they are abandoned in turn for others appearing more feasible."[39]

The capriciousness of some frontal patients is unrelated to short-term memory, which is usually preserved. These patients are often able to remember the instructions for a sequence of actions, which they nevertheless seem incapable of carrying out. What happens is best described as *distraction*.

In one instance, reported by Luria, a frontal patient was sent to his ward on an errand, as part of an examination. But on seeing a group of patients coming toward him, he turned and followed them. He got sidetracked from his intended mission.[40] Now, it is important to notice here that this behavior is not any different in form from normal everyday instances of misplaced intentions. You started to write a letter, but the telephone rang, and then someone dropped by, and only much later do you realize you didn't write the letter. What is different about the frontal patient is the ease with which he gets sidetracked.

Another manner in which frontal patients can get sidetracked is that the original plan is replaced by some habitual stereotyped action. One patient, when asked to light a candle, struck a match, and then put the candle in his mouth to smoke it, as he would a cigarette.[41] This performance may be a further instance of a tendency toward *perseveration* shown by frontal patients and discussed earlier in relation to the card-sorting test. One unfortunate man who was working in the carpentry shop of the hospital, continued to plane a piece of wood until it was completely gone, at which time he continued planing the bench.[42] All of these curious behaviors can be understood as difficulties in the initiation, formulation, or completion of a plan of action.

What kind of mental device is this thing we have been calling a plan? A simple situation illustrates. Assume you want to go to the corner store to buy some bread. You have a goal (the purchase), and you have a pretty good idea of how to accomplish the goal. This "pretty good idea" is the plan. It contains many little subgoals, such as finding money, walking to the store, etc. If you worked like a computer, the plan would be represented in a program, a list of instructions which controls the order of a sequence of operations to be performed.*

Each of the constituent operations of a plan may itself be a pretty complicated affair. For example, finding your wallet involves programming the searching movements of the eyes and the hands, and coordinating the search with pattern recognition processes. Search programs must also make use of a process which scans stored representations of the spatial layout of the house.

Each of these subprograms or subplans is nested within the main plan; it is not activated until the proper place in the sequence. You do not have to enumerate these activities in your main plan, simply name them ("find wallet"). The subplans will unfold at the proper time. This procedure is referred to as a *hierarchical process,* and it is a cardinal principle in writing good computer programs. Purposeful behavior is organized hierarchically, even though we may be consciously aware of only fragments of our behavior plans.

The behaviors contained in a plan are said, in everyday language, to be *intended*—guided by the intention to reach the goal. Reaching a goal involves the execution of a number of actions in a sequence, some of the actions quite complicated in themselves. Locating your wallet or purse, finding your jacket, putting it on, opening the front door, exiting, closing the door behind you, walking down the front steps, etc. At any point in the sequence, things occur: a newspaper photograph catches your eye, you remember that you have to wash the dishes. Any of these events could easily untrack you, setting you off on a new course of action, keeping you from getting the bread. Except for your intention.

*This metaphor of a computer program guiding purposeful action was first advanced in a delightful and influential book called *Plans and the Structure of Behavior,* by Miller, Galanter, and Pribram (New York: Henry Holt and Co., 1960). The treatment here owes much to their analysis.

A computer has intentions of sorts. When the execution of a computer program is interrupted by external inputs which need to be processed, then the execution of the program is held in abeyance by a place-holding mechanism, an electronic finger which later returns the program to the spot where it was interrupted. What could human intentions be made of? A recent discovery opens up the possibility that we can find a physical counterpart to an intention, and that it might originate in the frontal lobes.

The candidate for a physiological intention mechanism is a certain brain wave, visible in the EEG during periods of mental expectancy. It was first described in 1964 by W. Grey Walter and his colleagues at the Burden Neurological Institute in Bristol, England.[43] Walter called this brain wave the *contingent negative variation,* or *CNV*—a slow negative shift in electrical potential which occurs whenever two stimuli are paired in time, so that the first signals the arrival of the second. In this case, we say that the second stimulus is "contingent" on the first, hence the name of the wave. (See **Figure 5–8.**) It has since acquired the informal name of "expectancy wave," since this appears to be the crucial psychological condition for its occurrence.[44]

The CNV is recorded most clearly from the front portions of the scalp and seems to originate in the frontal cortex, sweeping backward toward other cortical regions.[45]

The CNV wave, or something like it, could turn out to be the physical basis of an intention, a place-holder in the hierarchical execution of a plan. It could function in some as-yet-unknown manner to prevent distraction—something like a gremlin, perched on your shoulder, constantly nagging, "Don't forget about buying the bread."

Damage to the frontal lobes of the brain creates problems in maintaining intentions. Frontal patients are often described as "stimulus bound," meaning that they are at the whim of momentary interests and are highly distractible. Distractibility also seems to be the reason why Jacobsen's frontally lesioned chimps could not perform the delayed-reaction task.

One way to accomplish the place-holding aspect of inten-

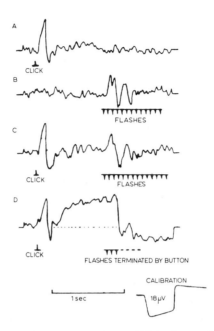

FIGURE 5-8. The contingent negative variation (CNV), observed in the EEG during moments of expectancy. (a) and (b) Cortical responses evoked by click and light flashes presented alone. (c) Clicks are paired contingently in time with flashes, but nothing is required of the subject. (d) Clicks are paired contingently with flashes, and the subject must press a button to terminate the flashes. The CNV appears in anticipation of the flashes (an upward deflection is electrically negative). Actually, an overt response is not necessary for the CNV to appear. All that is required is for the subject to anticipate and pay attention to the second stimulus. (From W. G. Walter, <u>Progress in Brain Research</u>, 1968, 22, pp.364–377. Reproduced with permission of the publisher.)

tion might be through the regulation of orienting responses (see Chapter 3). If orienting responses were suppressed during the execution of a plan, then there would be less probability of distraction by interesting stimuli.[46] Portions of the frontal cortex are anatomically linked to orienting and habituation systems elsewhere in the brain, and orienting reactions in monkeys are grossly altered following lesions to their frontal lobes.[47]

Another way of looking at the distractibility of frontal patients might be to regard it as a failure of memory: they seem incapable of remembering their intentions. However, this must be a very special kind of memory, for their immediate memory capacities (digit span—the longest number they can repeat back) and long-term memories (their home address) are usually unimpaired.

The idea of a separate intention memory is supported by a well-known psychological phenomenon known as the *Zeigarnik effect*. Zeigarnik demonstrated that memories for uncompleted tasks are especially strong. She gave her subjects a series of 20 simple tasks to perform, each task taking several minutes to complete. Half of the tasks, randomly chosen, were interrupted, with no opportunity for the subject to complete them. The subject was allowed to work undisturbed on the other half of the tasks. At the end of the series, the subject was asked to recall as many of the 20 tasks as possible. Zeigarnik found that people are able to recall the interrupted tasks much more easily than the ones they were allowed to complete.[48]

The neuropsychological significance of the Zeigarnik effect is that it shows the special nature of memories for intentions. Intentions make use of a special "quick-access" intention memory, some storage device in the brain which has special priority in consciousness.[49]

Inner Speech and Mental Organization

One way in which language influences human thought is as a code for the representation of plans, a type of inner speech. In this regard, language is a particularly effective code, because it embodies a great deal of knowledge about the world. Language can thus condense a plan to a manageable size. Consider the following internal monologue: "Tomorrow I have to go to the library . . . then meet Fred for lunch . . . then pick up the kids and take them to the doctor's." Concealed in these concise statements are a multitude of subplans which are waiting to unfold at the proper time: find wallet, find notebook, find keys, lock door, walk to car . . . . The act of naming an activity ("go to library") is extremely economical.

Of course, not all plans are verbal plans; if they were, how could a chimpanzee (or a young child) organize its behavior in such elegant ways? A chimp breaking off a blade of grass to use as a termiting rod shows a remarkable degree of foresight.[50]

In the last chapter we discussed how damage to the speech-generating area in the left frontal lobe produces the symptoms of Broca's aphasia—the inability to articulate speech, but with preserved ability to understand the speech of others. This aphasia was traditionally viewed as a difficulty in the translation of auditory speech images into speech-producing motor programs, though, it was noted, the situation is certainly more complicated than that. One of the complications is the link between frontal speech areas and the generation of inner speech. There is some reason to believe that the frontal speech area is also intimately connected with the organization of behavior and the planning functions of the frontal lobes.[51]

The use of inner speech plans in children was studied by the Russian psychologist L. S. Vygotsky, in his classic work on cognitive development.[52] Vygotsky found that an important stage comes about when individual actions of the child can be directed by verbal instructions from others. At a later stage, the child substitutes his own verbalizations for those of others. Finally, these verbalizations are suppressed, as the child apparently develops the ability of inner speech.

Young children often talk continuously to themselves while playing alone, but only later do they internalize this type of thinking. At about the time that children learn to internalize this speech (age 5 or so), they can be seen speaking instructions silently to themselves at critical moments during problem-solving.[53] Physiological studies show that even in adults, miniature movements of the lips, tongue, and vocal tract can be detected during the solving of difficult problems.[54] Inner speech apparently develops with the close participation of the motor end of the language system.

Alexander Luria extended Vygotsky's work in his study of the regulative functions of speech in children. He observed that a 15-month-old child will respond appropriately to "give me a teddy bear." However, if a brightly colored toy rooster has been placed next to the bear, he will suddenly change the plan and grab the rooster. The distraction of the attractive new toy overrides this intention. Similarly, if an 18-month-old child who started to put some rings on a stick is instructed to take the rings off, he may redouble his efforts at mounting the rings, not out of defiance, apparently, but out of an incomplete revision of the original plan of action.

At this stage, the child's behavior can be *initiated* by verbal instruction, but it cannot as easily be maintained or reprogrammed. Luria pointed to the parallel between these young children, whose frontal lobes are not yet fully functional, and the behaviors of frontal patients. There are several aspects to the problem:

1. There may be a simple disruption of verbal control by more powerful forces, such as the orienting reflex. Just like the child being distracted by the colorful toy rooster, frontal patients are easily sidetracked.

2. There may be a failure for the verbal instruction to establish control or to break through an ongoing plan. This was seen in the earlier examples of *perseveration* of motor stereotypes in frontal patients. The plan is apparently incapable of arresting the ongoing stereotype in order for the main sequence to continue. This is analogous to the child's perseveration in putting the rings on the stick.

3. There may be a failure to check the outcomes of action with the plan. Luria relates the case of an unfortunate woman with a frontal injury who failed to notice that she was boiling a mop instead of the spaghetti.[55]

This failure to monitor the outcome of actions can give rise to a dissociation between the verbal plan and the behavior, even when the patient can remember the former. Here is an excerpt from Luria's examination of a 43-year-old woman who had a tumor of the left frontal lobe:

Examiner: Shake hands 3 times.
Patient: (Shakes hands many times.)
Examiner: What are you supposed to do?
Patient: Shake hands 3 times.
Examiner: Do it.
Patient: (Shakes hands many times in a row.)[56]

The language capabilities of the human brain provide an efficient means of controlling and organizing thought and behavior. The impairment of this ability can be devastating to mental organization.

Acting for the Future

With impaired ability to form plans, Phineas Gage appeared to others to be an aimless wanderer. Unable to maintain his intentions, he appeared capricious. Without stable programs to furnish a context to his actions, Gage became childlike.

It is interesting to note in this regard that the frontal cortex matures rather late in child development, not becoming fully functional until the fifth or sixth year. As Luria suggested, some of the behavioral characteristics of childhood can be understood in terms of undeveloped frontal planning functions: such things as spontaneity, distractibility, and lack of discipline.

Why did frontal lobotomy work in many cases to alleviate the obsessions, anxieties, and depressions of psychiatric patients? Could it be that Moniz was right—that the great civilizing influence of the frontal lobes carries with it certain dangers of overcontrol? New evidence for Moniz's view comes from some interesting variations in the CNV which have been found in groups of psychiatric patients. Patients with chronic anxiety tend to have very low CNV's in the standard testing situation, possibly because their normal CNV baseline level is so high that there is little room for increase—a kind of "ceiling effect." However, since the CNV has been shown to decrease in normal subjects if they are distracted during the expectancy task, another possiblity is that the anxious patients are distracted and cannot maintain a high state of expectancy. It is difficult at present to decide between these two opposite interpretations. Obsessive and compulsive psychiatric patients, on the other hand, show exaggerated CNV's, persisting beyond the point of the second signal (which normally terminates the CNV; part (d) of Figure 5–8). The enhanced CNV in these patients may represent a physiological basis for these mental disorders.[57]

Are the mechanisms which enable us to postpone attending to the here-and-now also capable of destroying a more idyllic state of mind? This idea, in various non-neurological forms, enjoys a long history. For example, it is embedded in the Judaic creation story, where Adam and Eve were forced to leave Eden after tasting of the fruit of knowledge—human knowledge, laced with foresight.

Through planning, the immediate demands of the present can be held in abeyance while you coordinate and sequence your thoughts and actions on behalf of things yet to come. One of the evolutionary achievements of the human brain is an extraordinary capability for anticipating the future, for acting and for formulating plans of action in order to meet the future advantageously.

But, as in the story of Eden, we may pay a price for the mental machinery which permits us to build chairs and cities and rockets—and to engage in all the other complicated sequences of behavior in which present acts are performed on behalf of the future.

Recommended Readings

MEMORY AND ITS BIOLOGICAL BASIS

KLATZKY, R. L. *Human Memory.* San Francisco: W. H. Freeman, 1975.

BARBIZET, J. *Human Memory and Its Pathology.* San Francisco: W. H. Freeman, 1970.

PRIBRAM, K. H., and D. E. BROADBENT (eds.). *Biology of Memory.* New York: Academic Press, 1970.

FRONTAL LOBES, EXPECTANCY, AND PLANNING

LURIA, A. R. *Higher Cortical Functions in Man.* New York: Basic Books, 1966.

WARREN, J. M., and K. AKERT (eds.). *The Frontal Granular Cortex and Behavior.* New York: McGraw-Hill, 1964.

MILLER, G. A., E. GALANTER, and K. H. PRIBRAM. *Plans and the Structure of Behavior.* New York: Henry Holt and Co., 1960.

Consciousness and Brain Processes

This book started out as a discussion on the relationship of mental experience to the physical brain. This ancient philosophical question, which Schopenhauer called the "world-knot,"[1] was exhumed and found to be not entirely dead. The survey of contemporary neuropsychological knowledge on this issue,

6

which forms the substance of the book, has shown complex relationships of many different parts of the brain to conscious perception, thought, and action. It is now time to sum up what importance these research findings have for understanding the mind–body question.

The Localization of Conscious Functions in the Brain

Some approaches to the physical basis of conscious awareness rest on trying to find specific brain structures which support various aspects of conscious experience. Thus, the cerebral cortex has most often been regarded as the substrate of human consciousness,[2] because it underlies evolutionarily newer or "higher" cognitive capabilities. Descartes had no trouble locating the interaction point of soul in the body. He reasoned that the place must be the pineal body, a small cone-shaped structure at the back of the brainstem, because it was the only structure known to him which was not bifurcated into a right and left half. Since the soul was a unity, according to traditional philosophy and common sense, its locus of interaction with the body must lie in the pineal (see Figure 1–1, page 8).

In slightly more modern terms, we might ask if it is possible to localize the physical correlate of conscious experience. Conceptually, this does not present any greater problems than the localization of conscious functions to the brain as a whole (i.e., the modern view that conscious functioning is somehow subserved by structures of the brain, and not of the heart or the big toe). The question is whether a finer localization is possible, and this is a question of how the brain works. Does it work in a spatially discrete manner, where particular memory representations or particular cognitive processes are accomplished by the activities of local networks of nerve cells? Or does it operate more broadly, or "wholistically," through electrical field forces which emerge from the interactions of millions or billions of neurons?

Brain theorists continue to be in controversy on this point.[3] The nineteenth-century discoveries of the existence of diferent expressive and receptive centers for language formed the most impressive evidence for localization. These findings almost immediately came under attack from other neurologists who claimed that the conclusions were overenthusiastic. Pierre Marie, a French neurologist, reexamined the brains on which Broca had based his conclusions and asserted that the lesions which produced loss of speech were more extensive than Broca had claimed.[4] The controversy continues today in disclaimers about the lack of separability of frontal and posterior speech areas.[5]

In this century, the anti-localizationist or "wholistic" view came to be associated with several prominent names in neurology and psychology, most notably the Gestalt school.[6]

The concept of "mass action," a term describing wholistic brain functioning, is due to Lashley, the investigator who concluded, from his classical experiments on removals of cortex in rats, that memories were stored "equipotentially" in brain areas (see Chapter 2). The memory performance of which Lashley's rats were eventually capable depended upon the total amount (not on which part) of cortex remaining in the relevant region of the brain, and this, Lashley argued, demonstrated "mass action" of large brain regions in cognitive functioning.

The modern consensus is somewhere in between the two extremes of localization versus wholism.[7] Brain damage in man shows local consistencies, but it is also widely recognized that many different deficits can follow damage to the same regions in different patients. Part of the dispute lies in the uncertainties of neurological data, coming in many cases from patients in whom the total extent of brain damage is inaccurately known. Also, since the brain is a highly interconnected organ, it is difficult to evaluate the effects of damage in one area to the normal functioning of other areas.

This problem was elaborated by the British psychologist Richard Gregory, in a paper highly critical of localization research. Gregory argued that it is impossible to evaluate the effects of a specific lesion without a theory of how the parts of the brain function together. Take the case of an unknown machine which we try to understand by selectively removing parts, one at a time. When we remove a certain part—say, the gas tank—and the machine stops, then we might naively conclude, if we had never seen anything like an automobile before, that the machine's mechanism for producing motive power was the gas tank. Gregory pointed out that this difficulty is not encountered if we already know something about the complex mechanisms involved in internal-combustion engines. In the case of the brain, this state of knowledge, which presumes the existence of a well-developed and specific theory, has not yet been achieved, so the interpretation of brain-lesion data is difficult.[8]

Despite widespread skepticism about being able to localize complex psychological functions (such as naming or speaking), the fact is that localization is the most common explanatory principle used in neuropsychology today. Localization is the principle supporting the division of receptive aphasias from expressive disorders. Anatomical localization of function is also the principle behind the division of the mind into "analytic" and "synthetic" domains, corresponding to left- and right-hemisphere functioning.

This state of theorizing, everyone agrees, is a very primitive form of science, because functional connections almost certainly cut across anatomical units. The brain is a highly interconnected organ. What is needed is to understand which neurons work together, when, and under what conditions, and how they function to accomplish higher cognitive achievements, like seeing a face or writing a letter. In the meantime, localization serves as a rough explanation of sorts. If you don't know exactly *what* something is, it is at least helpful to know *where* it is.

For one thing, localization can lead to further discoveries. The localization of visual function to the occipital cortex, an achievement of nineteenth-century neurology, led to the discovery in this century of the functions of feature-detecting neurons in that region (see Chapter 2). Localization is also useful insofar as it may furnish a *structural description* of the pieces of a chunk of cognitive machinery. The localization of expressive and receptive language areas forms the basis for most current theories of how language processes are organized in the brain. Given the ongoing dispute about the localizability of cognitive functions in the brain, it should not be surprising that on the more specific issue of the localization of conscious functions there are conflicting views. On one side of this question are those who say that the cerebral cortex, or just the left hemisphere, or the reticular activating system is the seat of conscious experience. In the other camp are wholists, who stress that consciousness comes about, somehow, as the integral product of activity all over the brain—that there are many different neural substrates to conscious experience, some specifically human, others shared with other animals, and that a conscious experience could arise from activity related to any brain center.

An interesting compromise speculation is that only certain *forms* of neuronal activity result in consciousness, whereas others don't. This is the view of Karl Pribram, who feels that the physical substrate of awareness is not to be found in the well-known neural impulses (spike potentials), but rather in a less-well-understood class of electrical events, the slow, graded post-synaptic potentials (see Chapter 1).[9] Unlike spike impulses, which are rapid and are propagated over long distances from one neuron to another, there are slower electrical changes which occur locally in the branches of a neuron's dendritic tree. In some brain areas, particularly in certain layers of the cerebral cortex, the dendritic trees of neurons are dense and closely intermingled. In these jungles of neural fibers (the "dendritic feltwork" is how it has been described), electrical changes occur very slowly, compared with those of the propagated axonal spikes; they wax and wane in a continuous graded manner, as opposed to the all-or-none discharge of the spikes. The time scale of the dendritic slow potentials may be closer to the flow of conscious experience. Also, the complex interactions of local dendritic slow waves might form the basis for something like a neural hologram (see Chapter 2), a distributed, information-rich, and damage-resistant process which, according to Pribram, is just the sort of thing which may ultimately be found to be linked with consciousness. Although very little is known about the workings of slow, graded dendritic potentials, there are others besides Pribram who believe that these neural events will be found to be of importance in understanding the workings of the brain.

Another theory of consciousness which cuts across anatomical divisions is the *efference theory*.[10] This theory states that conscious experience is correlated with discharges of neurons in the motor or output systems of the brain (from *efferent,* referring to neural activity flowing out from the brain to the periphery, as opposed to *afferent,* sensory or inward-flowing neural activity). There is some limited evidence for this view, most of it demonstrating that efferent nerve impulses are important (if unconscious) influences on the construction of conscious experience.[11]

One attractive aspect of the efference notion is the consideration from automata theory (the theory that deals with the building of robots) that intelligent mobile machines need to have some executive process which runs the motor system, in order to coordinate groups of mutually exclusive impulses so that the machine doesn't go left with one leg and right with another. This is what Michael Arbib, a cybernetic theorist, calls "resolving the redundancy of potential command."[12] Arbib's example is the frog, shown in Figure 6–1. This frog sees two flies at once in equally salient portions of its visual space. There is a conflict, because there are two places to snatch at. A balancing of the two tendencies would be maladaptive, because the frog would then snatch at the "average fly," which is to say no fly. Frogs, unfortunately, are said to do this sometimes, but no matter: what is needed for more complex organisms, according to Arbib, is a supervisory system which chooses a single course of action for the whole motor system. This system would, perhaps, be one explanation for the evolution of consciousness as a unified executive process.

FIGURE 6-1.   A frog snapping at an "average" fly. (After M. Arbib, The Metaphorical Brain, New York: John Wiley and Sons, 1972. Reprinted with permission of the publisher.)

Among the neuroscientists who believe that consciousness can be roughly localized in the brain, the main point of dispute concerns cortical versus subcortical contributions. It is to this issue which we turn next.

Is the Cortex the Seat of Consciousness?

The evidence reviewed in Chapters 4 and 5, that the cerebral cortex is the distinguishing feature of the evolution of the brains of higher mammals, has led to the common assumption that the cortex must, therefore, be the seat of consciousness. The great proliferation of "uncommitted" cortex in man, which contains regions mediating language and other forms of human intelligence, underlines the association neuroscientists often make between *human* consciousness and cortical functioning.

This view may be unduly anthropocentric, a holdover from earlier days when, for reasons related to the prevailing theology, consciousness was allied with Reason and was thought to distinguish man from animals. Today, however, most people have no difficulty seeing conscious designs in the behaviors of their pet dogs and cats. To adopt a simpler meaning of "consciousness" as some form of subjective *awareness* (rather than the loftier idea of "awareness of self"), we must be prepared to accept the possibility that there are more primitive forms, or at least differently evolved forms.

In Chapter 3 we discussed the finding that waking consciousness, as opposed to sleep or coma, is intimately tied to the workings of structures in the brainstem. There it was noted that the separate contributions to consciousness of brainstem and cortical systems were difficult to disentangle, since they worked together: the RAS served to activate the cortex, which would otherwise be somnolent.

It seems curious, therefore, that scientists have taken sides on the issue of a cortical versus a subcortical substrate of consciousness. One modern version of the cortical theory is the *language-accessibility* view, discussed in Chapter 4. This type of theory states that human consciousness is largely associated with language processes localized, for the most part, in the left cortical hemisphere of the brain.

A recent champion of the other view—the view that consciousness is a property of the brainstem system—was the Mexican neurophysiologist Raúl Hernández-Peón.[13] He was impressed by the facts of RAS "gating" of sensory impulses, and found that sensory impulses from a cat's ear are suppressed at the level of the brainstem when the cat looks at a mouse. This would give the brainstem RAS the role of a general regulator of attention. "Attention" and "consciousness" are two closely related concepts. William James put it this way: "My experience is what I agree to attend to."[14]

Another advocate of the consciousness/brainstem view was Wilder Penfield, the late Montreal neurosurgeon who carefully charted the conscious reports of awake surgical patients while he electrically stimulated the surfaces of their exposed cortex. (During brain surgery, it is sometimes essential to have the patient awake during the procedure so that landmarks on the cortical surface can be established—for example, by finding the spot which yields a tingling sensation in the right thumb. Since the brain itself is insensitive to pain, the surgery can be accomplished under local anesthesia.) Penfield documented the thousands of brain sites stimulated in his many patients.[15] Cortical stimulation of sensory areas resulted in hearing something, seeing something, feeling something, etc., depending on the particular cortical area stimulated. The sensations which resulted were mostly very primitive and chaotic, not well-integrated percepts like visions of tables and chairs, but rather flashes, stars, tiny dots of light, and the like. Stimulation of motor cortex produced bodily movement. The rest of the cortex, the "uncommitted" parts, were usually silent to electrical stimulation. This fact—that stimulating most of the newer cortex produced few conscious effects—was one reason why Penfield came to believe that the cortex is not the seat of consciousness.[16]

Penfield speculated that the neural substratum of consciousness might lie in the upper brainstem, which includes the higher regions of the RAS. In Penfield's view, the cortex evolved as an "elaboration" device, something which provided added computational abilities but which was not essential to conscious functioning—just as an added bedroom will make a house more useful without really being essential for keeping its inhabitants sheltered. Penfield's work is most widely known for his finding that memories can be activated by an electrode placed on the surface of the cortex. He found that some cortical points, particularly in the right temporal lobe of epileptic patients, can play back an experience in great detail, as if it were tape-recorded. In one of these flashbacks, whenever a particular point was stimulated, a patient heard an orchestral symphony from a concert she had attended years earlier. Another patient was taken back to the kitchen of her childhood home and witnessed everyday happenings whith a vividness that made her feel she was actually there.

Originally, Penfield believed that these memory flashbacks were being recreated by neural activity at the point of electrical stimulation, on the temporal cortex. However, he ultimately concluded that the neural counterparts to these memories must lie elsewhere, because most cortical areas were found to react to direct stimulation by becoming functionally incapacitated. Thus, stimulation of Broca's area causes temporary aphasia. (This effect might happen because the stimulating electrode is not subtle enough to mimic the normal activity of the brain tissue, and so swamps the cortical area.) Penfield concluded that his patients' memory flashbacks were being produced by electrical activity elsewhere in the brain, triggered by the gross electrical stimulus applied to the cortex. His guess was that the locus of these memories was in the upper brainstem.

Penfield didn't dispute the importance of the cortical systems in human *thought processes* (most of which are probably unconscious operations) but he regarded the brainstem as all-important for conscious awareness. His reasons for this view were basically those of Hernández-Peón: that even massive removals of cortex do not seem to completely abolish awareness, while tiny lesions in the brainstem produce irreversible coma. Both Penfield and Hernández-Peón pointed to the evidence from "anencephalic monsters"—humans born without any cerebral cortex. These unfortunate beings are not capable of much learning and so do not develop any significant understanding of their environments. Yet, they do alternate cycles of sleep and wakefulness, and when awake they can cry and smile. So they appear to have some form of primitive awareness. Similarly, a normal newborn baby, whose cortex is not yet functional, shows brief periods of wakefulness throughout the day.

Despite the strong stands taken by some scientists on a cortical versus a subcortical locus for consciousness, it seems premature to decide this issue. Although lesions to the brainstem can dramatically abolish waking consciousness, it is also true that cortical destruction profoundly alters experience.

Human consciousness appears to be the product of complex interactions between old and new parts of the brain. It seems reasonable, therefore, to regard conscious awareness as an evolving natural phenomenon, shared in parts by many different species, but with unique qualities at different stages of evolution.

The Evolution of Consciousness

The question of awareness in animals has intrigued humans for some time. Descartes viewed animals as purely mechanical devices, because they were without souls. During this century, scientists have for the most part accepted the behaviorist position that intelligent behavior can be understood in purely physical (behavioral) terms.[17] A precursor to this point of view was that of the nineteenth-century biologist Lloyd Morgan, who wrote: "In no case may we interpret an action as the outcome of the exercise of a higher psychical faculty, if it can be interpreted as the outcome of the exercise of one which stands lower on the psychological scale."[18] Morgan was merely applying a well-known scientific principle, the principle of parsimony in scientific explanation: never accept a complicated explanation as true if a simpler one will suffice.

Recent findings on animal behavior, however, have reopened the issue. Donald Griffin, a biologist at Rockefeller University, argues that there is no reason to deny at least some conscious awareness to animals who communicate complicated messages to one another (as honeybees have been found to do) or who seem to possess complicated maps of their environments (as do bats), or who seem to act intentionally. Griffin believes that the evolutionary continuity of consciousness is more likely than its having arisen suddenly with our own species.[19]

The neurologist Jason Brown has recently proposed a theory of consciousness based on brain evolution.[20] The theory relies on the notion of *structural levels* of cognition in the brain, originally described by another brain theorist, Paul MacLean. The notion is illustrated in Figure 6–2. In this figure are depicted three main evolutionary stages in the development of the mammalian brain. The brainstem system was achieved at the level of reptiles (living reptiles have only rudimentary forebrains, and their sensory and motor functions are regulated by centers in the higher brainstem, including the thalamus—see

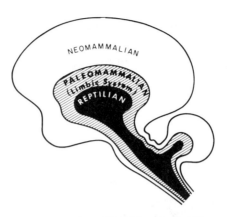

FIGURE 6–2. MacLean's conception of the "triune brain." Three evolutionary stages in the development of the mammalian brain are schematized. The reptilian brain includes the upper brainstem and thalamus. The limbic system developed out of the brainstem in primitive mammals, and the cortex (neocortex) of the forebrain developed out of the limbic system in higher mammals. (From P. D. MacLean, <u>Journal of Nervous and Mental Disease,</u> 1967, 144, pp. 374–382. Reproduced with permission of Williams & Wilkins Co., Baltimore.)

Figure 5–2). These animals are governed largely by instincts—genetically pre-programmed perceptual-motor sequences, such as emotional displays, territorial defense behaviors, nest-building, and so on. Reptilian consciousness, according to Brown, is at the sensory-motor level, centered on the body itself and not differentiated from external space. This is a preliminary form of consciousness.

The earliest mammals, most of them now extinct, evolved the primitive forebrain, which contained the capability to represent and remember experiences, and so to go beyond purely instinctive behaviors. The expanded forebrain of early mammals consisted of the newly evolved *limbic system,* discussed in Chapter 5 in relation to memory. The limbic system in humans includes the hippocampus and other subcortical structures in a highly interconnected system, receiving inputs from bodily control centers in the upper brainstem (see Figure 5-3). MacLean called this system the "visceral brain," because of its close connections to control centers for drive and emotion.[21]

For early mammals, the limbic system was the only fore-brain, and it was largely a primitive cortex. This primitive limbic cortex ("archicortex") is present in the human brain, but it was enveloped by the mushrooming newer cortex ("neocortex") of higher mammals. It also was stretched and folded inside the brain in the course of subsequent evolution to form the hippocampus, but some limbic cortex still survives in the human brain on the inside and underside surfaces of the cerebral hemispheres. These structures form a border ("limbus") between the newer cortex of higher mammals and the upper brainstem of reptiles.

Although it is linked strongly with emotional processes and with such drives as sex and aggression, the limbic brain also has cognitive functions. For one thing, sensory inputs from vision and hearing have recently been discovered leading into this region.[22] Also, as discussed in the previous chapter, there are strong links between the hippocampus and cognitive memory.

Brown believes that the cognitive achievement of the limbic brain is the production of *images,* images which form the basis both of perception and of hallucination. Brown makes this connection because it is sometimes found that hallucinations in man are associated with disorders of the limbic system. For example, stimulation of the hippocampus during surgery can produce fully formed visual hallucinations.[23] Also, recent theories of schizophrenic hallucinations involve imbalances of chemical transmitter substances in the limbic system.[24] Structures in the limbic system are believed to be the sites of action of many psychotropic drugs, including anti-psychotic tranquilizers (e.g., Thorazine) and hallucinogens (e.g., LSD).

According to Brown, it is at the level of the limbic brain that external objects become mentally distinguished from the organism's own body. This ability to distinguish internal from external space is helped by the limbic achievement of perceptual imagery. Images enable the leap from the mind of a lizard to the mind of an anteater. Limbic consciousness is the consciousness of the dream.

The next level in brain evolution, the *neocortical brain,* was achieved with higher mammals (horses, dogs) whose forebrains expanded backward and enveloped the limbic structures within the mantle of the cerebral neocortex. The level of cognition achieved with these higher mammals, according to Brown, was a level of *object recognition*—the conception of permanent objects in a well-articulated external space. It is at the point of "object consciousness" that awareness takes a familiar form. This is a consciousness of "external reality."

The advantage of this kind of awareness is that it provides an efficient coding system. According to Harry Jerison, a U.C.L.A. researcher on brain evolution, an animal's consciousness of enduring external objects is a kind of mental shorthand for all the different, but simultaneous, pieces of sensory data about these objects. The concept of an "apple" is a handy way for a brain to represent the combination of smells, tastes, and sights which usually occur together in time whenever we come across one of these things.[25]

The next structural level of consciousness, in Brown's theory, is found only in humans. This is the level of the *asymmetrical brain,* by which is meant the language and visuo-spatial centers which evolved asymmetrically in the neocortex of the left and right hemispheres (see Chapter 4). These asymmetric brain regions give rise to "symbolic consciousness," an awareness which involves the manipulation of symbols, or things which stand for other things. At the level of the asymmetrical brain, consciousness of external objects, achieved at the neocortical brain, is abstracted into symbols. The functional advantage of this evolutionary achievement is the capability for manipulating these symbols, and thus to think abstractly. The stages of Brown's theory are summarized in Table 6–1.

By the Brown/MacLean theory, these levels, which coexist in the human brain, do not operate independently. Rather they are systems which develop out of one another, "serving to transform cognition to successively more differentiated states."[26]

Table 6–1.
The Brown/MacLean Theory of Structural Levels of Cognition

LEVEL	STAGE OF EVOLUTION AT WHICH LEVEL WAS ACHIEVED	FUNCTION
Brainstem	Reptiles	Sensory-motor: a preliminary form of consciousness, bound up with instinctive acts
Limbic	Lower mammals	Imagistic: Images enable the first stage in differentiating objects from self
Neocortical	Higher mammals	Representational: objects conceived as enduring entities in an articulated extrapersonal space
Asymmetrical/ Neocortical	Humans	Symbolic: manipulation of language and other symbols, forming the basis for abstract thought

Awareness or consciousness, rather than being a property of only one part of the brain, has different manifestations at each different level. What results is that consciousness becomes a function of the highest form of brain organization of which the organism is momentarily capable.

The appeal of the Brown/MacLean idea comes from its apparent ability to explain many kinds of brain damage syndromes and other forms of psychopathology. For example, the amnesias and memory dissociations discussed in Chapter 5 can be seen as instances of regression to lower, or evolutionarily older levels of cognitive organization, as the result of blockage or destruction of higher levels. The patient H. M.'s ability to remember a motor skill, while not consciously remembering the learning experience, would be a reflection of the fact that lower levels of brain functioning (which mediated the motor skill) are not accessible to the consciousness of the higher cortex. This would be true for H. M., even though the higher symbolic capabilities, which would permit the recollection of the events in question, were partially impaired.

The phenomena of the Freudian "unconscious mind" are also seen by Brown as manifestations of different evolutionary levels of brain organization. The unconscious, by this view, is a relative term. What is conscious at the limbic level may be unavailable at the cortical level.

The details of this theory are sketchy, and it's not clear, for example, how it can predict very precisely what kinds of effects on consciousness will follow a blow on the head or the removal of a certain brain area. What happens to limbic, hallucinatory consciousness in the normal brain? To what extent does it underlie the conscious thoughts of wakefulness? Despite these objections, the theory is appealing because it is one of the few attempts by brain scientists to incorporate the facts of brain evolution into a discussion of conscious awareness.

The Emergence of Consciousness

The question of exactly how consciousness relates to the physical brain is not clearly a neurological question. Philosophers have traditionally regarded this issue as a philosophical one, one in which empirical evidence (scientific findings about how the brain works) will reveal no solutions to the "world knot." Nonetheless, many neuroscientists, especially later in their careers, tend to venture into theories and speculations of the mind–brain relationship. Occasionally, it is not clear whether a particular theory of this type is to be taken as a philosophical or a scientific statement. Such is the recent theory of Roger Sperry, the discoverer of split-brain phenomena.[27] Sperry's theory states that consciousness derives from the functional properties of higher-level brain processes (yet to be discovered) which "emerge" from the neural activity of lower-order brain events, and which then control or exert a causative influence on the lower-order processes of which they are composed.

The idea of emergence in evolution is not a new one.[28] Basically, the idea is that the evolution of more and more complex forms of matter produces more and more complex "levels" of operation. At each stage (the atomic level, the molecular level, the cellular level, etc.) new qualities emerge which are not predictable on the basis of scientific laws applying to the lower-level constituents. The example usually given is the emergence of chemical and physical properties of molecules from the combination of constituent atoms: just as the properties of water emerge from the joining of atoms of hydrogen and oxygen, so by Sperry's theory does conscious experience arise out of the complex interplay of highly organized brain processes. Just as the properties of water are not easily predictable from the properties of hydrogen and oxygen, the properties of experienced consciousness are not predictable by the physical brain events from which they arose. They are " 'different from and more than' the collected sum of the neuro-physico-chemical events out of which they are built."[29] They interact at their own level as dynamic entities, and they obey their own laws, presumably psychological laws.

This much of the theory appears to be philosophy. It is a statement similar in kind and alternative to the ones, discussed in Chapter 1, which assert that the mental and the physical are in such and such a relation to one another—two separate and parallel realms of existence (Leibniz), or confusions of language (Ryle), or two ways of talking about the same things (identity theory). The scientific import of Sperry's theory is in his description of a superordinate brain process "different from but more than" some constituent lower-order processes.

The way in which Sperry describes the influence of this higher "conscious" brain process is as an envelope.

The subjective mental phenomena are conceived to influence and to govern the flow of nerve impulse traffic by virtue of their encompassing emergent properties. Individual nerve impulses and other excitatory components of cerebral activity pattern are simply carried along or shunted this way and that by the prevailing overall dynamics of the whole active process (in prin-

ciple—just as drops of water are carried along by a local eddy in
a stream or the way a molecules and atoms of a wheel are carried
along when it rolls down hill, regardless of whether the individual
molecules and atoms happen to like it or not).[30]

The notion of a superordinate brain process, correlated with
the events of conscious awareness, is a scientific hypothesis.
Although the knowledge and tools aren't currently available to
detect such a process, if it exists, one can imagine a group of
scientists someday being able to do so. Could these scientists of
the future chart the evolution of the superordinate brain process
in other animals? Would the physical correlate of human consciousness be found in frogs? In worms? What kinds of physical
properties would be found associated with the living tissue
which supports this "conscious" brain process?

Some writers have suggested that it is organized *complexity*
which gives rise to conscious processes. The neurophysiologist
John Eccles pointed out that the human central nervous system
is of a much higher level of complexity than any other organized
system in the known universe! "Evidently the unimaginable
organized complexity of the cerebrum has caused the emergence of properties which are of a different kind from anything
that has been as yet related to matter with its properties as
defined in physics and chemistry."[31]

Sperry disavows complexity *per se* as being the matrix of
consciousness. However, there are reasons to believe otherwise.
In Chapter 3 it was shown that the times when a living human's
consciousness is temporarily absent are times when the activity
of higher brain centers are uncomplex in informational terms:
deep sleep and coma. In these cases, the neurons of the cerebral
cortex idle in patterns of slow synchrony. This is opposed to the
active state shown when these areas are excited and more
differentiated.

The second link between complexity and consciousness
comes from the psychological and physiological facts of habituation and automatizing, also discussed in Chapter 3. It was

argued there that long-range changes in attention to objects in one's environment (changes in perceptual consciousness) were related to the complexity of operation of the brain analyzers involved. When you don't hear the constant ticking of the clock, it appears that this is so because the brain mechanisms which process this information operate in a stereotyped manner.

Another piece of evidence suggesting complexity as a determinant of consciousness comes from the results of electrical brain stimulation. When a surgeon touches an electrical probe to the surface of the brain on the area where the body's skin senses are represented, there will result a consciously perceived tingling in some area on the skin—in the right forearm or left toe or lower back, depending on the specific brain site stimulated. However, the conscious feeling does not immediately follow the electrical brain stimulation. There is a brief period, a delay of only a half-second or so, before the awake patient can indicate a tingling sensation. This time is much longer than simple reaction times for stimuli applied directly to the skin surface, so there appears to be an "incubation period," a time during which the cortical excitation generated by the electrode is propagated to cells which somehow produce the conscious experience.[32]

One possible interpretation of this finding is that the neurons underlying the conscious perception lie elsewhere than in the cortex. However, another likely interpretation of the "incubation period" is that the initial excitation, generated in perhaps a few thousand local cortical cells, must be propagated and articulated, by relays of neurons, to many millions of cells before any conscious effect occurs. The spatio-temporal patterning of the activities of these millions of cells must be extremely intricate. (The celebrated English biologist Sir Charles Sherrington described the brain's intricacy of operation as an "enchanted loom."[33]) The incubation period for cortical stimulation of conscious experience may reflect the association between consciousness and neurophysiological complexity.

If organized complexity is all that matters, then it might be possible, as was suggested by the philosopher and theologian

Teilhard deChardin, that a global consciousness could emerge as a property of groups of brains (groups of people) who communicated closely enough.[34] Sperry doubts this possibility, because he doesn't think it likely that individual human brains could interact closely enough, in terms of physical proximity, to satisfy the physical conditions necessary to form a super-super-ordinate conscious process.[35] Still, the speculation is titillating.

There is a science fiction story in which a computer develops a willful consciousness when it exceeds a certain level of complexity and interconnectedness. The computer, which integrates information from subordinate computers, forming a nationwide network, has control over telecommunications, transportation, financial, and electronic library systems. In the story, this machine system finally exceeds some threshold of complexity and decides to take over![36]

By a law of physics, the universe is like a watch, winding down from its present state, in which there are islands of organization in the cosmos (atoms, planets, galaxies), to a state where energy is scattered uniformly throughout space. The evolution of life forms represents a high degree of complexity in these temporary organizations of energy. The most complexly organized entity known to man—the most complex of all these doomed reversals of the cosmic trend—is the human brain. The key to a scientific understanding of the mind–brain relationship may lie in science's ability to comprehend such complexity.

Recommended Reading

GLOBUS, G. G., and G. MAXWELL (eds.). *Consciousness and the Brain.* New York: Plenum Press, 1976.

Notes

CHAPTER 1

1. Siodmak, C. *Donovan's Brain*. New York: Triangle Books, 1944.

2. Watson, J. B. *Behaviorism*. New York: W. W. Norton, 1924.

3. Hilgard, E. R. *Theories of Learning*. New York: Appleton-Century-Crofts, 1956.

4. Malmo, R. B. *On Emotions, Needs, and Our Archaic Brain*. New York: Holt, Rinehart, & Winston, 1975.

5. Raphael, B. *The Thinking Computer: Mind Inside Matter*. San Francisco: W. H. Freeman, 1976. Also, Feigenbaum, E. A., and J. Feldman (eds.). *Computers and Thought*. New York: McGraw-Hill, 1963.

6. Turing, A. M. "Computing Machinery and Intelligence." *Mind*, 1950, 59, 433–460.

7. Samuel, A. L. "Some Studies in Machine Learning Using the Game of Checkers." in Feigenbaum and Feldman, *Computers and Thought.*

8. Some numbers which are *much* smaller than 10^{120} are 10^{16}–the total number of words uttered by all men since the beginning of human speech; 10^{20}–the number of grains of sand on the beach at Coney Island; 10^{30} –the number of snow crystals necessary to form the ice age. (From Kasner, E., and J. R. Newman. *Mathematics and the Imagination. New York: Simon & Schuster, 1940.)*

9. Newell, A., and H. Simon. "GPS, a Program that Stimulates Human Thought." In Feigenbaum and Feldman, *Computers and Thought.*

10. Turing, "Computing Machinery and Intelligence."

11. Ryle, G. *The Concept of Mind.* New York: Barnes & Noble, 1949.

12. It is interesting to note in this regard that the demise of Behaviorism in psychology during the 1960's was accompanied by renewed interest in the age-old topic of mental imagery.

13. Malcolm, N. *Problems of Mind: Descartes to Wittgenstein.* New York: Harper & Row, 1971.

14. Wittgenstein, L. *Philosophical Investigations.* New York: Macmillan, 1953. Also, Malcolm, *Problems of Mind.*

15. Sarbin, T. R. "Ontology Recapitulates Philology: The Mythic Nature of Anxiety." *American Psychologist,* 1968, 23, 411–418.

16. Whorf, B. L. *Language, Thought, and Reality.* Cambridge, Mass.: M.I.T. Press, 1956. Also, Cole, M., and S. Scribner. *Culture and Thought.* New York: John Wiley & Sons, 1974.

17. Part of this dispute could derive from a type of blindness people seem the have about differences in cognitive styles. One assumes that everyone else's mind works the same as one's own. If you are a visualizer, you may assume that everyone thinks in terms of vivid images. If you are a writer who deals with abstract material, such as a philosopher, you might think that all other people have the same kind of constant internal dialogue which dominates

your own thought processes, and you might be tempted to conclude that others are merely naive or unobservant if they describe their thinking in other terms.

18. Place, U. T. "Is Consciousness a Brain Process?" In Chappell, V. C. (ed.), *The Philosophy of Mind.* Englewood Cliffs, N.J.: Prentice-Hall, 1962. Also, Ornstein, J. *The Mind and the Brain.* The Hague: Martinius Nijhoff, 1972.

19. Shaffer, J. A. "Recent Work on the Mind-Body Problem." *American Philosophical Quarterly,* 1965, 2, 97.

20. Monroe, Robert. *Journeys Out of the Body.* New York: Doubleday and Co., 1973.

21. James,W. *The Principles of Psychology.* New York: Henry Holt & Co., 1890.

CHAPTER 2

1. Cornsweet, T. N. *Visual Perception.* New York: Academic Press, 1970.

2. Julesz, B. *Foundations of Cyclopean Perception.* Chicago: University of Chicago Press, 1971.

3. Schneider, G. E. "Two Visual Systems." *Science,* 1969, 163, 895–902.

4. Köhler, W. *Gestalt Psychology.* New York: Liverwright, 1929. Also, Boring, E. G. *A History of Experimental Psychology,* 2nd ed. New York: Appleton-Century-Crofts, 1950.

5. Von Senden, M. *Space and Sight: The Perception of Space and Shape in Congenitally Blind Patients Before and After Operation.* London: Methuen, 1960. Also, Gregory, R. L. *Eye and Brain,* 2nd ed. New York: World University Library, 1973.

6. Neisser, U. *Cognitive Psychology.* New York: Appleton-Century-Crofts, 1967.

7. Bruner, J. S. "On Perceptual Readiness." *Psychological Review,* 1957, 64, 123–152.

8. Lettvin, J. Y., H. R. Maturana, W. S. McCulloch, and W. H. Pitts. "What the Frog's Eye Tells the Frog's Brain." *Proceedings of the Institute of Radio Engineers,* 1959, 47, 1940–1951.

9. The pioneering work of David Hubel and Torsten Wiesel at Harvard in the late 1950's and early 1960's demonstrated the nature of the early stages of information-processing in the visual cortex. Hubel and Wiesel studied the receptive fields of single cells in the primary visual cortex of cats and monkeys and also in the adjacent secondary, or prestriate, visual cortex. Their results have since been confirmed in man by surgeons probing with micro-electrodes the exposed cortex of patients undergoing brain surgery for clinical purposes. Hubel and Wiesel's research is described in Hubel, D. H. "The Visual Cortex of the Brain." *Scientific American,* November 1963.

10. This facetious example is due to Harris, C. S. "Orientation-Specific Colour Adaptation: A Consideration of 4 Possible Models." Paper presented at the meeting of the Canadian Psychological Association, St. Johns, Newfoundland, 1971.

11. Weisstein, N. "Beyond the Yellow-Volkswagen Detector and the Grandmother Cell: A General Strategy for the Exploration of Operations in Human Pattern Recognition." In Solso, R. C. (ed.), *Loyola Symposium on Cognitive Psychology.* Potomac, Md.: Erlbaum, 1974.

12. Selfridge, O. G., and U. Neisser. "Pattern Recognition by Machine." *Scientific American,* August 1960.

13. Campbell, F. W., and J. G. Robson. "Application of Fourier Analysis to the Visibility of Gratings." *Journal of Physiology* (London), 1968, 197, 551–566. Also, Pollen, D. A., J. R. Lee, and J. H. Taylor. "How Does the Striate Cortex Begin the Reconstruction of the Visual World?" *Science,* 1971, 173, 74–77.

14. Harmon, L. D., and B. Julesz. "Masking in Visual Recognition: Effects of Two-Dimensional Filtered Noise." *Science,* 1973, 180, 1194–1197.

15. Lashley, K. S. "In Search of the Engram." In Symposium of the Society of Experimental Biology, No. 4: *Physiological Mechanisms in Animal Behavior.* New York: Cambridge University Press, 1950.

16. Lashley, K. S. "Patterns of Cerebral Integration Indicated by the Scotomas of Migraine." *Archives of Neurology and Psychiatry,* 1941, 46, 331–339.

17. Leith, E. N., and J. Upatnieks. "Photography by Laser." *Scientific American,* 1965, 212, 24–35.

18. Mager, H. J., O. Wess, and W. Waidelich. "Sequential Associative Information Storage and Reconstruction in a Holographic Circuit." *Optics Communications,* 1973, 9, 156–160.

19. Pribram, K. H. "Some Dimensions of Remembering." In Gaito, J. (ed.), *Macromolecules and Behavior.* New York: Appleton-Century-Crofts, 1966. Also, Westlake, P. R. "The Possibilities of Neural Holographic Processes within the Brain." *Kybernetik,* 1970, 7, 129–153. Also, Julesz, B. and K. S. Pennington. "Equidistributed Information Mapping: An Analogy to Holograms and Memory." *Journal of the Optical Society of America,* 1965, 55, 604.

20. Pribram, K. H. *Languages of the Brain.* Englewood Cliffs, N.J.: Prentice-Hall, 1971.

21. Julesz, *Foundations of Cyclopean Perception.*

22. Luria, A. R. *The Working Brain.* New York: Basic Books, 1973.

23. This controversy is discussed in Gardner, H. *The Shattered Mind.* New York: Alfred A. Knopf, 1975. See also, Brown, J. *Aphasia, Apraxia, and Agnosia: Clinical and Theoretical Aspects.* Springfield, Ill.: Charles C Thomas, 1972.

24. Ekman, P. *Darwin and Facial Expression: A Century of Research in Review.* New York: Academic Press, 1973.

25. Fantz, R. L. "Visual Perception from Birth as Shown by Pattern Selectivity." *Annals of the New York Academy of Sciences,* 1965, 118, 793–814.

26. Yin, R. K. "Face Recognition by Brain-Injured Patients: A Dissociable Ability?" *Neuropsychologia,* 1970, 8, 395–402.

27. Boring, E. G. *Sensation and Perception in the History of Experimental Psychology.* New York: Appleton-Century-Crofts, 1942.

28. White, B. W., *et al.* "Seeing with the Skin." *Perception and Psychophysics,* 1970, 7, 23–27.

29. Alternative explanations for a successful vision-substitution are
     possible. One explanation would be that in learning to use the
     vision-substitution system, functional connections between so-
     mato-sensory cortex and visual centers on the occipital lobe
     become established. The ability to recognize letters traced on
     one's back would seem to evidence the proposition that some
     connections of this sort normally exist, since it seems unlikely that
     the somato-sensory system would reduplicate the feature extrac-
     tors or other complicated mechanisms which we know must
     underlie visual pattern recognition of letters. The crucial test
     might be to see whether vision-substitution works on people who
     are blind because of destruction of their visual cortex.

30. This situation is similar to Feigl's imaginary "autocerebroscope."
     Feigl, H. *The Mental and the Physical.* Minneapolis: University of
     Minnesota Press, 1967.

31. It was pointed out by the physicist Ernst Mach that Newton's
     theoretical concepts of "uniform speed" and "absolute time" were
     defined in terms of each other. Uniform speed describes the
     motion of an object which traverses equal distances in any equal
     time intervals. To measure time intervals, you must use a clock,
     which to Newton was a system in periodic motion, such as a
     pendulum. To get around the difficulties with clocks in the real
     world, which move nonuniformly due to such things as friction,
     Newton defined "absolute time." Absolute time was "time which
     flows equably"—meaning a clock in absolutely *uniform motion.* But
     here is the circularity, since uniform motion must be defined
     again in terms of equal distances in equal time intervals. See Pap,
     A. *An Introduction to the Philosophy of Science.* New York: The Free
     Press of Glencoe, 1962.

CHAPTER 3

1. Shagass, C. "Electrical Activity of the Brain." In Greenfield, N.
    S., and R. A. Sternbach (eds.), *Handbook of Psychophysiology.* New
    York: Holt, Rinehart & Winston, 1972.

2. Treatments of research on the reticular activating system can be
    found in Thompson, R. F. *Foundations of Physiological Psychology.*
    New York: Harper & Row, 1967; Brodal, A. *The Reticular For-*

mation of the Brainstem, Anatomical Aspects and Functional Correlations. London: Oliver & Boyd, 1957; Magoun, H. W. *The Waking Brain,* 2nd ed. Springfield, Ill.: Charles C Thomas, 1963.

3. French, J. D. "The Reticular Formation." *Scientific American,* May 1957.

4. Broadbent, D. E. *Perception and Communication.* New York: Pergamon Press, 1958. Also, Lindsay, P. H., and D. A. Norman. *Human Information Processing.* New York: Academic Press, 1972.

5. Adrian, E. D. "The Physiological Basis of Perception." In Delfresnaye, J. F. (ed.), *Brain Mechanisms and Consciousness.* Oxford: Blackwell, 1954.

6. Berlyne, D. F. *Conflict, Arousal and Curiosity.* New York: McGraw-Hill, 1960. Berlyne has shown that higher vertebrates are motivated to behave in ways which increase novelty. He believes that there are inborn needs or drives to seek and investigate.

7. This story was originally told by Karl Pribram ("The Neurophysiology of Remembering." *Scientific American,* January 1969), who called it the "Bowery El Phenomenon."

8. Unger, S. M. "Habituation of the Vasoconstrictive Orienting Reaction." *Journal of Experimental Psychology,* 1964, 67, 11–18.

9. Sharpless, S., and H. H. Jasper. "Habituation of the Arousal Reaction," *Brain,* 1956, 79, 655–680.

10. Sokolov, E. N. *Perception and the Conditioned Reflex.* New York: Macmillan, 1963.

11. *Ibid.* The exact relationship of the "neuronal model" to other cortical activities has not yet been determined.

The localized cortical arousal of the orienting reaction does not exhaust the brain mechanisms of attention, which are not necessarily a unitary process. Attention refers to the selectivity of perception, and selectivity occurs at many levels in the nervous system. For example, Raúl Hernández-Peón and his colleagues found attentional effects very close to peripheral sense organs. They investigated the nerve signals produced in the auditory pathway of cats by repetitive click sounds. These nerve signals were dramatically reduced when the cat was distracted by looking at a mouse, which the experimenters placed nearby in a glass jar. These attentional effects at peripheral levels in the nervous system seem to be governed by efferent (outflowing) fibers in the sensory pathways. Interestingly enough, the efferent influences appear to have their origin in the reticular formation. As with localized cortical arousal during orienting, the attentional "switch" involves the reticular formation. (Hernández-Peón, R. "Neurophysiologic Aspects of Attention." In Vinken, P. J., and G. W. Bruyn (eds.), *Handbook of Clinical Neurology, Vol. 3.* Amsterdam: North Holland, 1968.)

12. Furst, C. J. "Automatizing of Visual Attention." *Perception and Psychophysics,* 1971, 10, 65–69.

13. The theme of return to de-automatized, childlike perception also recurs in mystical treatments of rebirth.

"Except ye be converted, and become as little children, ye shall not enter into the kingdom of heaven."

Matthew, XVIII, 3

Aldous Huxley, writing of his first experiences with the psychedelic drug mescaline, revived the image of the "cleansing of the doors of perception." Huxley talked of the brain as a great "reducing valve," which functioned ordinarily to filter out the barrage of sensory informtion. Mystical experiences, including those induced by psychedelic drugs, were said to open the valve. This is implicit in the popular notion that these experiences "expand consciousness." (Huxley, A. *The Doors of Perception.* New York: Harper & Row, 1954.) An interesting treatment of these matters, from the standpoint of psychology, can be gotten in Ornstein, R. *The Psychology of Consciousness.* San Fransisco: W. H. Freeman, 1972.

14. This idea seems to have had its origins in an influential theory, by Donald Hebb, on the importance of eye-movement commands to the perception of shape. (Hebb, D. O. *The Organization of Behavior.* New York: John Wiley & Sons, 1949.) It was reported soon after the discovery of REM/dream relationships that a correlation existed between the eye-movement patterns of REM and the content of the dream (Dement, W. C. "An Essay on

Dreams: The Role of Physiology in Understanding Their Nature." In *New Directions in Psychology II.* New York: Holt, Rinehart & Winston, 1965.)

15. Dement, W. C. *Some Must Watch While Some Must Sleep.* San Francisco: W. H. Freeman, 1972.

16. Rechtschaffen, A. In McGuigan, F. J., and R. A. Schoonover, (eds.), *The Psychophysiology of Thinking.* New York: Academic Press, 1973.

17. Cells in the mid-brain, closely related to the reticular formation, have axons which project to motor neurons in the spinal cord (motor neurons are cells which stimulate a muscle to contract). During REM sleep, these mid-brain cells strongly inhibit the spinal motor neurons and keep them from responding to signals from the cortex.

18. Gardner, R., *et al.* "The Relationship of Small Limb Movements During REM Sleep to Dreamed Limb Action." *Psychosomatic Medicine,* 1975, 37, 147–159.

19. See Rechtschaffen (footnote 16) for a critical review of this research area.

20. Dement, W. C., and N. Kleitmann. "Cyclic Variations in the EEG During Sleep and Their Relation to Eye Movements, Body Motility, and Dreaming." *EEG & Clinical Neurophysiology,* 1957, 9, 637–690.

21. Foulkes, D. "Theories of Dream Formation and Recent Studies of Sleep Consciousness." *Psychological Bulletin,* 1964, 62, 236–247.

22. *Ibid.*

23. Dement, *Some Must Watch While Some Must Sleep.* The picture presented here is somewhat complicated by the fact that sometimes vivid REM-like dreams will be reported by subjects who had just been woken from a slow-wave sleep period. For this reason, Dement says that it is only the *phasic* components of the REM state (twitches, PGO spikes, REM's, etc.) which are the actual correlates of dream thought. These phasic components can occasionally spill over to periods of slow-wave sleep, as they

apparently do for some people when deprived of REM sleep. The REM period itself is not a time of continuous rapid eye-movement, but rather these and other phasic events come in bursts, superimposed on a tonic background of EEG arousal and EMG suppression.

24. Oswald, I. *Sleeping and Waking.* Amsterdam: Elsevier, 1962.

25. Guilleminault, C., M. Billiard, J. Montplaisir, and W. C. Dement. "Altered States of Consciousness in Disorders of Daytime Sleepiness." *Journal of Neurological Science,* 1975, 26, 377–393. Narcolepsy should not be confused with epilepsy; although both are episodic brain disturbances, they appear to differ, at least in brain locus, and probably in mechanism. Epileptic attacks usually involve higher brain areas, whereas narcolepsy is some kind of disruption of the normal functioning of sleep centers located in the brainstem.

26. The alternation of cycles of REM and slow-wave sleep is under the control of centers in the brainstem, intimately related to the RAS. One of these sleep centers is the system of related structures, the *Raphé nuclei,* which controls the stages of slow-wave sleep. A tiny electrical pulse stimulating this area will initiate slow-wave sleep in animals. Another group of cells, the *locus coeruleus,* controls REM sleep. Studies of these brain circuits have led physiologists to discard an earlier theory that sleep was brought on by a passive inactivation of the reticular formation. It is now known that the various types of sleep come about by active inhibition exerted on the reticular formation and other areas by the sleep centers. (See Morgane, P. J., and W. C. Stern. "Chemical Anatomy of Brain Circuits in Relation to Sleep and Wakefulness." In Weitzman, E. D. (ed.), *Advances in Sleep Research, v. 1.* New York: Spectrum Publications, 1974.)

27. Jouvet, M. "Monoaminergic Neurons and Sleep Regulation and Function." In Petre-Quadens, O., and J. D. Schlag, *Basic Sleep Mechanisms.* New York: Academic Press, 1974.

28. Blakemore, C. "Developmental Factors in the Formation of Feature Extracting Neurons." In Worden, F. G., and F. O. Schmitt (eds.), *The Neurosciences: Third Study Program.* Cambridge, Mass.: M.I.T. Press, 1974.

29. Bloch, V., and W. Fishbein. "Sleep and Psychological Functions: Memory." In Lairy and Salzarullo, *The Experimental Study of Human Sleep*. Amsterdam: Elsevier, 1975.

30. Kripke, D. F. "Ultradian Rhythms in Sleep and Wakefulness." in Weitzman, *Advances in Sleep Research, v. 1.*

31. Dement, W. C. "The Effect of Dream Deprivation." *Science*, 1960, 131, 1705–1707.

32. Cartwright, R. D., L. J. Monroe, and C. Palmer. "Individual Differences in Response to REM Deprivation." *Archives of General Psychiatry*, 1967, 16, 297–303.

33. Zarcone, V., G. Gulevitch, T. Pivik, and W. Dement. "Partial REM Phase Deprivation and Schizophrenia." *Archives of General Psychiatry*, 1968, 18, 194–202.

34. Johann Wolfgang von Goethe, the eighteenth-century German poet and scientist, said that the "madman is a waking dreamer." For an interesting modern experimental approach to this question, see Dement, W. C., *et al.* "Some Parallel Findings in Schizophrenic Patients and Serotonin-Depleted Cats." In Siva Sankar, D. V. (ed.), *Schizophrenia—Current Concepts and Research*. Hicksville, N.Y.: PJD Publications, 1969.

35. Cartwright, R. D. *Night Life*. Englewood Cliffs, N.J.: Prentice-Hall, 1977.

36. Oswald, *Sleeping and Waking*.

37. *Ibid*. Also, O'Hanlon, J. F., and J. Beatty. "Concurrence Between Electroencephalographic and Performance Changes During Simulated Radar Watch." In Mackie, R. R. (ed.), *Vigilance II: Relationships Among Theory, Physiological Correlates and Operational Performance*. New York: Plenum Press, 1977.

38. Jasper, H. H. "Unspecific Thalamocortical Relations." In Field, J., H. W. Magoun, and V. I. Hall, (eds.), *Handbook of Physiology: Neurophysiology, II*. Washington, D.C.: American Physiological Society, 1960.

39. Barber, T. X. *LSD, Marihuana, Yoga, and Hypnosis*. Chicago: Atherton–Aldine, 1970.

40. Boring, E. G. *A History of Experimental Psychology*, 2nd ed. New York: Appleton-Century-Crofts, 1950.

41. Hilgard, E. R., and J. Hilgard. *Hypnosis in the Relief of Pain*. Los Altos, Calif.: William Kaufman, 1975.

42. Sarbin, T. R., and R. W. Slagle. "Hypnosis and Psychophysiological Outcomes." In Fromm, E., and R. E. Shor (eds.), *Hypnosis: Research Developments and Perspectives*. Chicago: Atherton–Aldine, 1972. See also Ulett, Apkiner, and Itil, in the same volume, for a different view.

43. Barber, T. X. *LSD*, pp. 119–120.

44. Hull, C. L. *Hypnosis and Suggestibility: An Experimental Approach*. New York: Appleton-Century-Crofts, 1933. See also Hilgard, E. R. *Hypnotic Susceptibility*. New York: Harcourt, Brace & World, 1965.

45. Perky, C. W. "An Experimental Study of Imagination." *American Journal of Psychology*, 1910, 21, 422–452. Recently, this area of research was revived by Sydney J. Segal (*Imagery: Current Cognitive Approaches*. New York: Academic Press, 1971). The assimilation of projected pictures into the visual image is illustrated by Segal's report. In some cases, subjects were asked to imagine a skyline scene but were shown a faintly projected picture of a tomato—and several subjects reported imagining a skyline with a round red sunset.

46. Sarbin, T. R., and W. C. Coe. *Hypnosis: A Social Psychological Analysis of Influence Communication*. New York: Holt, Rinehart & Winston, 1972.

47. Orne, M. T. "The Nature of Hypnosis: Artifact and Essence." *Journal of Abnormal and Social Psychology*, 1959, 58, 277–299.

48. Barber, T. X. *LSD*.

49. Sinclair-Greben, A. H. C., and D. Chalmers. "Evaluation of Treatment of Warts by Hypnosis." *Lancet*, 1959, 2, 480–482.

50. Barber, T. X. *LSD*.

51. Rosenthal, R., and L. Jacobson. *Pygmalion in the Classroom*. New York: Holt, Rinehart, & Winston, 1968.

52. Barber, T. X., *et al.* (eds.). *Biofeedback and Self-Control, 1970.* Chicago: Aldine-Atherton, 1971. Also, Stoyva, J., *et al.* (eds.). *Biofeedback and Self-Control,* 1971. Chicago: Aldine-Atherton, 1972. Also, Shapiro, D., *et al.* (eds.). *Biofeedback and Self-Control, 1972.* Chicago: Aldine-Atherton, 1973.

53. Barber, T. X. "Who Believes in Hypnosis?" *Psychology Today,* July 1970.

54. Dement, W. C., and M. Mitler. "New Developments in the Basic Mechanisms of Sleep." In Usdin, G. (ed.), *Sleep Research and Clinical Practices.* New York: Brunner-Mazel, 1973.

55. Tart, C. *Altered States of Consciousness.* New York: John Wiley & Sons, 1969. Also, Naranjo, C., and R. Ornstein. *On the Psychology of Meditation.* New York: Viking Press, 1971.

56. Wallace, R. "Physiological Effects of Transcendental Meditation." *Science,* 1970, 167, 1751–1754.

57. Pagano, R. R., R. M. Rosen, R. M. Stivers, and S. Warrenburg. "Sleep During Transcendental Meditation." *Science,* 1976, 191, 308–310.

58. Kasamatsu, A., and T. Hirai. "An Electroencephalographic Study on the Zen Meditation (Zazen)." *Folio Psychiatrica & Neurologica Japonica,* 1966, 20, 315–336.

59. Naranjo and Ornstein, *On the Psychology of Meditation.*

60. James, W. *The Principles of Psychology,* Vol. 1. New York: Dover, 1950 (first published in 1890).

CHAPTER 4

1. Köhler, W. *The Mentality of Apes.* New York: Harcourt, 1925.

2. Goodall, J. *In the Shadow of Man.* Boston: Houghton Mifflin, 1971.

3. Penfield, W. "Speech, Perception, and the Uncommitted Cortex." In Eccles, J. C., *Brain and Conscious Experience.* New York: Springer-Verlag, 1966. The uncommitted cortex used to be thought of as "association cortex," based on the behaviorist model of higher brain function as an associative connection across the

cortex between a sensory event (stimulus) and a motor output (response). This idea is basically one of the brain as a telephone switchboard. It is now realized that the functioning of these areas is extraordinarily complicated, and the more neutral term "uncommitted" is in general use.

4. Jerison, H. *Evolution of the Brain and Intelligence.* New York: Academic Press, 1973.

5. Strokes, or cerebrovascular accidents, are blockages of cerebral blood vessels which deprive selective brain regions of oxygen and nutrients. The brain cells in the affected area die and are not regenerated. The effects of strokes are usually more localized than those of brain tumors, which may create pressure in areas far removed form the site of the tumor. For this reason, stroke patients often provide the most precise clinical data available on the nature of cortical functioning.

6. Gregory, R. L. "The Brain as an Engineering Problem." In Thorpe, W. H., and O. L. Zangwill, (eds), *Current Problems in Animal Behaviour.* Cambridge: Cambridge University Press, 1961.

7. Wilson, E. O. *Sociobiology.* Cambridge, Mass.: Harvard University Press, 1973.

8. von Frisch, K. *Bees: Their Vision, Chemical Senses, and Language.* Ithaca, N.Y.: Cornell University Press, 1950.

9. Wilson, *Sociobiology.*

10. Chomsky, N. *Language and Mind.* New York: Harcourt, Brace & World, 1968.

11. Some writers take exception to the idea of uniqueness of human language based on any one property alone. For example, Hockett argues that propositionality, which he calls "open-ness," is shared by the dance system of the honeybee, since it is possible for a worker to report on a location never reported before by a bee or its co-workers. (Hockett, C. F. "Logical Considerations in the Study of Animal Communication." In Lanyon, W. E., and W. N. Tauloga (eds.), *Animal Sounds and Communication.* Washington, D.C.: American Institute of Biological Science, 1960.)

12. Gardner, R. A., and B. T. Gardner. "Teaching Sign Language to a Chimpanzee." *Science,* 1969, 165, 664–672.

13. Ploog, D., and T. Melnechuk. "Are Apes Capable of Language?" *Neurosciences Research Program Bulletin,* 1971, 9, 600–700.

14. Linden, E. *Apes, Men, and Language.* New York: E. P. Dutton, 1974. In a related project, David Premack has taught the use of a sign language to a chimpanzee. The chimp constructs statements through the manipulation of plastic symbols on a magnetic board. His subject, a chimp named Sarah, has become proficient in constructing well-formed sentences whose meaning depends on word order. (Premack, D. "Language in a Chimpanzee?" *Science,* 1971, 172, 808–822.)

15. Griffin, D. R. *The Question of Animal Awareness.* New York: Rockefeller University Press, 1976.

16. Even the memory images we have for *written* language, language taken in by means of the visual system, are coded into sounds. For example, in trying to remember letters of the alphabet shown to them, people tend to confuse letters that sound alike, rather than letters that look alike. (Conrad, R. "Errors of Immediate Memory." *British Journal of Psychology,* 1959, 50, 349.)

17. Luria calls these regions "tertiary cortex," in contrast to primary and secondary cortex, which are tied to specific sensory and motor systems (see Chapter 2). (Luria, A. R. *The Working Brain.* New York: Basic Books, 1973.)

18. Geschwind, N. "Disconnection Syndromes in Animals and Man." *Brain,* 1965, 88, 237–294; 585–644.

19. Brain lesions to this region can also produce more general cognitive deficits, often an inability to understand complex spatial relationships, to perform mathematical calculations, and to understand sentences expressing relations ("on top of" or "father's sister"). To understand what all these seemingly disparate cognitive abilities have in common is a challenging puzzle. See Luria, A. R. *Higher Cortical Functions in Man.* New York: Basic Books, 1966.

20. Geschwind, N., and W. Levitzky. "Human Brain: Left-Right Asymmetries in Temporal Speech Region." *Science,* 1968, 161, 186–187. Also, Wada, J. A., R. Clarke, and A. Hamm. "Cerebral Hemispheric Asymmetry in Humans." *Archives of Neurology,* 1975, 32, 239–246.

21. Robinson, B. W. "Vocalization Evoked from Forebrain in *Macaca Mulatta.*" *Physiology and Behavior,* 1967, 2, 345–354.

22. Penfield, W., and L. Roberts. *Speech and Brain Mechanisms.* Princeton, N.J.: Princeton University Press, 1959.

23. The comparison between the effects of animal and human brain stimulation should be interpreted cautiously, since the two types of data are not quite comparable. In the monkeys, stimulation of the brain produces vocalization, while in human surgical patients, stimulation produces arrest of ongoing speech.

24. This is an earlier, behaviorist view of language competence, expressed most forcefully by Skinner, B. F. *Verbal Behavior.* New York: Appleton-Century-Crofts, 1957.

25. In practice, of course, the number of comprehendible sentences is limited because of memory limitations. People lose track of very long sentences.

26. Chomsky, N. *Syntactic Structures.* The Hague: Mouton, 1965.

27. Lenneberg, E. H. *Biological Foundations of Language.* New York: John Wiley & Sons, 1967.

28. Brown, J. *Mind, Brain, and Consciousness.* New York: Academic Press, 1977.

29. Gardner, H. *The Shattered Mind.* New York: Alfred A. Knopf, 1975.

30. Ibid.

31. Aphasiologists make the distinction between this kind of *literal* or "phonemic" *paraphasia,* where the substitution is by sound ("spoot" for "spoon") and *verbal paraphasia,* where there is a substitution of one word for another, sometimes related in meaning ("knife" for "fork"). Neologisms are literal paraphasias where there are several incorrect sounds ("tarripoi").

32. Caramazza, A., and R. S. Berndt. "Semantic and Syntactic Processes in Aphasia." *Psychological Bulletin,* in press.

33. Brown, *Mind, Brain, and Consciousness.*

34. Liberman, A. M. "Perception of the Speech Code." *Psychological Review,* 1967, 74, 431–461. Also, Sokolov, A. N. *Inner Speech and Thought.* New York: Plenum Press, 1972.

35. Caramazza, A., and E. G. Zurif. "Dissociation of Algorithmic and Heuristic Processes in Language Comprehension." *Brain and Language,* 1976, 3, 572–582.

36. Geschwind, N. "The Organization of Language and the Brain." *Science,* 1970, 170, 940–944.

37. Lenneberg, *Biological Foundations of Language.*

38. There are some initial gains in recovery of speech made by adult aphasics, but this appears mostly due to reduced swelling and increased blood supply to the regions surrounding the destroyed tissue. Generally speaking, symptoms not recovered in three to five months following a stroke or other injury are usually irreversible. *(Ibid.)*

39. For a discussion of what happens when a person who speaks more than one language becomes aphasic, see Critcheley, M. "Aphasia in Polyglots." *Brain and Language,* 1974, 1.

40. Brown, J. W., and J. Jaffe. "Hypothesis on Cerebral Dominance." *Neuropsychologia,* 1975, 13, 107–110.

41. For a discussion of these issues, see Leman, G., in Bannister, D. (ed.), *The Evaluation of Personal Constructs.* New York: Academic Press, 1968; also, see Griffin, *The Question of Animal Awareness.*

42. Gazzaniga, M. S. *The Bisected Brain.* New York: Appleton-Century-Crofts, 1970.

43. Sperry, R. W. "Hemisphere Deconnection and Unity in Conscious Awareness." *American Psychologist,* 1968, 23, 723–733.

44. Smith, A., and C. W. Burklund. "Dominant Hemispherectomy." *Science,* 1966, 153, 1280–1282. Also, Austin, G. M., and F. C. Grant. "Physiologic Observations Following Total Hemispherectomy in Man." *Surgery,* 1955, 38, 250–258.

45. The separate abilities of the two hemispheres have also been revealed by a technique which knocks out, temporarily, one hemisphere at a time. The method is to inject a strong sedative drug (sodium amytal) into the artery which supplies blood to one side of the brain, the left or right internal carotid artery. This *sodium amytal test* is usually restricted to assessing hemisphere functioning in patients about to undergo surgery. The results of sodium amytal testing confirm conclusions reached from data on split-brain patients and on people with brain damage restricted to one side or another. This is a fine example of how converging information from several sources serves to validate scientific hypotheses.

46. Nebes, R. D., and R. W. Sperry. "Hemisphere Deconnection Syndrome with Cerebral Birth Injury in the Dominant Arm Area." *Neuropsychologia,* 1971, 9, 247–259.

47. Split-brain patients are probably not typical of most people, as a result of years of abnormal brain functioning related to the epilepsy. If the brain damage causing the seizures was long-standing, especially if it occurred before the brain was fully matured, then left-hemisphere language capabilities could have been taken over by both hemispheres as a compensation for damage on the left.

48. Searleman, A. "A Review of Right Hemisphere Linguistic Capabilities." *Psychological Bulletin,* 1977, 84, 503–528. Zaidel, however, reports greater right-hemisphere ability to understand meanings of abstract words. (Zaidel, E. "Lexical Organization in the Right Hemisphere." In Buser, P., and A. Rougeul-Buser (eds.), *Cerebral Correlates of Conscious Experience.* Amsterdam: Elsevier, 1978.)

49. Van Lancker, D. "Automatic and Propositional Speech." In *Cerebral Dominance,* UCLA Brain Information Service Conference Report #34 (1973). This right hemisphere capability for emotional expression, together with some other evidence, has led some to speculate that the right hemisphere may be specialized for the cortical contribution to emotions. The other evidence is the observation that patients with right-hemisphere brain damage, but not those with left-hemisphere damage, frequently show inappropriate emotional reactions, usually an overly jocular manner. However, most of the evidence on emotional specialization

is too sketchy at present to allow any firm conclusions. See Galin, D. "Implications for Psychiatry of Left and Right Cerebral Specialization." *Archives of General Psychiatry,* 1974, 31, 572–583.

50. Gott, P. S. "Language after Dominant Hemispherectomy." *Journal of Neurology, Neurosurgery, and Psychiatry,* 1973, 36, 1082–1088.

51. Bever, T. G., and R. J. Chiarello. "Cerebral Dominance in Musicians and Nonmusicians." *Science,* 1974, 185, 537–539.

52. Bogen, J. E. "The Other Side of the Brain II: An Appositional Mind." *Bulletin of the Los Angeles Neurological Society,* 1969, 34, 135–162.

53. White, M. J. "Laterality Differences in Perception." *Psychological Bulletin,* 1969, 72, 387–405. Also, Kimura, D., and M. Durnford. "Normal Studies on the Function of the Right Hemisphere in Vision." In Dimond, S. J., and J. G. Beaumont (eds.), *Hemisphere Function in the Human Brain.* New York: John Wiley & Sons, 1974.

54. Jerison, H. J. "Evolution of the Brain." In Wittrock, M. C., *et al., The Human Brain.* Englewood Cliffs, N.J.: Prentice-Hall, 1977.

55. Levy-Agresti, J., and R. W. Sperry. "Differential Perceptual Capabilities in Major and Minor Hemispheres." *Proceedings of the National Academy of Sciences* (U.S.A.), 1968, 61, 1151.

56. Ornstein, R. E. *The Psychology of Consciousness.* San Francisco: W. H. Freeman, 1972.

57. Teuber, H.-L. "Why Two Brains?" In Schmitt, F., and F. Worden (eds.), *The Neurosciences: Third Study Program.* Cambridge, Mass.: M.I.T. Press, 1974.

58. Liberman, A. M., *et al.* "Perception of the Speech Code." *Psychological Review,* 1967, 74, 431–461.

59. Studdert-Kennedy, M., and D. Shankweiler. "Hemispheric Specialization for Speech Perception." *Journal of the Acoustical Society of America,* 1970, 48, 579–594.

60. Semmes, J. "Hemispheric Specialization: A Possible Clue to Mechanism." *Neuropsychologia,* 1968, 6, 11–26. See also Hewes, C. "Primate Communication and the Gestural Origin of Language." *Current Anthropology,* 1973, 14.

61. Bruner, J. S. *On Knowing: Essays for the Left Hand.* New York: Atheneum, 1965.

62. Bogen, "The Other Side of the Brain II." Also, Hoppe, K. D. "Split Brains and Psychoanalysis." *Psychoanalytic Quarterly,* 1977, 45, 220–244.

63. Austin, M. D. "Dream Recall and the Bias of Intellectual Ability." *Nature,* 1971, 231, 59.

64. Goldstein, L. *et al.* "Changes in Interhemispheric Amplitude Relationships in the EEG During Sleep." *Physiology and Behavior,* 1972, 8, 811–815.

65. Kocel, K., *et al.* "Lateral Eye Movement and Cognitive Mode." *Psychonomic Science,* 1972, 27, 223–224. Also, Kinsbourne, M. "Eye and Head Turning Indicates Cerebral Lateralization." *Science,* 1972, 176, 539–541.

66. Penfield and Roberts, *Speech and Brain Mechanisms.*

67. Bakan, P. "Hypnotizability, Laterality of Eye Movements and Functional Brain Asymmetry." *Perceptual and Motor Skills,* 1969, 28, 927–932.

68. Bogen, J. E., *et al.* "The Other Side of the Brain IV: The A/P Ratio." *Bulletin of the Los Angeles Neurological Society,* 1972, 37, 49–61.

69. Galin, D., and R. Ornstein. "Individual Differences in Cognitive Style." *Neuropsychologia,* 1974, 12, 367–376. Also, Dumas, R., and A. Morgan. "EEG Asymmetry as a Function of Occupation, Task and Task Difficulty." *Neuropsychologia,* 1975, 13, 219–228.

70. Mischel, W. *Personality and Assessment.* New York: John Wiley & Sons, 1968.

71. This item is from a test purporting to measure general intelligence. Zaidel found that both hemispheres in split-brain patients have competence for these problems, but they may go about solving them in characteristically different ways. (Zaidel, E. "Concepts of Cerebral Dominance in the Split Brain." In Buser and Rougeul-Buser, *Cerebral Correlates of Conscious Experience.*)

72. Bogen, J. E., and G. M. Bogen. "The Other Side of the Brain III: The Corpus Callusum and Creativity." *Bulletin of the Los Angeles Neurological Society,* 1969, 34, 191–220.

73. Ornstein's widely quoted treatment of the subject identifies the left hemisphere with the thought of the technological, rational West, and the right hemisphere with the thought of the intuitive and mystical East (Ornstein, *The Psychology of Consciousness*). Professor E. K. Sadalla of Arizona State University has remarked that this identification of left with Western thought and right with Eastern thought holds especially if one is facing north (personal communication).

74. See Neisser, U. "The Multiplicity of Thought." *British Journal of Psychology,* 1966, 54, 1–14.

75. Sperry, R. W. "Brain Bisection and Consciousness." In Eccles, *Brain and Conscious Experience.*

76. Sperry, "Hemisphere Deconnection and Unity in Conscious Awareness."

77. The transfer of memories from one side of the brain to the other and the interhemispheric access of memory are documented in a remarkable series of experiments with cats. Sperry, R. W. "Cerebral Organization and Behavior." *Science,* 1961, 133, 1749–1757.

78. Eccles, J. C. *Facing Reality.* New York: Springer-Verlag, 1970.

79. Heilman, K. M., and R. T. Watson. "The Neglect Syndrome." In Harnad, S., *et al., Lateralization in the Nervous System.* New York: Academic Press, 1977.

80. Gardner, *The Shattered Mind.*

81. A third possibility is that the left hemisphere's persistent attempts to use language, even when damaged, avoids a complete inactivation of that half of the brain, so that it can continue to signal to the right that something is missing. When the right hemisphere is damaged, however, it may be more susceptible to inactivation and so would be unable to signal its ignorance to the intact left. See Bowers, D., and K. M. Heilman. "Material Specific Hemispheric Arousal." *Neuropsychologia,* 1976, 14, 123–127.

82. Galin, D., and R. Ornstein. "Lateral Specialization of Cognitive Mode: An EEG Study." *Psychophysiology,* 1972, 9, 412–418.

83. Levy, J., C. Trevarthen, and R. W. Sperry. "Perception of Bilateral Chimeric Figures Following Hemispheric Deconnection." *Brain,* 1972, 95, 61–78.

84. Sperry, "Hemisphere Deconnection and Unity in Conscious Awareness."

85. Galin, "Implications for Psychiatry of Left and Right Cerebral Specialization."

86. Freud, S. *Collected Papers,* Vol. 4. London: Hogarth Press, 1948.

87. Despite its wide influence, Freud's theory of the unconscious has not recently been held in wide repute among psychologists. Partly, this is because of logical confusions over the meaning of the notion of the unconscious, and partly it is due to difficulties in bringing the concept into the research laboratory.

The Freudian unconscious is a curious sort of theoretical entity. It is never directly observed, but—like subatomic particles in physics—it is hypothesized to exist because it explains certain observed phenomena. Unlike electrons and positrons, however, the theory of the unconscious doesn't really predict anything about human behavior, although after the fact, it can explain a great deal. For this reason, Freud's theories have come into disfavor among scientifically minded psychologists. If a man says that he wants to break off an unhappy relationship but continues to send his lady flowers and keeps asking her out, then you might describe him as unconsciously desiring to continue the friendship. But you might also say, more parsimoniously, that he had conflicting intentions, without hypothesizing a complicated psychic netherworld.

There is one notion of unconscious thought with which few psychologists would quibble: that unconscious thought is constituted of all the cognitive brain activities which don't reach the level of awareness. These would include such things as the perceptual-motor control of well-practiced golf swings, the brain activities aroused by habituated sounds, or unattended voices. These all can be regarded as "thought," since they produce intelligent effects. Perhaps most cognitive brain activities are unconscious in this sense. Freud called these things "preconscious," distinguishing them from truly unconscious thoughts—because preconscious thoughts had the potential for becoming conscious, but just weren't at any particular moment in time. Truly unconscious thoughts were actively kept from consciousness.

The attempt to bring unconscious thoughts into the scientific laboratory has met with a surprising amount of controversy, reminiscent, in some ways, of the academic disputes over ESP experiments. This research tends to revolve around the question of whether there can be "unconscious perception." A good review of this research can be found in Dixon, N. F. *Subliminal Perception*. London: McGraw-Hill, 1971.

88. Wittgenstein, L. *Tractatus Logico-Philosophicus*, trans. by D. F. Pears and B. F. McGuiness. Atlantic Highlands, N.J.: Humanities Press, 1974 (first published 1922).

CHAPTER 5

1. Hebb, D. O. *The Organization of Behavior*. New York: Wiley-Interscience, 1949.

2. Verzeano, M. "The Activity of Neuronal Networks in Memory Consolidation." In Drucker, C., and J. McGaugh, (eds.), *Neurobiology of Sleep and Memory*. New York: Academic Press, 1977.

3. Gerard, R. W. "What Is Memory?" *Scientific American*, September 1953.

4. Eccles, J. C. "Possible Synaptic Mechanism Subserving Learning." In Karczmar, A. C., and J. C. Eccles (eds.), *Brain and Human Behavior*. New York: Springer-Verlag, 1972.

5. Landis, C., and F. A. Mettler. *Varieties of Psychopathological Experience*. New York: Holt, Rinehart & Winston, 1964.

6. Penfield, W. "Speech, Perception and the Uncommitted Cortex." In Eccles, J. C., *Brain and Conscious Experience*. New York: Springer-Verlag, 1966.

7. John, E. R. *Merchanisms of Memory.* New York: Academic Press, 1967.

8. Jerison provides an interesting discussion of the evolutionary origins of human mentality. (Jerison, H. J. *Evolution of the Brain and Intelligence.* New York: Academic Press, 1973.)

9. Lashley, K. S. "In Search of the Engram." In Symposium of the Society of Experimental Biology, No. 4: *Physiological Mechanisms in Animal Behavior.* New York: Cambridge University Press, 1950.

10. It is necessary to point out that equipotentiality holds only within specified regions of the cortex. Visual memories are not lost with damage to the frontal parts of the brain, even though other mental functions may be impaired. (See Meyer, V. "Psychological Effects of Brain Damage." In Eysenck, H. (ed.), *Handbook of Abnormal Psychology.* New York: Basic Books, 1961.)

11. Thompson, R. F. *Introduction to Physiological Psychology.* New York: Harper & Row, 1975.

12. See Chapters 2 and 4.

13. Bloch, V., and W. Fishbein. "Sleep and Psychological Functions: Memory." In Lairy, G. C., and P. Salzurullo, (eds.), *The Experimental Study of Human Sleep.* Amsterdam: Elsevier, 1975.

14. Barbizet, J. *Human Memory and Its Pathology.* San Francisco: W. H. Freeman, 1970.

15. A similar difficulty in consolidating memories occurs as a part of *Korsakoff's syndrome,* a degenerative brain disease found among chronic alcoholics. Korsakoff's patients present a slightly different, less pure form of memory impairment. A review of this area can be found in a work by Talland. The brain injury comes about from a deficiency in thiamine (Vitamin B1); the hippocampus and related structures (especially the mammilary bodies) are especially susceptible to damage from B1 deficiency. (Talland, G. *Deranged Memory.* New York: Academic Press, 1965.)

16. Milner, B., S. Corkin, and H.-L. Teuber. "Further Analysis of the Hippocampal Amnesic Syndrome." *Neuropsychologia,* 1968, 6, 215–234. H. M. could occasionally learn a new thing or two:

Kennedy's face on a coin (H. M.'s operation was in 1954) and the plan of his new house, but not where to find the lawnmower. There are other interpretations of H. M.'s disability besides consolidation. For example, his problem could be with retrieving memories which were actually stored. (For the controversy surrounding this issue, see Warrington and Weiskrantz, *Nature,* 1970, 228, 628–630; Cermak and Butters, *Brain and Language,* 1974, 1, 141–150; Marslen-Wilson and Teuber, *Neuropsychologia,* 1975, 13, 353–364.)

17. Starr, A., and L. Phillips. "Verbal and Motor Memory in the Amnestic Syndrome." *Neuropsychologia,* 1970, 8, 75–88.

18. Douglas, R. J. "The Hippocampus and Behavior." *Psychological Bulletin,* 1967, 67, 416–442.

19. Bloch and Fishbein, "Sleep and Psychological Functions."

20. Hebb, D. O. *Textbook of Psychology,* 3rd ed. Philadelphia: W. B. Saunders, 1972.

21. Pribram, K. H. "The Limbic Systems, Efferent Control of Neural Inhibition and Behavior." *Progress in Brain Research,* 1967, 27, 317–336.

22. Pribram, K. H., and L. Kruger. "Functions of the 'Olfactory Brain.'" *Annals of the New York Academy of Sciences,* 1954, 58, 109–138.

23. Heath, R. G., S. B. John, and C. J. Fontana. "The Pleasure Response." In Kline and Laska (eds.), *Computers and Electronic Devices in Psychiatry.* New York: Grune & Stratton, 1968.

24. Kolb, L. C. *Noyes' Modern Clinical Psychiatry,* 7th ed. Philadelphia: W. B. Saunders, 1968.

25. Cases such as these are dramatic enough to have become the basis for several popular books and movies. The most famous was the case reported by Thigpen and Cleckly, which later served as the basis for a movie. (Thigpen, C. H., and H. M. Cleckly. *The Three Faces of Eve.* New York: McGraw-Hill, 1957.

26. Landis and Mettler, *Varieties of Psychopathological Experience.*

27. James, W. *The Principles of Psychology.* New York: Dover, 1950 (first published 1890).

28. Overton, D. "State-Dependent or 'Dissociated' Learning Produced with Pentobarbital." *Journal of Comparative and Physiological Psychology,* 1966, 57, 3–12.

29. Brown, J. *Mind, Brain, and Consciousness.* New York: Academic Press, 1977.

30. Harlow, J. M. "Recovery from the Passage of an Iron Bar Through the Head." Proceedings of the Massachusetts Medical Society. Boston: Clapp, 1869.

31. The frontal lobes are actually composed of other regions besides this newly evolved *prefrontal cortex* (also called frontal "granular cortex). Among the other regions is the motor cortex, which controls the production of voluntary actions, located on the posterior upper surface of the frontal cortex, in front of the Rolandic fissure. Damage to this area results in paralyses or other movement disorders.

The other evolutionarily older frontal areas are located on the medial (central-facing) and orbital (underneath) surfaces of the frontal lobes. These areas, when damaged, give rise to disorders of arousal (passiveness, listlessness) or of affect (euphoria).

It should be understood that discussions of frontal-lobe functioning in this section refer more accurately to the new "prefrontal" cortex. However, the functions of all the frontal regions may interact, and their physical proximity makes it difficult to analyze the effects of brain damage to one area independently from effects of possible damage to a neighboring region.

A more comprehensive treatment of frontal-lobe functioning can be found in Luria, A. R. *Higher Cortical Functions in Man.* New York: Basic Books, 1966.

32. Teuber, H.-L. "The Riddle of Frontal Lobe Function in Man." In Warren, J., and K. Akert, *The Frontal Granular Cortex and Behavior.* New York: McGraw-Hill, 1964.

33. Jacobsen, F. C., J. B. Wolfe, and T. A. Jacobson. "An Experimental Analysis of the Functions of the Frontal Association Areas in Primates." *Journal of Nervous and Mental Disease,* 1935, 82, 1–14.

34. Frontal lobotomy was also used to alleviate intractable pain in cases of terminal cancer. The curious result was that unlike certain more modern brain operations performed for this purpose—operations which destroy lower brain pathways to block incoming pain impulses—frontal lobotomy did not do away with the subjective experience of pain. The lobotomized patients claimed to feel the pain just as much as before the operation. They just didn't seem to care about it. (See Barber, T. X. "Toward a Theory of Pain." *Psychological Bulletin,* 1959, 56, 430–460.)

35. Freeman, W., and J. W. Watts. *Psychosurgery in the Treatment of Mental Disorders and Intractable Pain.* Springfield, Ill.: Charles C Thomas, 1950.

36. The cavalier use of lobotomy for the treatment of mental disorders has declined also in response to public outcry against visions of unwilling patients being turned into docile and passive vegetables. More skeptical observers have suggested that the real reason for the decline of lobotomy was the development, during the 1950's, of powerful chemical tranquilizing drugs, which also make psychiatric patients more manageable.

    The ethical issues involved in lobotomy and newer forms of "psychosurgery" are discussed in Chorover, S. L. "The Pacification of the Brain." *Psychology Today,* 1974, 7, 59–69.

37. Hamlin, R. M. "Intellectual Function after Frontal Lobe Surgery." *Cortex,* 1970, 6, 299–307.

38. Milner, B. "Effects of Different Brain Lesions on Card Sorting." *Archives De Neurologie,* 1963, 9, 90–100.

39. Harlow, "Recovery from the Passage of an Iron Bar Through the Head."

40. Luria, A. R. *The Working Brain.* New York: Basic Books, 1973.

41. Luria, *Higher Cortical Functions in Man.*

42. *Ibid.*

43. Walter, W. G., *et al.* "Contingent Negative Variation: An Electric Sign of Sensorimotor Association and Expectancy in the Human Brain." *Nature,* 1964, 203, 380–384.

44. Cohen, J. "Cerebral Psychophysiology: The Contingent Negative Variation." In Thompson, R. F., and M. Patterson, *Bioelectric Recording Techniques*, Part B. New York: Academic Press, 1974.

45. Walter, W. G. "The Contingent Negative Variation." *Progress in Brain Research*, 1968, 22, 364–377.

46. The reader should be aware that this interpretation of the significance of the CNV is speculative. The more usual speculation is that the CNV acts to sensitize or prime cortical tissue, so that the cortex is made ready to act upon the expected stimulus. (Walter *et al.* "Contingent Negative Variation," 1964.) This theory has some points in its favor. For one thing, the electrical negativity of the CNV probably comes about by a depolarization of millions of cortical neurons, which would probably have the effect of lowering the firing threshold of these cells. Second, the CNV has been found to be related to performance: it is highest on trials when reaction to the expected stimulus is fastest.

It is difficult at the present time to decide between alternative theories. A major problem is that the CNV cannot easily be studied over longer time intervals than those provided in standard experimental situations (typically several seconds). This limitation is due to technical difficulties in recording very slow waves in the EEG and in distinguishing these changes from such artifacts as chemical or mechanical drifts at the junction of the electrode and the skin.

In any event, it would seem that to build a purposeful machine such as the human brain, one would have to incorporate some kind of intention mechanism of the type described in this chapter. Whether or not the CNV is actually related to that mechanism is a question for future research.

47. Greuninger, W., and J. Greuninger. "The Primate Frontal Cortex and Allostasis." In Pribram, K. H., and A. R. Luria, *Psychophysiology of the Frontal Lobes*. New York: Academic Press, 1973.

48. Zeigarnik, B. "Uber das Behalten von Erledigten and Unerledigten Handlungen." *Psychologische Forschung*, 1927, 9, 1–85.

49. Miller, G. A., E. H. Galanter, and K. H. Pribram. *Plans and the Structure of Behavior*. New York: Holt, Rinehart & Winston, 1960.

50. On chimp tool use, see Goodall, J. *In the Shadow of Man.* Boston: Houghton Mifflin, 1971. On long-term behavioral organization in infants, see Huttenlocher, J. "The Origins of Language Comprehension." In Solso, R. (ed.), *Theories in Cognitive Psychology.* Potomac, Md.: Erlebaum, 1974.

51. Luria, A. R. *Traumatic Aphasia.* The Hague: Mouton, 1970.

52. Vygotsky, L. S. *Thought and Language.* Cambridge, Mass.: M.I.T. Press, 1962 (originally published in 1934).

53. Luria, A. R. *The Role of Speech in the Regulation of Normal and Abnormal Behaviour.* Oxford: Pergamon Press, 1961.

54. Sokolov, A. N. *Inner Speech and Thought.* New York: Plenum Press, 1972.

55. Luria, *Higher Cortical Functions in Man.*

56. Luria, A. R., K. H. Pribram, and E. D. Homskaya. "An Experimental Analysis of the Behavioral Disturbance Produced by a Left Frontal Arachnoidal Endothelioma." *Neuropsychologia,* 1964, 2, 257–280.

57. Weinberg, H. "The Contingent Negative Variation: Its Clinical Past and Future." *American Journal of EEG Technology,* 1975, 15, 51–67.

CHAPTER 6

1. Globus, G. G. "Unexpected Symmetries in the 'World Knot.'" *Science,* 1973, 180, 1129–1136.

2. Magoun, H. "Darwin and Concepts of Brain Function." In Delfresnaye, J. F. (ed.), *Brain Mechanisms and Consciousness.* Oxford: Blackwell, 1954.

3. Meyer, V. "Psychological Effects of Brain Damage." In Eysenck, H. (ed.), *Handbook of Abnormal Psychology.* New York: Basic Books, 1961. Also, Pribram, K. H. *Languages of the Brain.* Englewood Cliffs, N.J.: Prentice-Hall, 1971; Eccles, J. C. *Social Research,* 1972, 39, 753–757.

4. Gardner, H. *The Shattered Mind.* New York: Alfred A. Knopf, 1975.

5. See Chapter 4.

6. Head, H. *Aphasia and Kindred Disorders of Speech.* New York: Hafner, 1963. Also, Goldstein, *Language and Language Disturbances.* New York: Grune and Stratton, 1948.

7. Luria, A. R. *Higher Cortical Functions in Man.* New York: Basic Books, 1966.

8. Gregory, R. L. "The Brain as an Engineering Problem." In Thorpe, W. H., and O. L. Zangwill (eds.), *Current Problems in Animal Behaviour.* Cambridge-Cambridge University Press, 1961.

9. Pribram, K. H. *Languages of the Brain.* Englewood Cliffs, N.J.: Prentice-Hall, 1971.

10 Festinger, L., *et al.* "Efference and the Conscious Experience of Perception." *Journal of Experimental Psychology,* 1967, Monograph Supplement 74 (4, whole No. 637).

11. *Ibid.*

12. Arbib, M. *The Metaphorical Brain.* New York: John Wiley & Sons, 1972.

13. Hernández-Peón, R. "Neurophysiologic Aspects of Attention." In Vinken, P.J., and G. W. Bruyn (eds.), *Handbook of Clinical Neurology, Vol. 3.* Amsterdam: North Holland, 1968.

14. James, W. *The Principles of Psychology.* New York: Henry Holt & Co., 1890.

15. Penfield, W. "Speech, Perception, and the Uncommitted Cortex." In Eccles, J. C., *Brain and Conscious Experience.* New York: Springer-Verlag, 1966. Also, Penfield, W., and L. Roberts. *Speech and Brain Mechanisms.* Princeton, N.J.: Princeton University Press, 1959.

16. Penfield, W. *The Mystery of the Mind.* Princeton, N.J.: Princeton University Press, 1975.

17. Watson, J. B. *Behaviorism,* New York: W. W. Norton, 1924.

18. Morgan, C. L. *An Introduction to Comparative Psychology.* London: Scott, 1896.

19. Griffin, D. R. *The Question of Animal Awareness.* New York: Rockefeller University Press, 1976. See also an earlier treatment by the German biologist Jacob von Uexküll, in his monograph on the *Umwelten,* or "Subjective worlds," of animals. Von Uexküll provides some fanciful descriptions of what it might be like to be a dog, or a fly, based on considerations of their sensory systems and their behaviors. ("A Stroll Through the Worlds of Animals and Men." In Schiller, C. H. (ed.), *Instinctive Behavior.* New York: International University Press, 1957.)

20. Brown, J. *Mind, Brain, and Consciousness.* New York: Academic Press, 1977.

21. MacLean, P. D. "Psychosomatic Disease and the 'Visceral Brain.'" *Psychosomatic Medicine,* 1949, 11, 338–353.

22. MacLean, P. D. "The Triune Brain, Emotion, and Scientific Bias." In Schmitt, F. O. (ed.), *The Neurosciences: Second Study Program.* New York: Rockefeller University Press, 1970.

23. Horowitz, M., and J. Adams. "Hallucinations on Brain Stimulation." In Keup, W. (ed.), *Origin and Mechanisms of Hallucinations.* New York: Plenum, 1970.

24. Snyder, S. H. *Madness and the Brain.* New York: McGraw-Hill, 1974.

25. Jerison, H. J. "Evolution of the Brain." In Wittrock, M. C., *et al., The Human Brain.* Englewood Cliffs, N.J.: Prentice-Hall, 1977.

26. Brown, *Mind, Brain, and Consciousness.*

27. Sperry, R. W. "Mental Phenomena as Causal Determinants in Brain Function." In Globus, G. G., and G. Maxwell, *Consciousness and the Brain.* New York: Plenum Press, 1976.

28. For example, see Morgan, C. L. *Emergent Evolution.* London: Williams & Norgate, 1923.

29. Sperry, R. W. "A Modified Concept of Consciousness." *Psychological Review,* 1969, 76, 532–536.

30. *Ibid.*

31. Eccles, J. C. *Facing Reality.* New York: Springer-Verlag, 1970.

32. Libet, B. "Electrical Stimulation of Cortex in Human Subjects." In Iggo, A. (ed.), *Handbook of Sensory Physiology*, Vol. 2. New York: Springer-Verlag, 1973.

33. Sherrington, C. S. *Man—On His Nature*. Cambridge: Cambridge University Press, 1940.

34. Teilhard deChardin, P. *The Phenomenon of Man*. New York: Harper & Row, 1959.

35. Sperry, "Mental Phenomena as Causal Determinants in Brain Function."

36. Clarke, A. C. "Dial 'F' for Frankenstein." *Playboy*, January 1965.

Glossary

alexia. The inability to read, associated with organic brain damage; a form of aphasia.

alpha waves. Synchronized waves (8–13 cycles per second) which appear in the EEG during wakefulness and which indicate that the underlying brain tissue is momentarily idling.

analgesia. The state of not being able to feel something which is ordinarily painful.

angular gyrus. The cortical area destroyed in cases of anomia, lying at the intersection of the temporal, occipital, and parietal lobes.

anomia. The inability to name objects; one type of aphasic symptom.

aphasia. The variety of language disturbances which can result from brain damage.

artificial intelligence. The science of creating machines and machine programs which manifest thought-like or perceptive behaviors.

axon. Fiber of a neuron which transmits electrical action potentials.

basic rest-and-activity cycle (BRAC). The alternation between periods of activity and rest hypothesized to occur in 90-minute cycles throughout the day.

Behaviorism. The school of psychology which held that observable behavior was the proper scientific subject matter of psychology, since mental events are not publicly observable.

brainstem. A series of bumpy enlargements which form the upper end of the spinal cord; it includes the thalamus, pons, and medulla.

Broca's aphasia. Speech disorder characterized by relatively intact comprehension but impaired speech output.

Broca's area. Area of the brain in the left frontal cortex. Brain lesions associated with expressive disorders tend to be near Broca's area.

cerebellum. The structure at the back of the brainstem which is primarily concerned with the coordination of movement.

cerebral cortex. The outer, convoluted layer of the forebrain hemispheres, consisting of densely packed cells; it underlies higher cognitive functions.

cerebral hemispheres. The two large halves of the forebrain which sit upon the evolutionarily older brainstem and which contain the cerebral cortex, subcortal centers, and large tracts of connecting nerve fibers.

coma. State of continual sleep, induced by lesions of the brainstem's reticular activating system (RAS).

commissurotomy. See split-brain operation.

consolidation period. A period of time during which new memories exist only in a dynamic electrochemical form; memories must remain undisturbed for a time in order to be consolidated as permanent structural engrams.

contigent negative variation (CNV). A slow negative shift in electrical potential which occurs whenever two stimuli are paired in time, so that the first signals the arrival of the second. It appears in the EEG during periods of mental expectantcy.

corpus callosum. The large cable of nerve fibers which connect the two cerebral hemispheres, functioning to transmit information between the hemispheres and to coordinate their activities.

déjà vu. The experience of feeling that the present moment, in all its exact details, has been lived before.

delta waves. EEG brain waves with a frequency of 1.5 to 4 cycles per second, characteristic of deep sleep.

dendrites. Parts of a neuron; the branched fibers which receive stimulation from other neurons.

dis-habituation. A reoccurence of the orienting reaction to a stimulus which had previously been habituated.

dissociation. The separation from conscious access of certain coherent groups of memories, such as memories relating to emotionally painful experiences.

electroconvulsive shock (ECS). A psychiatric treatment for depression, involving the passing of a strong electrical current across the brain.

electroencephalogram (EEG). "Brain waves"; a recording of the electrical oscillations of large groups of nerves, usually obtained from electrodes on the surface of the scalp.

electromyogram (EMG). A recording of the electrical activity of the muscles.

EMG suppression. The phenomenon whereby the muscles of the body become flaccid and paralyzed during REM sleep; it is characterized by a flattening of the electromyogram (EMG).

encephalization. The progressive increase in brain size relative to body size in animal evolution.

engram. The permanent physical memory trace in the brain.

epipenomenalism. The position that mental events are merely secondary to underlying brain events and hence do not reflect anything important about the brain's operations.

equipotentiality. Lashley's principle that within a functional region of the cortex any piece of tissue is equal to any other in its ability to mediate a learned behavior.

forebrain. The two cerebral hemispheres of the brain, containing the cerebral cortex. The forebrain evolved as a characteristic of the brains of mammals.

fovea. An area, in the center of the retina, which is packed very densely with receptors and provides for the clearest vision.

fugue. State of mental confusion accompanying flight from a stressful situation, often in the form of aimless wandering.

global aphasia. The inability to understand or produce any form of language, either spoken or written.

grammar. Hypothetical linguistic process by which a speaker determines word order and sentence structure.

habituation. The process whereby a repeated stimulus loses its ability to evoke an orienting reaction.

hippocampus. A structure of the limbic system, associated with learning and cognitive memory.

hologram. An optical recording technique which uses a laser beam to record and reproduce entire wave fronts of light.

hypnagogic images. Intense, successive visual images which often occur during the transition between waking and sleeping.

identity theory. A philosophical theory which holds that mental processes and physical brain processes are identical.

interactionism. Descartes' position on the mind–body problem which holds that there is a causal interaction between mind and body which occurs at a particular place in the brain.

introspection. The method of looking inward to discover knowledge about the contents of the mind.

Korsakoff's syndrome. A degenerative brain disease involving the limbic system, in which the consolidation of memories is impaired.

lateral eye movements (LEM's). A shifting of the eyes either left or right during problem-solving, apparently due to the selective activation of one hemisphere over the other.

limbic system. An interconnected group of nerve centers of the forebrain at the border (or "limbus") of brainstem and cerebral hemispheres.

lobotomy. The severing of the nerve fibers running between the frontal cortex and other brain centers.

locus coeruleus. The control center for REM sleep; a group of brainstem cells connected to the RAS.

materialism. A class of philosophical theories which dispense with the duality of mind and matter by holding that the universe is composed only of physical objects and their relationships.

medulla (medulla oblongata). Lower portion of the brainstem, containing reflex centers for the control of blood circulation and breathing.

micro-electrodes. Extremely fine-tipped metal or glass electrodes less than one micron at the tip, which enable the sensing of electrical activity emanating from single neurons.

narcolepsy. A brain disorder characterized by episodes of an uncontrollable need to fall asleep in the middle of the day.

neuronal model. Circuits of neurons in the cortex which model or match patterns of incoming sensory stimulation; theorized by Sokolov to explain habituation.

neurons. The electrically active cells of the brain and spinal cord, composed of cell body and of fibers (called axons and dendrites) extending away from the cell body.

operational definition. A definition in terms of the operations which one would perform to determine the presence or absence of the quality being defined.

optic disc.   The area on the retina where blood vessels enter and where nerve fibers exit; this area lacks rods and cones and hence is blind.

optic tectum.   The area located on the back of the brainstem which, like the visual cortex, receives fibers from the optic nerve. An evolutionary older visual brain which, in mammals, functions to locate objects in the periphery of the visual field and to guide head and eye movements toward them.

orienting reflex.   The set of physiological changes evoked by surprising or novel stimuli.

paraphasia.   The substitution of inappropriate or nonsensical words which might sound like the intended words.

pattern vision.   The identification of visual objects or forms by brains and machines; pattern recognition.

phasic characteristics.   Brief and irregular physiological events; in REM sleep, such events as rapid eye movements and muscle twitches (vs. tonic characteristics).

phoneme.   Basic sound unit of speech.

placebo.   A drug which is physiologically inert but which has effects due to the user's expectations.

pressure phosphene.   A sensation of light which is caused by mechanical pressure on the neural tissue in the retina.

prestriate cortex.   The secondary visual areas which surround the primary (or striate) cortex, and which have important roles in pattern vision.

propositionality.   The inventive property of human language whereby words can be recombined to make an indefinitely large number of meaningful statements, or "propositions."

prosopagnosia.   A rare form of visual agnosia, resulting from damage to occipital and posterior temporal cortex in the right hemisphere, in which faces or familiar persons, possibly including one's own, cannot be recognized.

psychophysical parallelism. Leibniz's solution to the problem of the mind–body relationship, which holds that the physical and mental, as independent and self-contained realms, function in "pre-established harmony." thus giving the appearance that the two are causally related.

pure alexia without agraphia. A rare aphasic disorder characterized by the inability to comprehend written speech, but with all other language functions essentially intact, including the ability to write.

Raphé nuclei. The control center for slow-wave sleep, located in the brainstem and connected to the RAS.

rapid eye movements (REM's). Rapid flicks of the eyes beneath the eyelids which occur during active sleep (see REM sleep).

RAS. See reticular activating system.

receptive field. The place in the visual field from which a given visual neuron responds to stimulation.

REM sleep. Active sleep, characterized by rapid flicks of the eyes beneath the lids (rapid eye movements), a desynchronized EEG pattern, EMG suppression, and increased body temperature and heart rate.

reticular activating system (RAS). The system located in the brainstem that sends streams of impulses to the thalamus and cortex to control wakefulness and attention.

reticular formation. A finger-sized mass of tissue, located along the axis of the brainstem, which drives the reticular activating system.

retrograde amnesia. Loss of memory for events that occurred just prior to a blow or shock to the brain.

scotoma. A blind spot in the visual field.

simultagnosia. A form of visual agnosia in which one object may be perceived if presented alone, but not if it is introduced with another object in the visual field.

slow-wave sleep. Quiet sleep or deep sleep, during which the cortex appears to be resting, and body temperature, breathing, and heart rate all drop to their lowest levels.

sodium amytal test. The technique of injecting the sedative drug sodium amobarbitol into the carotid artery leading to one side of the brain, to knock out functioning in that half in order to reveal the separate abilities of the other half.

solipsism. The philosophical position that only one mind actually exists (that of the solipsist) and that all else is delusion.

spatial-frequency spectrum. The composition of a picture or visual scene in terms of its component "waves" of brightness.

spike potentials (action potentials). Electrical impulses which are transmitted down the axon of a nerve cell, transmitting excitation to other nerves.

split-brain operation (commissurotomy). The severing of all direct connections between the two hemispheres of the forebrain, most importantly the corpus callosum.

state-dependent memory. Memories which can be recalled only in a specific, altered brain state in which the memory was acquired.

striate cortex. The area of the visual cortex of the brain which receives information directly from the eye. Also called the "primary visual cortex."

synapse. The cleft between two connecting neurons, where transmission of electrical information from one nerve cell to another occurs, by means of the release of chemical transmitter substances.

syntax. Grammar.

thalamus. Enlargement at the top of the brainstem which contains relay centers for messages to and from the forebrain.

theta waves. Rhythmic EEG brainwaves (4 to 8 cycles per second), which appear at the onset of sleep.

tonic characteristics. Physiological events which occur over a long period of time; in REM sleep, such characteristics as EMG suppression, increase of the heart rate and breathing rate, and elevation of temperature (vs. phasic characteristics).

Turing's Test. A test proposed to enable one to decide whether a particular machine possesses "intelligence." The machine, placed in one room, and a human being placed in another room, are each interrogated via teletype. If the machine and the human cannot be distinguished, the machine passes the test.

uncommitted cortex. Newly evolved areas of the cortex of the forebrain not specifically committed to sensory or motor functions.

unilateral spatial neglect. Type of brain damage to the occipital and parietal regions of one side of the brain leading to a condition in which the person will not notice that he is blind in the opposite visual half-field or that he cannot feel the opposite side of the body.

visual agnosia. A perception deficit, caused by lesions to pre-striate cortical areas, in which visual objects are sensed but identification of these objects cannot occur by visual means alone.

Wernicke's aphasia. Form of aphasia in which outward forms of speech are preserved, but speech is mostly meaningless, and comprehension of spoken and written speech is extremely faulty.

Wernicke's area. The cortical region for the perception of speech, lying next to the area on the temporal lobe which receives and analyzes auditory information.

Zeigarnik effect. The phenomenon of especially persistent recall of tasks which are interrupted or left unfinished.

Index

visual cortex, 38–39, 40, 51–52, 62, 69, 70, 125, 135, 140–41; damage to, 64–65. *See also* Striate cortex
visual neurons: tuning of, 47–52
visuo-spatial thinking, 143–46, 149, 150, 152, 161
von Senden, M., 41–42
Vygotsky, L. S., 192

waking and wakefulness, 75, 76–93, 204; alpha waves in, 78–79, 115; characteristics of, 76, 115; degrees of, 76; variations in, 93. *See also* Consciousness; Orienting reaction; Sleep
Walter, W. Grey, 189
Watson, John, 10, 11

Wernicke, Carl, 133–34, 135
Wernicke's aphasia, 130, 132–33, 134, 136, 137
Wernicke's area, 125–26, 127–28, 130, 131, 134, 146
Whorf, Benjamin, 23–24, 136
Wittgenstein, Ludwig, 21–25, 27, 114
"word salad," 131, 134

Yin, Robert, 67

Zeigarnik, B., 191
Zeigarnik effect, 191
Zen and brain activity, 114–15